THE NEW OPTIONS MARKET

THE NEW OPTIONS MARKET

FOURTH EDITION

Max Ansbacher

John Wiley & Sons, Inc.
New York • Chichester • Weinheim • Brisbane • Singapore • Toronto

Library of Congress Cataloging in Publication Data:

Ansbacher, Max G.
    The new options market / Max Ansbacher.—4th ed.
      p. cm.—(Wiley trading advantage)
    Includes index.
    ISBN 0-471-34880-5 (cloth : alk. paper)
    1. Options (Finance) I. Title. II. Series.
    HG6024 .A51 2000
    332.64'5—dc21   00-020122

This book
is dedicated to
my father Heinz
and in loving memory
of my mother Rowena

CONTENTS

PREFACE TO THE
FOURTH EDITION

I have now been working as an options professional for 25 years and I am more convinced than ever that there is nothing in the securities world that can bring investors and speculators so much fun, excitement, challenge, profit, heartbreak, and diversity as options. Options offer literally infinite possibilities when one multiplies all the strategies, strike prices, and durations by all the stocks and stock indexes that exist.

In fact, the world of options is so diverse that to say that people are in options is to tell us absolutely nothing about what they are doing. Are they using every bit of spare cash they have to buy calls on a hot new stock which they have heard from a top source is going to come out with blockbuster earnings next week? Or are they taking in a little extra cash from a stock portfolio by selling covered calls? Are they using intricate spreads to capitalize on short-term price variations in options? Have they decided to take on the risks of selling uncovered options because they believe that that is the best way to make money from options? Or are they taking most of the risk out of their stock portfolios by buying puts on them? And this just brushes the surface of the possibilities.

In this book we will outline every one of these strategies in clear, simple language and provide detailed examples so that you will be able to see exactly how they each work. We will then explain how you can make money from them and how you can lose money. And then I will give you my own rules of strategy, which represent what I have learned from my years in the business about how to shift the odds in your favor as much as possible so that you have the best probabilities of being a winner.

There are no complicated mathematical formulas in this book. Although a Nobel prize was awarded to the men who created the basic option price valuation formula, I believe that in many cases the market forces know more than mathematicians about how to price options. Therefore, I believe that some common sense about the likely future moves of stocks and indexes can serve the nonprofessional trader just as well as or in most cases better than complex mathematics.

In revising my previous edition, I have been struck by two thoughts. The first is that the examples concerning specific stocks had become ludicrous with the passage of time. The very first example in the book was RCA, which hasn't existed as a separate company in over a decade. Other examples were for stocks selling at $11 a share. Polaroid was often mentioned, but whoever talks about it today? Yet in the 1980s it was the Yahoo! of its time.

The second point that hit me was that not only are all the basic descriptions of the options and how to use them still completely accurate, but my rules of strategy are still right on the mark. I have added some comments on the rules of writing uncovered options, which I have developed in my recent involvement with that strategy, but basically the strategies are as true today as they were 25 years ago.

I would like to express my appreciation to Laurence Goellner for his valuable assistance in preparing the manuscript of this revised edition.

My female readers should note that, like so many other authors, when I mention an option buyer and write that "he" does something, I am not trying to imply that only men trade options. Rather I am simply following the English language which doesn't seem to have a nongender-specific pronoun for a person. Women are certainly included as options traders and professionals, and I have changed many phrases from the previous edition that had referred to "all the men on Wall Street" and so forth.

Like the works of Shakespeare, options can contain almost all the elements of human emotions. They can be exhilarating, satisfying, depressing, exciting, vexing, delightful, surprising, dull, worrisome, or pleasing. It is my modest hope that with the help of this book you will also find them to be profitable.

INTRODUCTION

On April 26, 1973, the directors of the Chicago Board Options Exchange held their breaths and crossed their fingers. For on that date, when they opened the first exchange in the world's history to deal in stock options, they took on a large risk. If they could have foreseen that in the next 17 months the stock market would fall into one of the deepest and longest declines in its history, and that because of declining stock exchange volume many brokerage firms would be driven out of business, it is questionable whether they would have dared to open the new exchange.

Even without this foreknowledge, however, there were plenty of reasons for doubt. The traditional market in puts and calls had been part of the American investment scene since almost the turn of the century, but it had never caught on with the investing public. Many professional Wall Streeters therefore predicted flatly that the new exchange, limited at first to calls on just 16 stocks, would be a disastrous flop.

But in less than a year the outcome was clear. The CBOE became the biggest success in the shortest time of any financial exchange that has ever existed in the United States! In the first days of the CBOE its directors were overjoyed when it traded 1,600 calls a day. The volume quickly grew to 5,000—to 10,000—to 20,000 calls a day. At this point the baby CBOE, then trading calls in 32 stocks, was actually trading options on more shares per day than the venerable American Stock Exchange was trading on all its 1,000+ listed stocks.

By now the press was beginning to sit up and take notice. In a front-page story the *Wall Street Journal* hailed the CBOE as "a glittering success, attracting flocks of individual investors." *New York* magazine wrote, "Options are well on their way to becoming the next financial bandwagon." Even as the stock market declined further and drove more of the public away, *Fortune* noted that the new options could lead the individual investor back to Wall Street.

ASTOUNDING VOLUME GROWTH

Volume on the CBOE continued to rise ever higher, to 30,000 options a day, and by October 1974 the CBOE began to have 40,000 options days. The increasing volume forced the CBOE to move to larger quarters, where it would have five times more trading floor space. Then the American Stock Exchange announced that it, too, would be offering options on 20 additional stocks; later the Philadelphia, Pacific, and Midwest stock exchanges began trading options also. Today these five exchanges routinely trade 1,500,000 options or more a day, options based on over 1,300 underlying stocks and over 42 different indexes.

What made this astounding growth even more amazing was that the institutional investors, who had come to dominate the stock markets in the 1970s, were, by and large, conspicuous for their absence from the options exchanges. This meant that at a time when the public was fleeing the stock market it was moving into the new options markets in unprecedented numbers.

What explains this sudden explosive growth? What had happened was that by simply making some basic changes in calls, the new options exchanges had made buying and selling options as easy as buying and selling stocks. The prices for both were now listed in the major newspapers every day, and both had the liquidity that investors require so that they can get into and out of investments quickly.

With the obstacles of the traditional puts and calls now overcome, the public was able to realize the advantages that options offer to sophisticated investors. These unique advantages are:

Leverage. When an investor buys 100 shares of a stock for $100 each and it goes up $10, he has made a profit of $1,000. But when he invests the same amount of money in calls of that stock and the stock goes up $10, he can make a profit of $10,000. If the stock goes up more, the disparity becomes even greater. Chapter 2, "Buying Calls," thoroughly explores the exciting potential of buying calls but concludes that the disadvantages often outweigh the advantages. Buying puts creates similar opportunities to make money when a stock declines, and Chapter 5 explores the many possibilities presented by puts.

Income. By selling calls on stocks that he owns, an investor can expect to generate an income of 10% to 20% a year on his investment.

And the additional options income comes without any more risk of loss than if the investor continued to own the stock without selling any calls. Chapter 3, "Selling Covered Calls," explains just what the drawbacks to selling calls are and how to wring out the highest possible annual income by selecting options offering the most profitable strike prices and durations.

High return. For those who don't mind taking unusually high risks, selling options on stock that one does not own can lead to returns of up to 40% of one's investment a year. The risk of loss, however, is high. Chapter 4, "Selling Naked Calls," weighs the potential high income against the risks and tells how you can reduce your potential loss in advance.

Sophisticated strategies. Since the options exchanges usually offer several options on the same underlying stock, shrewd investors can have a field day selling the short-term options and buying the long-term options on the same stock, selling the high strike price call and buying the low one, or doing just the reverse— selling the stock short and buying a call as the perfect insurance policy. The objective of these spreads and straddles is to make money for the investor within a broad range of stock prices; because of the large variety of options available, it is now possible to custom-tailor a hedge program to fit almost any investor's objectives. Even spreads and hedges have their drawbacks, however, and Chapter 6, on spreads, points them out—as well as the profit one may expect to earn.

These are the basic benefits that investors can derive from the informed use of stock options. By being aware of the brokers' commissions and the tax consequences that are described in detail in Chapters 7 and 8, the investor should be able to benefit greatly from the new options markets.

In short, I have written this book to give the intelligent investor everything one needs to know to start a profitable investment program in America's most exciting form of investing.

THE NEW OPTIONS MARKET

1

THE FUNDAMENTALS OF STOCK OPTIONS
Facts You Need to Know

There are two basic types of stock *options*, calls and puts. A *call* is the option people buy when they think that the price of a stock is going to go up. A *put* is what they buy when they think that it will go down. An easy way to remember which is which is provided by the sentence, "I call up my broker and then I put down the phone." Since calls are the more popular, we will discuss them first.

ELEMENTS OF CALLS

A call is the right to buy 100 shares of a certain stock or stock index at a stated price within a given period of time. For example, a call might be the right to buy 100 shares of stock in Ford Motor Company for the price of $60 per share at any time between now and the third Saturday in January. The price per share at which the call buyer has the right to purchase the stock or index is called the *strike price* or *exercise price*. Thus, if a call is the right to acquire a share for $60, that call would have a strike price of $60.

All options have very precise and definite time limits. They completely cease to exist once that time limit has passed. Since options literally expire upon the passage of that time limit, that time limit is called the *expiration date*. Expiration dates are referred to by the month in which they occur. No actual date is needed because the expiration date is always the Saturday following the third Friday of the named month. So when we talk about a May option, we mean an

1

option that expires on the Saturday following the third Friday in May. This usually turns out to be the third Saturday.

Options are available with a number of different expiration months. They are the two nearest-term months plus two additional months from quarterly cycles that start in either January, February, or March. For example, if it were now late September options would be trading that expire in October and November. Some stocks would also have options expiring in January and April, other stocks would have options expiring in February and May, and some would have options expiring in March and June. Thus, at any time, the shortest-duration option will vary from as little as a few minutes to one month and the longest-duration option will vary from just over six months (on expiration day) to nine months (when the new options have just been added). Even longer-term options are called LEAPS.

The acronym LEAPS stands for long-term equity anticipation securities. These options may extend for up to three years and three months from their original listing. They expire only in January on the regular expiration date. Except for their longer duration, they are just like regular options. In fact, once enough time has passed, they simply become regular options.

All options expire at 5:00 P.M. eastern time on the Saturday immediately following the third Friday of the named month, and this Saturday is the date you will see in the description of your option in the confirmation slip you receive from your brokerage firm and in its monthly statements. But this date is a technical one and of no importance to you. More important for you is the date by which your broker must receive your instructions to *exercise* your option. This will vary from firm to firm, but it cannot be later than 5:30 P.M. eastern time on the business day (normally Friday) preceding that technical expiration date. And even more important than the cutoff date for exercising an option is the last time it can be traded. Normally options on individual stocks trade until 4:02 P.M. eastern time, which is two minutes after the stock exchange closes, while options on stock indexes trade until 4:15. On the final day of an option, the expiring options on individual stocks stop trading at 4:00, and options on stock indexes stop trading at 4:10. Many brokerage firms require that orders for expiring options be entered at least 30 minutes before the final trading time due to the large influx of orders that often develops at the close.

Thus any call can be fully described by stating all of the following critical aspects, always given in the same order: first the name of the underlying common stock or stock index, then the expiration month, and finally the strike price. A call termed "Ford January 60" gives its owner the right to acquire 100 shares of Ford Motor Company common stock for the price of $60 per share at any time between now and the Saturday following the third Friday in January.

READING THE OPTIONS QUOTATIONS

Now that you understand the elements that define each option, it is an easy matter to read the prices in newspaper reports or other quotation sources. The first item is the name of the stock with the strike price. In some formats this is followed by three columns listing the price for the option of that strike price for each of the next three expiration months. The number below the name of the stock is its closing price on the stock exchange. This may or may not be the same number you will see for the close of the stock on the stock market pages of a newspaper, since the price in the options listing is the consolidated close, and may have taken place at a stock exchange other than the New York Stock Exchange (NYSE).

The *open interest* figure is the cumulative total of all the options that have been sold (or "written") to create new positions. When an option *writer* writes (sells) a new option, the open interest figure goes up by one and will continue to reflect that contract until the contract expires, the option is exercised, or the writer closes out the position by purchasing an identical option.

Certain Sunday newspapers and *Barron's* publish more complete reports of the week's activities, including the high and low prices of each option for the week. But all the important information is contained in the daily reports, even though in order to save space some newspapers do not report the volume figures for the individual options.

One note of caution is in order. One cannot rely on the figures to be a guide as to what you may do on the following day, because all the figures are closing figures; that is, they describe the final transaction of the day. Since some options have very little volume, the final transaction might have occurred at 2:00 P.M., when the stock was at $87, and by the time the stock market closed the stock might have sunk to $85. But of course the figure you will read in the newspaper for the option is the price when the stock was $87. Obviously, if the stock opens the next morning at $85, the price of the call will be less to reflect the decline in the stock. If you ask your broker after the market close, he should be able to tell you when the final trade for any option took place. He can also tell you what the closing *bid* and *asked* prices were for the option, which are accurate price indications of the closing stock price.

THE VALUE OF OPTIONS

The right to acquire a stock for a given price between now and some future date is almost always worth a certain amount of money. This is true whether the stock is currently priced at more or less than the strike price. The reason is that, even if the current price of the stock is below the strike price, there is a possibility that by the time the expiration date comes around, the price of the stock will have risen above the strike price. The owner of the call will then be able to purchase the stock at a bargain price. This is called exercising the call. The call owner can sell the stock immediately after exercising the call and make a cash profit of the difference between the strike price and the then market value of the stock.

For example, if on the third Friday in January the Ford stock used in our initial example was selling at $65 on the New York Stock Exchange, the owner of the call with a strike price of $60 would be able to acquire the stock by paying $60. He would then own stock worth $65. His profit on exercising the call and selling the stock would be $5, less what he originally paid for the call and his commissions. Thus, on its expiration date a call is worth the price of the stock minus the strike price with an adjustment for commissions. On the other hand, if the price of the Ford Motor Company stock was $60 or less on the expiration date of the call, then the owner of the call would have nothing of value. This is because the right to purchase the stock for $60 is worth nothing if anyone can do the same thing without owning a call. So he would not acquire the stock through his call; whatever he had paid for the call would be a complete loss.

The amount that a person pays to acquire an option is called the *premium*. In effect, this is the price of the option, but it is called a premium to distinguish it from the underlying common stock, which also has a price. Premiums can consist of two types. If the strike price of a call is above the current price of the stock or stock index, then the entire premium is said to be *future time value* because it will only be of any real value in the future (if the stock goes up over the strike price). If, however, the strike price is below the stock price, then a part of the premium is said to be *cash value*, because if you owned that call and exercised it today you would have something of value.

Here are examples. If a July 80 call has a premium of 4 and the underlying stock is now at $75, the entire premium of 4 is said to be future time value. If you owned that call and were to exercise it today it would not have any value. That would be true until the stock went over $80. On the other hand, if the stock is now $85 and the premium is 7, the call would have a value right now of 5 if you were to exercise it. For this reason, we say that 5 *points* of the premium represents cash value; the other 2 points are future time value. These two concepts are of great importance in deciding which options to buy or to sell, as we will see later.

Premiums of calls are quoted for individual shares, but the actual price of a call is the quoted premium multiplied by 100 because one call gives you the right to purchase 100 shares. Thus, when one reads that a Ford Motor Company call is selling for $2\frac{1}{4}$, this means that the premium on one share of Ford stock is $2.25, so the cost of purchasing one call is 100 times that: $225.

The same rule applies to stock index options. If a call on the Standard & Poor's 100 index, known as the OEX for short, has a premium of 16, you multiply this by 100 to get the actual amount you would pay to buy this call, namely $1,600. The value of the underlying security is 100 times the current price of the index. Thus if the OEX is at 700, one call on it represents a call on $70,000 worth of stock.

The person who buys a call must always pay cash for the full premium. There is no *margin* possible on a call, with the exception of LEAPS, because there is such a high probability that the call will soon be worth nothing, so that a brokerage house putting up the margin could quickly have no collateral for its margin loan. LEAPS are an exception, and brokerage firms are allowed to loan up to 25% of the current market value of options that have more than nine months until expiration.

BUYING OPTIONS—THE ADVANTAGES

Perhaps these definitions have left you slightly less than trembling with excitement. Your reaction might well be, so what? What's so exciting about the right to buy or sell a stock for a given price within a given amount of time?

The answer is that nothing else in the securities sphere offers as great an opportunity to make or lose a fortune in as short a period of time as stock options. You've heard the old adage that when the elephant sneezes, the mouse is knocked down by a hurricane. The option is the mouse and the underlying common stock is the elephant. When the common stock moves up by 5%, the call can move up by 100%. And that, in its simplest form, is what calls are all about.

Leverage

Options give a person the chance to make a large gain with a relatively small investment. They give the investor tremendous leverage. For a small investment, usually 10% of the price of the underlying common stock or less, the option purchaser gains the right to participate in the price increase or decrease of the underlying stock for a period of time, just as if he actually were an owner of the stock. The call owner differs from the stock owner in that he has to pay for the cost of the call, but he has his right for only a limited time, and he does not receive dividends. But, thanks to the liquidity of the options exchanges, a call buyer can always overcome the time limitation by buying another call when his first one expires.

Let us illustrate this leverage with an example, using our Ford call option with a strike price of $60 expiring in January. Suppose the current price of Ford stock on the New York Stock Exchange is, more or less by coincidence, also $60. If the expiration date in January is three months away from the date when the call is purchased, the premium (price) of the call might be 3, meaning you would pay $300 for the call). Now let us assume that you are considering purchasing 100 shares of Ford stock for a total price of $6,000.

You firmly believe, on the basis of everything you have read, that Ford is underpriced and that within the next three months it is pretty certain to go up to $70 a share. You intend to purchase the stock as a short-term investment only, and will sell the shares at the end of January. How much money could be made by buying the stock as compared to the call? If you buy 100 shares of the stock for $6,000, and the price of the stock does go up to $70 a share by the end of January, it would be worth an additional $10 a share and you would have a profit of $1,000.

On the other hand, if you invest the same amount ($6,000) in calls at a premium of 3 (i.e., at a cost of $300 each), you will be able to purchase 20 calls on a total of 2,000 shares. Now if the price of the underlying common stock goes up to $70 a share, the right to acquire the stock for only $60 will be worth $10 a share. In other words, your calls will have gone up in value from $3 a share to $10 a share. The calls that you bought for $300 each are now worth $1,000 each, and your original investment of $6,000 is worth a full $20,000. You have just made a 233% profit on a $6,000 investment in only three months. Compare this with the 16.66% profit you would have made by buying the stock.

If you want to figure out what this options profit would come to in annual terms, since three months are a quarter of a year, you multiply by four and find that you are making a profit at the rate of 932% a year! Pretty good. And this all from a stock that had a rise of only 10 points. By comparing the $1,000 profit you would have made on buying and selling the stock with the profit of $14,000 you would make by buying a call, you can understand what the excitement is all about.

And of course, had the stock gone up more, the difference in profit would have been even more sensational. If the stock had gone up 20 points to $80 share, the profit on the common stock itself would have been $20 a share for a total profit of $2,000. The purchaser of the call would have made a profit of $17 a share for a total profit of $34,000. That would be his net profit on a $6,000 investment in just three months.

But, you might wonder, aren't there any liabilities to be incurred in buying a call? What if you should be proven wrong and the price of the stock falls, or just stays where it is? Will you then have to come up with more money? This is a natural question for anyone who has tried to get a little more leverage from common stocks by buying them on margin, only to see the price of the stock fall and receive a call from his broker asking for more money immediately to protect his investment. With respect to a call, the answer to the liability question is a clear and emphatic "no." The buyer of an option can never be required to put up more money. The only liability he has is the cost of the option when he buys it. The only risk he faces is that it will expire when the price of the stock is at or below the strike price and the call becomes worthless. Then the call purchaser will have lost the entire premium paid for the call, but that is all he will have lost.

Protection from Stock Price Declines

And while we're on the subject of liabilities, this is a good time to look at the purchase of calls from another point of view, namely that of restricting your losses in case of a decline in the price of the stock. Suppose in our original Ford Motor Company example, you think that the stock is probably going to go up, but you know that if certain developments occur, the price is likely to go down. You could purchase the 100 shares for $6,000 as we mentioned before and pray hard that the price will go up and that your fears of a decline will not materialize.

Or in the alternative: You could decide to invest in calls that would give you a profit potential similar to the 100 shares. More specifically, you could decide to buy a single call for $300. If the strike price is $60, you would make $100 for every dollar the stock rises above $60 (less the premium of $300 that you paid). What this means is that you are obtaining leverage similar to a $6,000 purchase with an outlay of cash of only $300. In addition to conserving your capital, the big advantage comes if the price of the stock should go down.

Let us suppose that the price of the stock falls by $10, to $50 a share, during the period of the option. If you had purchased the stock for $6,000 it would now be worth only $5,000, for a loss in value of a full $1,000. On the other hand, by purchasing a call for $300 you limit your loss to just that $300. Thus you'd be ahead of the stock purchaser by $700. And remember, no matter how fast the stock falls in price and no matter how far it finally plummets, the $300 you paid for the call is the most that you can possibly lose. So the further the stock falls, the better the call purchaser does in relation to a person who bought the stock.

THE CALL SELLER

Since buying a call seems like such a wonderful way to make quick money in an upswing and such a great way to cut losses in a downturn, you might wonder who is stupid enough to sell you a call. After all, if you are going to buy one, it means that someone has to sell you one. And if you are going to make a 100% profit on your purchase, doesn't that mean that the person who sells you the call is going to lose an equal amount? If buying a call is such a wonderful investment, why would anyone ever sell one? Well, we will explore just how wonderful an investment buying a call is in more detail in Chapter 2. But right now, we'll explain that the seller of a call doesn't necessarily lose any money at all when the underlying stock goes up above the strike price.

In all probability the seller of your call is also the owner of the underlying stock. Thus, when the stock goes up and you make money on your call, he is losing money on the call he has sold you, but at the same time he is making money on the rise in the price of the stock he owns. In fact, the two equal each other and the gain in one completely cancels out the loss in the other so that the stock owner is not losing anything on the rise in the price, but rather is making money to the extent that the call was sold originally for more than its actual cash value. For example, if a stock were $42 a share, the option with a $40 strike price would have a cash value of $2, and if he sold it for $4, he would have a profit of $2.

He would, however, have made more money if he owned the underlying common stock and had not sold the call—thereby losing potential profits. But he doesn't mind this, because no matter what happens to the price of the stock, he gets to keep the entire premium as profit. The seller of a call figures that this compensates him for giving up some potential profit when the stock goes up. And remember, even when the stock goes up, he still has the profit of his premium, to the extent it exceeded its cash value.

EXERCISING THE CALL

When the expiration date for the option arrives and the price of the stock is above the call's strike price, the owner of the call can exercise the call, meaning that he directs his broker to buy in the stock at the exercise price. This, however, involves paying a commission. He must pay a commission on the purchase of the stock, and if he sells the stock immediately to realize a profit, he must pay another commission on that sale. But, the call owner has an alternative for a *closing transaction*. Instead of exercising his option he can sell it. Even on the last trading date for that option, there will be a buyer for it who will be willing to pay the approximate difference between the stock price and the strike price.

You might wonder who in the world would want to pay $7 for a call that is going to expire in one day. The answer is that for every person who owns an option—is *long* an option—there is a person who is *short* an option—who has sold an option that he didn't have in the first place. Unlike common stocks, which start out their existence by being issued by a corporation, an option is a creation of the options exchange itself. It is created simply by selling it short.

So, on the final few days of trading, if you own a call that is worth some money, that means someone sitting on the other side of the fence is short a call, which is going to cost either money or stock to redeem. When a call expires *in the money*—that is, when the stock is above the strike price—the seller of a call must either deliver the stock or close out the position by buying a call to offset the one that is short. If the call writer owns the shares, there is no problem. But a call writer who does not own shares may not wish to buy them just so they can be called away. He will therefore buy a call instead, to close out his position. This is why in the last few days of an option period there is often a frantic amount of trading in those calls that are in the money.

Exercising Index Options

Stock index options are handled differently. If you were to exercise a call to acquire a stock index and you received 100 or 500 different stocks in different quantities, including fractions of shares, you would have quite a mess on your hands. Therefore, options on stock indexes are exercised on a cash basis. This means that the actual value of the index is calculated and then the strike price is subtracted from that, and the difference is credited to the brokerage account of the person who is exercising the option.

For example, let's say you were long an October 1,300 call on the Standard & Poor's 500 stock index (SPX), and the index closed on the Friday of the expiration Saturday at $1,327.53. You decide to exercise the call. You would subtract the value of the strike price ($1,300 times 100 equals $130,000) from the value of the index itself ($1,327.53 times 100 equals $132,753). You would receive the difference, which is $2,753. This is clearly cleaner than receiving 500 stocks and then having to sell them.

SHORT SELLING A CALL

How much must a person pay if he decides to sell a call short? After all, there has been no expense incurred by the options exchange in issuing the call, and the call buyer has paid the full amount of the premium. What is there for the seller to pay? Yet it stands to reason that selling cannot be free to everyone who wishes to do so, because if the underlying stock goes up, the person who sells short may be called upon to deliver a large amount of money.

The answer is that the seller of a call must put up money, which is held in escrow by the exchange as the guarantee that he will fulfill his obligations upon expiration. The amount of margin that the exchanges require is computed under formulas that are discussed in Chapter 7. Normally the required margin is much greater than the amount of the premium received for the call. In addition, the margin must usually be *marked to the market* every day, which means that if the stock underlying a call you are short goes up today, you must deliver an additional amount for each call you are short to your broker. Because of this requirement for daily computations, most brokerage houses require that you maintain greater margin balances than are actually required. This also discourages rampant speculation and provides a degree of safety to the broker should the price of the call suddenly escalate. Instead of having your margin in cash, you can deposit the required number of shares of the stock.

So far, we have concentrated on calls. And yet calls are only half of the stock option picture. Puts make up the other half.

ELEMENTS OF PUTS

A put is the right to sell 100 shares of a particular stock or stock index at a certain price within a given time. It differs from a call only in that a call is the right to *purchase* a stock for a set price whereas a put is the right to *sell* a stock for a set price. For example, a put might be the right to sell 100 shares of Sears stock at $35 each at any time between now and the January expiration date. This would be denominated a "Sears January 35" put. If the price of the stock on the day before expiration was $30, the holder of the put would have the right to require the put writer to purchase 100 shares of Sears stock from the put holder for $35 each. He would "put" the stock to the put writer. Since he could acquire the shares for only $30 each just before exercising his put, the value of the put would be close to $500.

The owner of a put is under no obligation to exercise the put, and if the price of the stock goes up (against the expectations of the put buyer) the only liability faced is the loss of the premium paid. Thus, puts are very much like calls in that the purchaser has no liabilities and no potential losses other than the premium paid for the option. Because most investors expect that stocks will go up, there is usually not as great a demand for puts on individual stocks as there is for calls, and accordingly the premiums are generally less than for comparable calls. Interestingly, the reverse typically is the case for puts and calls on stock indexes.

As with a call, the buyer of a put traded on an exchange would not need actually to purchase the shares of stock and deliver them to the put seller in order to make a profit. The put owner will probably prefer to simply close out his put transaction by selling a put during the final period of its existence. Since he is the owner of a put, when he sells it he is out of the market, and the difference between the cost of the put and the selling price is his profit. This profit will normally be just about what he would have realized by actually purchasing the shares on the open market and delivering them to the put writer. Selling a put eliminates the need to have enough cash to finance the purchase of the stock and saves the commissions on the purchase and sale of the stock. Of course, a put owner who owns the underlying stock might prefer to deliver his shares for the strike price.

ADJUSTED STRIKE PRICES

In addition to the regular strike prices of 20, 35, 60, and so on, you may have noticed that some stocks have odd strikes, such as $46^5/_8$, $37^3/_8$, and so forth. These odd *adjusted strike prices* are the results of stock dividends paid on the shares of stock, or of stock splits. One of the features of listed options is that there is no adjustment made in the exercise price when the common stock pays a regular or special cash dividend. In a way, it could be said that this is unfair to the purchaser of a call option because the payment of a dividend will normally reduce the price of the stock by the amount of the dividend. The reason a dividend causes a stock price reduction is simply that if a company is going to pay a 50 cents dividend, the day before the dividend it has cash of 50 cents per share in its treasury, and the value of the stock reflects the value of this cash. After the dividend is paid out to the shareholders, the company's treasury is reduced by 50 cents per share, and therefore the shares, which represent the value of owning a part of the company, are worth 50 cents less than they were before the dividend was paid out. So the stock price will generally fall by 50 cents.

This means that the value of any call options that are in the money will fall by a related amount. But, while this may be unfair theoretically, it was felt that administrative convenience and the need to standardize options made this inequity unavoidable. And, in practice, the inequity is reduced by the fact that options tend to have unusually low premiums just before a stock goes *ex-dividend*.

But what happens when a stock declares a stock dividend of, say, 20% of the value of the stock? Now we have a more drastic situation. Let's assume that a shareholder owned 100 shares of stock before the stock dividend, each with a value of $100. Thus the value of his holdings was $10,000. Once there is a 20% stock dividend, he will own 120 shares, but his total holdings will not have changed in value by one bit, assuming the stock price does not go up. He still owns the same percentage of the company, and the company has not become worth any more or any less by issuing some additional shares. His holdings are still worth $10,000, but now consist of 120 shares; a little simple division will reveal that each share of stock is now worth only $83.33. So, if the stock closed at $100 before the ex-dividend date of the stock dividend and the price stays constant, it will open the next morning at $83.33. That's fine for people trading in the stock, but what about the guy who owns the $100 strike price option?

Obviously, unless something were done, his option would suddenly have lost almost all of its value when in fact there was no real decline in the price of the stock. So there had to be an adjustment of strike prices to reflect stock dividends, and that is what the odd strike prices are. When a stock goes ex-dividend after a stock dividend, the strike prices of all existing options are reduced proportionally, and in this example, a $100 strike price option would become an $83³/₈ strike price option. But that is not all.

Remember, in addition to lowering the price of each share, more shares were created. To reflect this fact, the number of shares in each option is increased. Instead of one of these odd strike price options being the right to buy 100 shares of stock, it becomes the right to buy 120 shares (or some other number). So be careful when you buy or sell these options. If you are a buyer, and your broker quotes you a price of $2, your cost of one option is going to be not $200, but $240 in this example, since the price per share is multiplied by the figure of 120 shares per option.

While this could be awkward, it is not as dangerous as the hazard faced by the option seller. Let's say you are a *covered call writer or seller*. After a stock split you buy 1,000 shares of the stock at $83³/₈. You proceed to sell 10 options with the $83³/₈ strike price for a $2 premium and sit back to reap your hoped for profits of $2 a share. You are happy to see the price of the stock go up smartly, and you wait to have the stock called away so you can go on to greener pastures.

The stock moves up to 100, and sure enough your stock is called away. All 1,000 shares. Plus 200 shares you don't own! To your horror you find that you were naked on 200 shares, which you must now buy in at the current price of $100 and deliver at $83³/₈. The moral is simple: If you see an odd strike price, or any option with the symbol "o" after it in your quote source, be sure to ask how many shares are included in each option. This also is crucial in spreads where you may wish to combine some regular strike price options with some odd-priced ones. Be sure that you get the right ratio of options.

As soon as there is a stock dividend, the options exchange will introduce new options with regular strike prices. Thus, in this case there would be that $83⅜ strike price option, and right below it would be the new $80 strike option. There often are some interesting spreads between the two, but please remember that you need 12 of the $80 options to offset 10 of the $83⅜ ones.

SPECULATIVE NATURE OF OPTIONS

There is one final point that belongs in this chapter on the basics of dealing in puts and calls: With the exception of selling calls when you own the underlying shares, this is a highly speculative business. That sounds like a pretty tame statement, especially for anyone who has read a number of prospectuses for newly issued shares. The Securities and Exchange Commission (SEC) makes stock issuers write "highly speculative" all over the prospectuses, sometimes even in red, in capital letters. Well, while new issues are considered speculative, dealing in calls is about five times more so. If you think that certain stocks are risky, let me tell you that they loom as solid as the Rock of Gibraltar in comparison to puts and calls.

When you buy a put or a call with the price of the stock near the strike price, there is a 50% chance that when the call expires it will be worth absolutely nothing—that's right, not one single penny. Whether you paid $200 for it or $1,000, the money you paid will have simply disappeared into thin air. And unlike the stock market, where that happens only occasionally when a company goes into bankruptcy or receivership, this is the norm for options. Remember, most of them become worthless!

So unless you are completely willing to kiss your money good-bye the minute you buy an option, you had better not invest in puts and calls. Or do it the only conservative way, which, as described in Chapter 3, is to be on the selling side when you own the underlying stock. Of course, you won't get rich overnight by this method, but as that chapter explains, you might be surprised at just how fast you will make money.

On the other hand, the person who sells puts or calls without owning the underlying stock—a *naked option writer or seller*—can face an almost unlimited risk. He not only must be prepared to lose the money that he puts up as margin when he sells his call, but he must also face the possibility that every day the price of that underlying stock may jump. If it jumps high enough, he will get an urgent call from his broker demanding more money to cover the margin requirements. If the money is not sent in, the position will be closed out by the brokerage firm at a large loss to the client. In Chapter 4, I explain how to reduce the risk as much as possible, but the risk is still there.

With the exception of covered call writing, this is not a game for the person who is trying to accumulate enough money to send three children to college in another five years. This is not the investment for the person who is concerned with building up a substantial nest egg to retire on in 10 or 15 years. This is not for the person who wants to get out of the job he is in and needs to accumulate some capital in order to start a business of his own. If you need to accumulate some money for a particular purpose that is important to you, then this is not the method for you. The one exception would be to sell calls on stock that you already own. And that method is one I do recommend in such a situation.

Selling and buying options (with the exception just noted) is for the person who has some extra money. It is for the investor who has made some money in the stock market and is now looking for a quicker, more exciting way to increase it; for the professional person who had a good year and now has more money in a savings account than he really needs; for the businessperson who has already made payments into a retirement plan, paid for disability insurance, made the mortgage payments, and put away something for a rainy day, and still has money left over; for the single person who works for a corporation that pays for retirement, Blue Cross, and disability insurance, and who figures that anything left over after paying current expenses is money that he can easily afford to lose. For these people, trading in options can be extremely rewarding, as this book will demonstrate.

But one cannot warn the reader often enough that trading in options is for only the speculative person who isn't going to miss the entire investment if it is lost. At this point it is worth reprinting the third paragraph of the Options Clearing Corporation (OCC) prospectus, which appears in boldface type on the first page:

> Both the purchase and writing of options involve a high degree of risk and are not suitable for many investors. Such transactions should be entered into only by investors who have read and understand this prospectus and in particular, who understand the nature and extent of their rights and obligations and are aware of the risks involved. An investor should not purchase an option unless he is able to sustain a total loss of the premium and transaction costs of purchasing the option, and should not write an option unless he is able to sustain substantial financial losses, or in the case of a call, unless he owns the underlying security.

Anyone contemplating trading in options is urged to read the entire prospectus. Having said that much, let me point out that if you can afford to lose your investment, there is no method I know of that can be more rewarding in as short a period of time than trading in options. While it is risky, experience shows that trading in carefully selected puts and calls can produce an extremely high income on the amount of the investment.

2

BUYING CALLS
Low Cost and
Potentially Large Profits

The fall of 1998 was not a good time for the New York Stock Exchange. The stock averages had been taking solid losses for months following the stunning news in August that Russia was repudiating virtually its entire foreign debt. This had brought about the virtual collapse of the Russian stock market and caused havoc in the third world's stock markets. Concern about these markets soon turned to worry about the domestic markets when word began to spread that a $4 billion hedge fund named Long-Term Capital Management was suffering severe losses.

The firm was headed by legendary bond supertrader John W. Meriwether, who had formerly run the powerful bond department at Salomon Brothers. In fact, that firm had been so successful under his leadership that the U.S. Treasury Department enacted a special regulation aimed at prohibiting Salomon from buying too large a percentage of the Treasury bonds that the Treasury auctioned periodically. Unfortunately, one of Meriwether's traders decided that with a little hanky-panky he could easily flout the regulation. When the violation was discovered, Meriwether was forced to resign. But with the reputation he had built up for himself, it was not too hard for him to attract large amounts of institutional money to Long-Term Capital. The firm was very profitable from its beginning as it engaged in what were basically hedged bets.

It was therefore a stunning shock to the financial world when the hedge fund announced in September 1998 that it had actually become insolvent. Because of the giant size of the fund, the New York

Federal Reserve Bank became concerned that the fund's possible bankruptcy would cause a massive panic that could bring down financial markets around the world. The Bank engineered a bailout of the hedge fund. But Wall Street wondered how many other hedge funds would be next, and pondered the fate of the stock markets.

It was not surprising that the Dow Jones Industrial Average had fallen by 20% from its high of 9,400. Many of the individual stocks had plummeted by a much greater amount. What had started as an overseas problem had soon triggered selling in the U.S. market as investors began to consider the negative impact that these events would have on the important U.S. export sector. The autumn was particularly bad for many of the technology stocks, which depended so strongly on export sales.

Within the technology sector, no area was more volatile, and hence more vulnerable to a downturn, than the Internet stocks. The Internet industry had been founded only a few years earlier when an electronic communications system developed by the U.S. Department of Defense and later used by libraries and scientists was opened up to the public. From then on the only limit was in the imagination of the public. The Internet became a place where a company with nothing but a few years of losses could issue an initial public offering (IPO) and take in hundreds of millions of dollars. Both the company and its top officers could live happily ever after.

While this business plan was worked successfully again and again by a multitude of entrepreneurs, it meant that the stocks of companies that had gone public were selling at very high prices without most of the fundamental economics, such as profits, which traditionally had given stocks their value. Internet companies did not have a history of being profitable; they did not have any history indicating that they could survive in a difficult economic or competitive environment; and at that time, in fact, they usually had very large losses. They were bought largely by individual investors who believed that the Internet would do for the United States in the twenty-first century what the railroad and the internal combustion engine had done for the country in the nineteenth and the twentieth centuries respectively.

Therefore, when stock prices started falling in the autumn of 1998, it was not surprising that the Internet stocks were falling with them. And because the reason for buying them was based on a conviction about the future rather than a business textbook analysis of fundamentals such as book value and profits, it was not surprising that they were falling even faster than others. As an example, on Thursday, October 1, 1998, when the Dow Jones Industrial Average lost 2.7%, the tech-heavy Nasdaq Composite fell 4.8%, and many Internet companies fared far worse. America Online was down 10.4% and Yahoo! suffered a 12.8% drop.

Among the Internet companies, none had come up faster and gone further than Amazon.com, which had the goal of nothing less than to become the Goliath of all Internet retailing. Under the leadership of Jeff Bezos, commonly thought to be the brightest of all the Internet entrepreneurs, Amazon.com had seen its sales of books explode exponentially and its stock price shoot up likewise. But in October the stock was off from its high of 144. In fact, on that Thursday it fell 8.1% to $102^5/_8$.

Things were so bad that Wall Street analysts were saying, "It's a classic lack of confidence in the market. When people want to get out, the floodgates open." And as the next week ended, Amazon.com limped to a close of $92^7/_{16}$. It would have been a very gutsy move to buy the stock at this point. Not only was the market in a strong downtrend, but Amazon.com was almost devoid of the factors that experts say give stocks their high prices. Furthermore, at $92^7/_{16}$, it was still far from cheap, and with the extremely fast moves in Internet stocks, who could have known whether the stock would fall much further?

But there was a way that one could have speculated on a possible resurgence of Amazon.com without risking a large amount of capital. On that day, Friday, October 9, 1998, there were calls trading on Amazon.com stock. Anyone who thought that the stock had a chance of going up could have bought a call without risking a large amount of money per share. For example, the call that many people would have chosen—because its strike price was just above the price of the stock and because it had a reasonable length of time left—was the January 100 call. It closed that day at a price of 15 per share of Amazon.com stock. We'll discuss the aspects of calls at greater length later, but for now it is enough to know that for every point that Amazon.com was above 100 at the option's expiration date on January 16, 1999, the call would be worth 1. If, for example, the stock closed at 110, the option would be worth 10, and if it closed at 115, it would be worth 15. At a price of 100 or less, the option would expire worthless. Would you have been willing to risk 15 per share to buy this call? (See Figure 2.1.)

If you had been a purchaser of this call, you would have had to believe that the stock would go from its price of $92^7/_{16}$ up to the strike price of 100, then up an additional 15 to cover the cost of the option, and then up some more to cover the commission in and out. This means that the stock would have to climb a full 25.35% up to 116 in

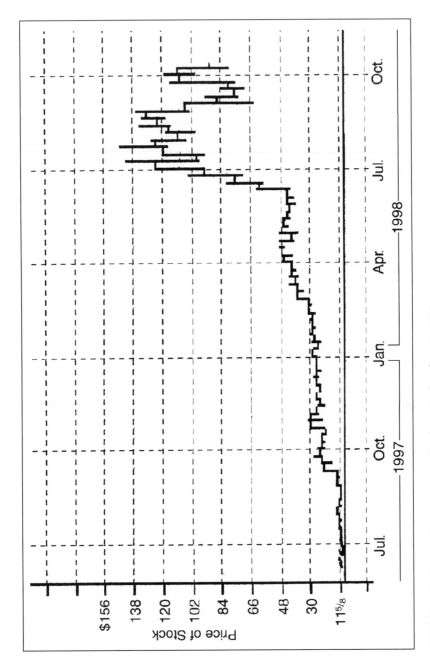

FIGURE 2.1 Chart of Amazon.com Stock up to October 9, 1998
Would you have risked $15 a share at that time to buy the January 100 strike price call?

order for the call buyer just to break even on the purchase! And it would have to do this in less than four months, because otherwise that call would become worthless on the expiration date with no extensions possible. Those who contemplated buying a January 100 call on Amazon.com presumably were aware of all this and firmly expected that it would climb to well over 116 so that they could make a profit to compensate for the enormous odds against them.

In fact, it was only the tremendous faith that some investors had in Amazon.com and its almost incredible past performance as well as its potential future growth that kept the option premium as high as 15. Just think for one minute. For a stock to climb 25% in less than four months, it would have to increase by an annualized rate of more than 75%! And yet investors purchased 844 of those calls on October 9, 1998.

But then the unexpected happened, as it almost always does on Wall Street. The hundreds of hedge funds that were supposed to follow Long-Term Capital into insolvency didn't do it. It seemed that with the exception of two or three very small funds, Long-Term Capital had a strategy that was unique unto itself. So the second shoe never dropped. Wall Street gave a sigh of relief. Then the international scene proceeded to get a bit better rather than worse. Then the very fear in overseas markets produced a flight to safety in U.S. Treasury bonds, which pushed down interest rates in the United States. This drop in interest rates then became a major bullish factor pulling up stock prices. Instead of crying on Wall Street, suddenly there was cheering that the world was not coming to an end, and indeed that the U.S. economy was in fact doing rather well, thank you.

As the markets rose, nothing climbed faster than the Internet stocks and for exactly the same reasons that they had fallen so fast earlier—namely, that since they were really a play on an uncharted future, there was no limit to how high stock traders could value them. Amazon.com was moving along right with all the others. In just four weeks the stock climbed up to $115\frac{1}{2}$ for a gain of 25%, which, as you may remember, was just shy of the price needed to break even at the expiration of the option. And how was the option doing? It was selling at a lot more than 15 because it still had those two months to go. The closing price was a big $35\frac{3}{8}$. So while the stock had gone up 25%, the option had actually increased by a whopping 136%. In just four weeks those who had purchased the option had more than doubled their money.

Then the news on Wall Street started getting even better. Long-Term Capital seemed like nothing more than a bad dream in the distant past. America was booming. Earnings were going up and the stock market loved it. By December 17th, just over two months later, Amazon.com had climbed 104% to 189. The option meanwhile had multiplied to an amazing 176 bid price, meaning that this is what it could have been sold for. That's an increase of 161 per share for a profit of 1,073%, which means that the option had grown by over 10 times its original price.

By now Wall Street was positively bubbling with enthusiasm for the stock market and the Internet stocks in particular. As one analyst said, "The public is in love with Internet stocks and believes that they are the way to play the future." A column on the *New York Times* editorial page said, "The Internet is the wonder of the era, the tool that is expected to change everything." Then Amazon.com did two things that lit a fire under its stock.

First it announced that it was expanding from selling books to also selling music compact discs (CDs) and cassette tapes. This gave proof to its followers that Amazon.com was not just an online bookstore, but that it had the key to becoming an important retailer in every field that it chose to enter. The future never looked brighter.

Second, Amazon.com announced that it was splitting its stock three for one. To a public that believed a stock split was a sure sign of future success, this was like pouring gasoline on a roaring fire. And to top it off, there were a lot of doubting Thomases who had thought that the stock was widely overvalued and had built up significant short positions. As the stock rose, these poor souls were forced to buy in their positions, further accelerating Amazon.com's dramatic ascent. But wait a minute. Did we forget the three-for-one split effective on January 5th? Sure, the price of the stock on January 15th was 140, but because of the split it was worth three times that amount, or 420. (See Figure 2.2.) So the shareholders had made a killing with their stock going from $92^7/_{16}$ to 420 in just three months for a profit of 354%.

How did the options holders fare? Taking into consideration the three-for-one split, the January 100 call closed with a bid of 315. So a transaction that cost 15 had grown to 315, for a gain of 2,000%. Every $1,000 that was paid to buy the Amazon January 100 call and was held until expiration became $21,000. This percentage may be a bit difficult to grasp, but the basic fact that on a comparatively small investment in calls one can very quickly make a great deal of money is one that everyone can easily comprehend.

Well, you might ask, what are the drawbacks? If you are an experienced hand at the stock market, you might ask whether the call purchaser would have had to put up some margin in case the underlying stock had gone down. No, the purchaser had to pay only the

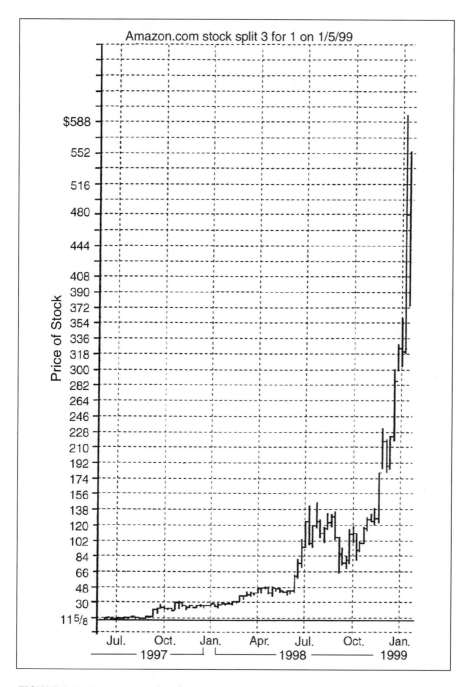

FIGURE 2.2 Amazon.com Stock through the Expiration of the January Calls
Amazon.com shareholders made a profit of 354%, but those who bought the
January calls made a profit of 2,200%.

cost of the call, nothing more, and no matter what happened to the stock, this was the most that he could lose.

Or, perhaps again if you are a stock market veteran, you are saying to yourself, well, that was a nice paper profit, but how many of the people who owned the Amazon.com January 100 calls on January 16, 1999, were lucky enough to sell at that very point in time? Didn't the stock fall subsequently, taking with it much of the profit? The answer is that this was no paper profit. Since the calls expired on that day, every single owner got out at just the right time.

No, there was no hitch. Everyone who bought a January 100 call on Amazon.com on October 9, 1998, and held it to expiration made an enormous profit without assuming any risk other than the possibility of losing the modest cost of 15 per share. And while this Amazon.com example is spectacular, it is by no means unique. Literally thousands of calls have doubled at various times, and many options have tripled and quadrupled. When you buy a call, the risk is limited to the small amount you pay for the option, but the profit, as we have seen, can be almost unlimited.

And now that I have shown you how easy it can be to make your fortune buying calls, I am going to summarize in one sentence the entire lesson of this chapter. It is by far the principal teaching of this entire book: Never, n-e-v-e-r, NEVER, N-E-V-E-R buy a call until you have carefully considered these three points: (1) there is a very good chance that you will lose all or most of your money; (2) there is a very good chance that you will lose all or most of your money; and (3) there is a very good chance that you will lose all or most of your money. Only after you have carefully and thoughtfully enunciated these three points to yourself should you ever buy an option, at any price. It doesn't matter how cheap the option is, or how long it has to run, or how deep in the money it is.

Whenever you buy an option you are engaging in an extreme form of speculation, which is to say you are gambling. If you want to gamble you are welcome to do so, but when you lose your money, remember that you should have known beforehand that it could happen. And if this still isn't enough to cool your ardor for buying options, just take a look at the actual results of option buyers in the past.

Let's look at an objective analysis of what actually would have happened to $100 that was used for buying call options on April 29, 1975, compiled as accurately as possible by Value Line. By August 1977 the amount had fallen to just $2. By December 1, 1977, it had shrunk to under $1. This was a period in which the stock market increased slightly. Interesting, isn't it? While this example is old, I don't think that the results would be very different today. Of course, this doesn't mean that history will repeat itself. Maybe option buyers in the next few years will go on to reap untold riches. But it does kind of make you pause and think, doesn't it?

THE GAMBLE OF BUYING CALLS

Why should you be very reluctant to buy a call? First let me state the obvious, which is that, like the purchasers of the January Amazon.com call described earlier, a certain number of call purchasers are going to have their stocks rise smartly, just as they expected that they would. They will make money, and a few will make a lot of money. But this does not mean that most people will win by buying calls, any more than the fact that at every horse race some people win their bets means that the way to make money is to bet consistently at the track. Or at a casino.

To understand why the consistent buyer of calls could be a loser in the long run, let's analyze just what buying a call means. It means that you are paying a premium for the right to participate in the rise of a stock within a specific period of time. This sentence contains many elements. Perhaps the most damaging is the final one, which limits a call to a specific period of time. Let's discuss just why this can be so adversely important.

Time Limits

You may be convinced that a stock is drastically undervalued, that its position is fundamentally sound, that technically it is ready for a big recovery, that its industry is in for tremendous growth, and that the market in general is about to experience a major upward thrust. You may be right. But before committing yourself to buying a call, ask yourself this question: If you are right, then why isn't the stock selling at a higher price today?

All the factors you mention for its increase in price are known to you today and are influencing you today. Surely, other potential buyers of the stock are also aware of them. And yet the stock is no higher than it was yesterday. So, why do you think that these same factors, which are public knowledge today and are not pushing the price of the stock up, are suddenly going to have a magical effect after you have purchased a call?

You might argue that others don't know how to properly evaluate the information that you have, and once they do, the price of the stock will surely rise. Now you are bringing in another factor, which is that it will take other investors time to appreciate the value of the stock at its present price. Once you concede that it may take some time, how can you possibly be sure that enough people will come to this realization within the life span of the option you are buying? Believe me, there is nothing sadder than to see the price of a stock rise dramatically above the strike price—one week after the option has expired!

So the first reason for not buying an option is that neither you nor anyone else can know that a stock will go up within a relatively short period of time. As a matter of fact, a number of studies have looked into how well professional securities analysts can forecast the rise of stock prices. AT&T conducted a particularly comprehensive survey a few years ago because it invests billions of dollars for its pension funds. If just one analyst or bank pension management team could do even a quarter of a percentage point better than another, it could mean millions of extra dollars for the fund. Many other surveys of less depth have been conducted over the years by economics professors and others. All have reached one conclusion: No one and no group of people, over the long term, has done any better than a purely random selection of stocks.

Unpredictability

Put in graphic terms, this unanimous conclusion of the studies means that, in the long run, all the Phi Beta Kappas, MBAs, and PhDs in economics wearing their expensive pin-striped suits in their elegant offices, with all the information that is available to them from every source including personal interviews with company presidents and reams of computer printouts, do not do one jot better at picking stocks than anyone could do by simply throwing darts at the stock market page of the newspaper.

Therefore, when you truly believe that a certain stock surely is going to go up, and that it will definitely go up within the next three months, remember that either you are the first person in the history of Wall Street who really could tell when a stock would go up (in which case you should be writing a book of your own instead of reading this one) or your feeling of certitude is simply misfounded. Chances are that it is the latter. Therefore, the first thing you must do is face up to your own limitations, and the most obvious one is that you do not know whether a stock will go up and you certainly do not know whether it will go up within the next three months.

Having disposed of your divine power of prophecy, we can proceed to the next argument made in favor of buying calls, which is that even if you can't pick a particular winner, the odds in favor of a call buyer are so great that given enough tries you will come out a winner. The reasoning is that most calls are so cheap and the potential reward so great that you can easily afford a number of losses, because you will more than make up for them on the big winners like Amazon.com.

STATISTICAL SUPPORT FOR OPTIONS BUYERS

There is some statistical support for this position (see Figure 2.3). A simulation of returns obtained from various strategies was conducted for the period July 1963 to December 1975 by Robert C. Merton of the Massachusetts Institute of Technology, Myron S. Scholes of the University of Chicago, and Mathew L. Gladstein of Donaldson, Lufkin & Jenrette Securities Corporation. During that period $1,000 invested in the Dow Jones Industrial Average would have grown to $2,226, and $1,000 invested in the 136 stocks that had exchange-listed options in December 1975 would have grown to $5,043, including reinvestment of all dividends. A strategy of investing 90% of the portfolio in commercial paper and the remaining 10% in the purchase of options produced significantly better results. By buying on-the-money options with this strategy, $1,000 using the Dow Jones stocks would have grown to $3,138 and using the original 136 optionable stocks $1,000 would have grown to $6,372. What was surprising about the study was that as the exercise price of the options purchased was increased, so that only options that were out of the money were purchased, the results were even better. When options 10% out of the money were purchased, the result on the 136 stocks was $11,178, and when options 20% out of the money were purchased, the result was a phenomenal $25,670!

The reason for these results was not that a profit was made on most of the options, and in fact a very large percentage of them were losers. Rather, the profit came from the relatively few options that were extremely profitable due to abnormally large increases in the price of the underlying stocks. This study indicated that by purchasing out-of-the-money options one could take advantage of these aberrational moves in stock prices and capture a large-percentage profit on the options.

A number of qualifications must be made. First, 90% of the money was kept in safe, short-term, interest-earning notes. Second, the period started with a long bull market. Third, it would be difficult for most investors to obtain the diversification necessary to get these results. Finally, it may take many years for the bull market situation to be duplicated. Certainly, if there is an unusually flat market, the results of

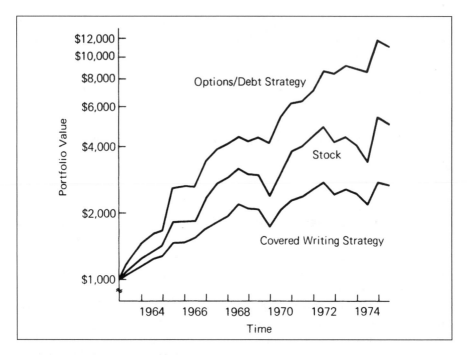

FIGURE 2.3 Results of a Simulation Study into Various Investment Strategies
The stock strategy was an equal dollar allocation to each of the 136 optioned stocks
at that time with all dividends reinvested. The covered writing strategy consisted of
continuously writing six-month calls that were 10% out of the money and rewriting
upon expiration. The options/debt strategy consisted of investing 90% of the money
in high-quality certificates of deposit and using the remaining 10% to purchase calls
that were 10% out of the money. No taxes or transaction costs were deducted.
Source: "A Simulation of Returns and Risk of Alternative Option Portfolio Investment
Strategies," R. C. Merton, et al. in the *Journal of Business* (April 1978). Reprinted by
permission of the University of Chicago Press.

this study would not be duplicated, because while stocks would remain
stable and the portfolio would increase from the interest yield, most of
the options that had been purchased would expire worthless, resulting
in a constant decline. Nevertheless, it is good to know that option buying, if done under the proper circumstances, has statistical support.

Breaking Even

It may be true that each call is not expensive, but one still must ask
what has to happen for a call buyer to make money. Let's take a simplified example in which the price of the stock happens to be exactly at

the strike price. What has to happen is that the price of the stock must move up enough to cover the premium plus the cost of the commission paid buying the call, plus the commission incurred in selling the call.

If a stock is selling at 25 with a strike price of 25, an option with a six-month duration might typically be selling at $2^{1}/_{2}$. In other words, for the buyer of the call to just break even, the price of the underlying stock must move up to about $27^{3}/_{4}$: It must move up to $27^{1}/_{2}$ just to cover the cost of the call, and up another $^{1}/_{4}$ point to cover the commissions on buying and selling, which will total approximately $^{1}/_{8}$ point each way if you bought three calls. Well, you might think, that doesn't seem so hard. After all, stocks frequently move up a point in one day in a good market, so why shouldn't this stock move up more than three points, which is only one point a month. Surely, that can't be very difficult.

Let's analyze that. In the first place, the trend of the stock market over about 50 years has been dissected, analyzed, and described about as much as anything else in the world. The conclusion is that over the long haul, which has included some pretty wild bull markets, the average annual increase in stock value, including dividends that were constantly reinvested, has been just over 8%. Now, note that this includes the reinvestment of dividends. If we assume that dividends have averaged only about 3% per year, this leaves us with an annual appreciation in the price of the stock of 5% a year.

But in trying to demonstrate the falsity of the call buyer's thinking let us take the facts most favorable to his case, as lawyers do when they are requesting a judge to grant them a summary judgment. So we will accept 8% as the average increase of all stocks over all the years. Although the past cannot predict the future, it is the only guide we have, so in the following discussion I will assume that the past growth rate will continue over a long period of time.

Returning now to our call buyer, his stock must rise from 25 to $27^{3}/_{4}$ in order to break even. This works out to an increase of exactly 11%. But the average increase of 8% is less than that. So from the start, the odds are stacked against the call buyer. Remember that with this required 11% increase the call buyer still wouldn't make a single dime. He has risked his money, the stock has gone up more in six months than the average stock does in an entire year, and he still hasn't made a thing.

Doubling Investment

Let us say that the call buyer expects to double his money. To do this, the call buyer in our example must net $2^{1}/_{2}$, so that he must sell his call for $5^{1}/_{4}$ to regain his original investment of $2^{1}/_{2}$ plus his profit plus the commissions of approximately $^{1}/_{4}$ point. Thus, the stock must rise to $30^{1}/_{4}$, an increase of 21%. Is it realistic to expect that a stock is going to shoot up by this amount? By a percentage that is well over twice what the average stock has actually gone up throughout recent history in an entire year?

By now you may be inclined to believe that buying a call is not such a sure thing. And remember the downside risk. Should the buyer be wrong and the stock stay right at 25, he will lose his entire investment! And if it goes down he will, of course, also lose his entire investment, but it will happen more quickly. In any event, from a purely mathematical viewpoint, there is an approximately 50% chance that the stock will either stay where it is or go down, and the call buyer will lose everything. And that is a pretty substantial loss to suffer in just six months. By way of comparison, it's pretty hard to think of many stocks that have done that in six months.

HOW TO END UP BROKE

One thing is pretty certain. If you continue to buy options with all your money, you are eventually going to end up broke. This is true regardless of any survey showing that option buyers end up making more money than others. The reason for this is simply a result of the highly volatile nature of options.

Let's assume that a solid, long-term bull market comes along, and you are buying three-month options. You triple your money in the first three months. You reinvest this in more options, and that investment also triples, so that now you have nine times your original investment. You reinvest this in more options, and this time they double. Now you have 18 times your original amount. You reinvest and the bull market goes on.

But this time, there is a brief lull in the upward rise in prices, as there is in every bull market. The stocks in which you have bought options fall back, but only slightly. Just enough to be below the strike prices of all your options on their expiration dates.

How much money do you have now? Back to only nine times what you started with? Just three times? Or just the small amount you originally had? No. You have absolutely nothing. And this is the insidious aspect of buying options. Because no matter how much money you speculate with in buying options, 100% of the money is at risk, able to be totally wiped out in a single option expiration period. And, furthermore, it can be said with almost absolute assurance that if you play the options game long enough in this manner, you will lose every penny you have invested in call options at that time.

This is the reason why all studies of option buying limit the amount of exposure so carefully to a given percentage of a person's total assets. By limiting your exposure, you will lose only that small percentage of your assets when the nearly inevitable shakeout in options takes place.

CALLS VERSUS STOCKS

One argument often cited in favor of buying calls is that doing so limits your risk in case of a downward slide by the stock. The argument is that by purchasing a call on 100 shares for, let us say, $5 per share, you are capturing the same upward potential as the person who buys the shares for $50 each. Since your total outlay is $500, whereas the stock buyer's is $5,000, the conclusion is that you are smart, because your total risk is only $500 while he is risking 10 times as much. Although this argument is true, it is also a deceptive method of comparing a stock purchase with a call purchase.

It is deceptive because you have not bought the same potential capital gains with your $500 worth of calls as the other person did with his $5,000 worth of stocks. If this were really the case, why would anyone buy stock at all? Can it be that everyone who buys stock is really a sucker paying 10 times as much as he could if he only knew the "secret" of calls?

There are some pretty savvy people making their livings on Wall Street, and they have more money invested in common stocks than in calls. Many of these professionals know more about puts and calls than you will ever know. Sure, they could all be wrong to prefer stocks, but it does kind of plant the seed of doubt in your mind, doesn't it?

Why do I say you don't get the same profit from calls as from stocks? For two very good reasons. The first is the premium. It's easy to overlook the premium because it's not very large in relation to the price of the stock, but it usually is very large in comparison to the actual gains made by the stock. If you are paying a premium that is 10% of the stock price for your call at the money strike price, and during its term the price of the stock goes up 10%, you have made nothing, while the owners of the stock have made nice 10% gains. Not bad for them, especially if they do it in only three months. But not good for you.

Furthermore, if the stock is purchased on margin of 50%, then a gain of 10% in the price of the stock is a gain of 20% on the investment, which looks good compared to the 0% on the call. But what if the price of the stock goes up by only 5%? The person who bought the stock has made a 5% gain. You, on the other hand, have suffered an enormous loss, equal to 50% of your investment! Now what were you saying about having the same right to participate in gains as if you had bought the stock?

The second reason why the purchase of a call is not equal to the purchase of stock is that the call buyer has only a limited time in which to make his gains. Let us take three months for an example. If the stock doesn't go up in three months, the call buyer has lost his entire investment.

He now has a choice. He can shrug his shoulders and walk away, having lost all the money he put up, or he can try to recoup it by buying another three-month call on the same stock. The temptation is very strong to try to recoup. Let us assume that he does purchase another call. Now his investment in premiums is 20% of the value of the stock.

Mathematically, there is no more chance that the stock will rise during the second period than there was that it would go up in the previous period. There certainly is no greater chance that it will go up more than before, and yet unless it leaps up by 20% the investor will be losing money. The call purchaser who does this for a whole year will have paid a premium of 40% by the final quarter and still will have only a call that is good for three months. Is there much chance that any stock will go up 40% in three months?

The purchasers of the stock, in contrast, have the perpetual right to enjoy its possible appreciation without putting up a single extra penny. It costs nothing to wait two, three, or more years for a stock to go up. And while waiting, instead of paying ruinously high premiums of up to 40% a year, they may be collecting handsome dividends that compensate them for their cash investment in the stock.

For these two reasons—premium cost and time limit—it is clear that buying a call on a stock does not give the same chance to benefit from a stock's appreciation as does buying the stock itself. Rather, the two are investments of different kinds. Both involve the same stock, but they are still completely different investments, just as renting a house for five years is quite different from owning it for five years, even though in both cases you can live in it for five years.

A Practical Comparison

To be meaningful, a comparison of one investment to another should compare investments of equal amounts. Thus, to determine whether a call really is a better risk against a downward stock price movement than is the stock, one should compare an investment of $1,000 in the stock with an investment of $1,000 in calls on the stock. (See Figure 2.4.) Now, comparing the two investments on an equal basis, it is obvious that buying a call is no protection against downside risk at all. In fact, it is exactly the opposite, because the owner of the call will lose 100% of the money invested if the stock goes down and will even lose everything if the stock stays right where it is! The owner of the stock, on the other hand, will still have his original purchase and is sitting pretty waiting for the move up in the next quarter.

So, when someone says that buying a call instead of a stock is a good way to hedge against a downward movement of the stock, I reply that buying a call is only a good way of protecting yourself from a price decline if you consider losing 100% of your investment a good

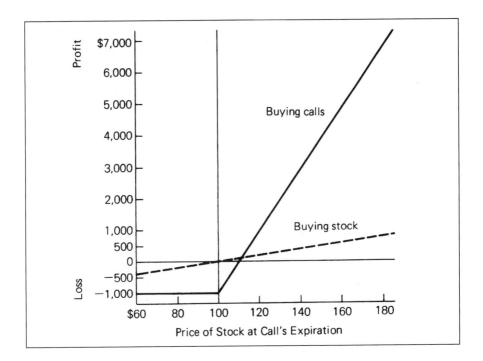

FIGURE 2.4 The Advantage of Buying Calls instead of Stock

Results of investing $1,000 in calls compared to an equal investment in stock (price of stock when purchased: $100; premium of 100 strike price calls: $10)

Chart shows the remarkable leverage calls provide, so that every $1 increase in the price of the stock above $110 provides an additional $100 profit, as opposed to only $10 for the stock ($1 for each of the 10 shares purchased). But note that if the stock is anywhere between $0 and $111, which is the most likely area, the stock buyer comes out ahead.

protection. As for me, I would rather protect my investment by retaining a good portion of it as the owner of stock—or retain a bigger portion of it by keeping the stock and the premium that I receive by selling calls on it.

Liquidity and Risk

Another argument that is made in favor of buying calls is that you can have the excitement of making a fortune from a small premium, while protecting yourself on the downside by selling out if the call should go down. Yes, you could cover yourself by selling out your position, but in my opinion this really doesn't help the buyer of a call very much. Here's why.

Let's say you pay 10 for a three-month call with a 100 strike price when the stock is at 100. Three weeks after you buy the call, the stock drops to 92 and your option is worth 5. Of course you can now sell your option and receive 5, thus limiting your loss to only 5. But you would be giving up a chance to make a large profit if the stock goes up over $100 in the next two months.

If you thought that the stock was worth more when it was selling for $100, you may think that it is worth a lot more now that it is only $92. It seems to me that you might as well hold on and hope that the price will go back up. You paid for a three-month call and you might as well get its benefit for the full duration.

Furthermore, when you bought the call for 10 you thought it was a reasonable price, one that merited your buying it rather than selling it. Now that it has declined by half to only 5, it certainly doesn't seem like a good price at which to sell it. It has been my experience as an options professional handling many option trades that, for these reasons, almost no one ever sells an option when it has gone down in price, and I'm not sure that one should try to break such a strong pattern. But if you have the discipline it may be a good idea.

RULES OF STRATEGY

But no matter what is written here, there will be some traders who will continue to buy calls as the easy way to get rich. Lured on by the apparent low cost and the potential ease with which their money could double, they will bravely ignore any odds against them. If you are one of these people, then at least give yourself as good a chance as possible. There are methods by which you can make certain you get the best odds possible. And you may very well end up making money. If there is a sustained strong bull market and you adhere to the following strategies, you probably will. Follow these rules of strategy and you will maximize your chances of making money by buying calls.

Strategy Rule Number 1: Never Buy a Call When Its Strike Price Is More Than a Few Points above the Stock Price

It is the consensus that only about 40% of the old *over-the-counter* (*OTC*) calls were ever exercised. Their strike prices were usually identical with or very close to the price of the stock. Now, if you add the burden of requiring the stock to go up substantially before it can even get beyond the point of complete worthlessness (that is, beyond the strike price), you have just decreased your probability of making money on the call.

The savings in the premium of the call are often not proportional to the increasing difficulty of the feat that your stock must perform during the limited life of the call. We can measure this by analyzing the premiums and chances of making money on a stock that has calls outstanding with different strike prices.

Let's take an actual example of a volatile stock that had four regular strike prices available (Table 2.1). The price of the stock was $49\frac{1}{2}$ and the intermediate-duration options had just four months to go and were selling at the following prices:

TABLE 2.1 Option Premiums at Different Strike Prices

Strike Price	Option Premium
50	$4\frac{5}{8}$
55	$2\frac{9}{16}$
60	$1\frac{1}{4}$
70	$\frac{3}{8}$

To the novice the calls with the highest strike price of 70 might seem like real bargains. Imagine being able to buy calls on 1,000 shares of a really volatile stock for only $375. Or for a little fun, just buy one option for $37.50 If the stock goes up to 71 you will more than double your money. And if it goes up to 74 you have multiplied your cost by 10! This could become another bonanza just like the one described in the beginning of this chapter.

Let's examine all the possibilities if the stock goes to various prices in increments of 5 on the call's expiration. Assume that a person spends up to $4,630 on options, which means that he could purchase 10 of the 50 calls, 18 of the 55s, 37 of the 60s, or 123 of the 70 calls. (See Table 2.2.) Ignoring commissions for the sake of simplification, here's what happens.

TABLE 2.2 Profit (or Loss) from $4,630 Worth of Calls

Price of Stock at Expiration	Strike Price 50	Strike Price 55	Strike Price 60	Strike Price 70
$50 or under	($4,630)	($4,630)	($4,630)	($4,630)
55	370	(4,630)	(4,630)	(4,630)
60	5,370	4,420	(4,630)	(4,630)
65	10,370	13,470	13,870	(4,630)
70	15,370	22,520	32,370	(4,630)
75	20,370	31,570	50,870	56,870
80	25,370	40,620	69,370	118,379

Now let's analyze these figures. Yes, they do show that if the stock goes up to 75 or higher, the purchaser of the 70 option is the biggest winner. But what are the chances of this happening? To start with, there is a 50% chance that the stock will go down rather than up or that after four months the stock will be just about where it was when the options were purchased, that is, just around 50. Even if it moves up, how many times does a stock move up 50% in price in four months? Even though it happens more often to stock prices than the statistical model of random distribution would suggest, it is still very infrequently. If you would like to know just how infrequent this is, just try to remember the last time you owned a stock that went up 50% in four months. Or better still, look through a chart book and write down the number of stocks that have done this. Except for the Internet stocks in 1997–1999, you will find very few such stocks.

In the 50% of the cases in which the stock ends up at 50 or lower, the purchasers of all the calls will lose all their money. But the purchaser of the 50 call will lose $1,000 less for every point rise in the price of the stock above 50, and when the stock reaches 55 he will actually have a modest profit of $370. But at 55 all the other call purchasers will still have a 100% loss.

If the stock really does well and gets up to 60, we have a different situation. Now the purchaser of the 50 option has a very nice profit of $5,370 for well over a 100% profit on his cost, and the buyer of the 55 option has a profit of $4,420 for almost a 100% profit, but the other two option buyers still have a complete loss. Even though the stock is up a solid 20% in four months, the stock might as well have gone down to 35 as far as they are concerned.

If the stock should do exceptionally well and get up to 65, we would find that the purchaser of the 50 option is making a profit of $10,370, the purchaser of the 55 option is making a profit of $13,470, and for the first time even the purchaser of the 60 option is making a significant gain of $13,870. But whoever purchased the 70 option still has a complete loss.

Right Stock, Wrong Option. Sad but true. Even though the purchaser of the 70 option was right in thinking that the stock would have an outstanding rise in four months, he still loses every dime he invested. Just imagine the dismay, disappointment, and perhaps disgust and bitterness when he realizes that as smart as he was in correctly predicting a very rapid upswing for the stock, as far as the effect on the dollar-and-cents return on his investment went, it might just as well have gone down 15 points. In short, he picked the right stock but destroyed himself by picking the wrong strike price.

If the stock should have a truly amazing rally and get all the way up to 70, then the purchasers of the 50, 55, and 60 options will really be in the chips. The 50 option will be producing a profit of $15,370, the 55 will produce a profit of $22,520, and the 60 option will produce a whopping profit of $32,370 on that initial cost of $4,630. Everyone will be cheering. Everyone, that is, except for the buyer of the 70 option.

With the stock at 70, he has correctly picked out what would be one of the outstanding winners in the stock market. Stocks that go up by 40% in four months don't come along very often. So the call purchaser can pat himself on the back as having picked the stock that probably is on everyone's lips as an outstanding performer. He can look at himself in the mirror when he gets up the morning and say that he sees the face of a pretty savvy guy, and he can tell all his friends at the club when the conversation turns to stocks that he not only thought four months ago that the stock was in for a good rise, but that he had the guts to put his money where his mouth was and that he actually bought calls on it. Yes, he'll be the envy of them all, and he can be pretty proud of himself.

The only thing he can't do is to spend the profits he made from being right. Because, you see, he lost 100% of his cost. So how smart was he after all?

I can hear people now saying that my example isn't really relevant because everyone knows that a call with a strike price 40% out of the money is a way-out investment, and that the smart investor puts only a little money in that kind of a call. It's sort of a lark: You put up some money that you can easily afford to lose and you forget about it until just before the expiration period. If the stock doesn't really go up, you lose your money. But so what? You knew in advance that you probably would, and that's why you invested only a small amount.

A Little of a Bad Thing. On the other hand, if the stock should surprise everyone and go over the strike price, wow! You get a free paid vacation or whatever else you want with your unexpected but very welcome bonanza. This no doubt describes the psychology of a person who buys such a call. It could be called the lottery syndrome. But it in no way changes the odds or makes it a better investment. What such a person is really saying is that he knows it's a risky investment and that's why he invested only a little in it. Here's my tip on how to improve that investment strategy: If you know that you are so unlikely to make a profit, then why not invest *very* little in it—specifically, nothing. A little of a bad thing is not necessarily a good thing.

Especially now, when option premiums are so much less than they used to be, there seems to be no need to reach for the far-out-of-the-money options, when anyone can afford to buy just slightly out-of-the-money options that will make a profit even if the stock goes up just a little bit.

This may seem to contradict the conclusion of the study by Merton, Scholes, and Gladstein referred to earlier in the chapter. There are, however, two important differences between the study and the typical investor. First, the study assumes an almost infinite diversification, that is, buying options on every one of the optionable stocks, so if any one goes up by 50%, you own it. Obviously this is not the case for most investors, and so, to make up for this lack of diversity it is my conclusion that it is necessary to own options that will make money from smaller price increases. And second, the study was based on a period that had great bull markets and times of tremendous volatility, two conditions that are not always going to be present in the stock market.

To summarize, it is hard enough to make money on a call, even when you buy a call with a strike price just about where the stock is. Historically there is almost a 50% chance that the stock you select will go down rather than up, and another 10% chance that it will remain so close to the strike price that you will barely cover the expenses of buying an on-the-money option. Thus, when the stock starts out at the strike price, the odds are 60 to 40 against you that you will make a profit on your cost. For every point that you require

the stock to climb before you can begin to recoup part of your investment, you are making the odds against you just that much worse.

The only advantage of a higher strike price is that the calls are
cheaper, but as the example in this section shows, that is a tricky
economy indeed. Since they are cheaper, you can make a higher-per-
centage profit if the stock exceeds that strike price than someone who
bought the lower strike price calls. But, in my opinion, the profit on a
successful call with a low strike price is high enough without making
it any more risky. Thus, Strategy Rule Number 1 is don't buy a call
when its strike price is significantly higher than the stock.

Strategy Rule Number 2: Never Buy a Call When Its Strike Price Is Significantly Lower Than the Stock Price

When you do buy a deep-in-the-money call you are giving a free insurance policy to the seller of the call, which can cost you heavily but
will help you only very little.

To illustrate this rule and the reasoning behind it, let's take another actual example. A stock was $24^3/_4$ and had options with about
seven weeks left before expiration with strike prices at 15, 20, and
25. The premiums were $10^3/_8$ for the 15 strike price call, $5^3/_4$ for the
20, and $1^{15}/_{16}$ for the 25. If you purchased calls worth $1,038, you
would get 100 of the 15 strike price, 180 of the 20, and 534 of the 25.

Let's see what happens to the purchaser of these calls on their
expiration date when the stock is at various prices, again ignoring
commissions for the sake of simplification. (See Table 2.3 and Figure 2.5.)

TABLE 2.3 Profit (or Loss) on Calls Purchased for $1,037

Price of Stock at Expiration	Strike Price 15	Strike Price 20	Strike Price 25
$15 or under	$(1,037)	$(1,037)	$(1,037)
20	(537)	(1,037)	(1,037)
25	(37)	(137)	(1,037)
27	163	223	31
28	263	403	565
29	363	540	1,099
31	563	900	2,167
33	769	1,260	3,235

If we were to carry the table and the figure out further, the 25 strike price call would continue to outgain the other two calls by an increasingly wide margin.

What this table and figure show is that if the stock moves up more than 3 points from its present level, the purchaser of the call with the strike price nearest the current level of the stock is going to be the winner. The more the stock moves up over 3 points, the more he is going to be ahead of the other calls.

Note that only in the over 20 and under 27 range is the 25 call really behind the other calls. Once the stock price falls below 20, all the calls, including the 15 strike price, are heavy losers. My conclusion would be to buy the 25 call, because if you don't expect the stock to move up at least 3 then you should not be buying the call in the first place.

The reason for the large difference in potential profit is clear. The purchaser of the call at the 25 strike price is paying strictly for the future time value of the option itself. You might say that he is buying a pure call. The purchasers of the calls at the other strike prices are buying an option—the right to gain if the price of the stock goes up—but they are paying a large portion of their money for the purchase of an interest in the current value of the stock (i.e., current cash value or *intrinsic value*). And this is what makes their calls so expensive and gives them so little upside profit potential.

Let me explain. Since the price of the stock is already at $24^3/_4$, a call with a 20 strike price is worth $4^3/_4$ if it is exercised today. And of course it could be exercised today, because a call can be exercised at any time until the expiration date. Therefore, the premium includes not only an option to profit by future gain on the price of the stock, but $4^3/_4$ to pay for the present value of the option due to the current price of the stock.

The premium for the 20 strike price call is $5^3/_4$, and of this $4^3/_4$ represents the stock's present value. Therefore, only $1 actually goes to buy the "pure option" part of the call. What benefit is the purchaser receiving from the other $4^3/_4$? The answer is clear. Absolutely nothing in terms of options. In effect, he is paying out money to buy that portion of the stock that is above the strike price. This greatly reduces his leverage, which of course is at cross-purposes with the very reason for purchasing calls at all. The only advantage is that the call with the lower strike price has a lower cost for the "pure option" part of the premium. That is, the 25 call costs $1^{15}/_{16}$, but the "pure option" part of the 20 call costs $5^3/_4$ (premium) minus $4^3/_4$ (present value of option), or just 1, which is about as much as the 25 call. But should the price of the stock go down, that lower cost is quickly transformed into a much larger loss per share.

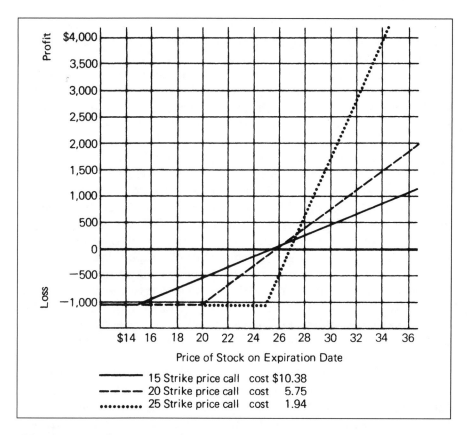

FIGURE 2.5 In-the-Money Options
Profit or loss on buying calls with different strike prices (price of stock when calls were purchased: 24³/₄
This chart illustrates that calls with strike prices substantially below the current price of the stock will not provide as good a profit to the call buyer as those with higher strike prices. See Strategy Rule Number 2.

These factors can be seen in even more extreme form in the case of the 15 strike call. With the stock at 24³/₄ and the strike price at 15, the difference between them is 9³/₄, which is the value of the option. Since the total premium is 10³/₈, the "pure option" part of the premium is 10³/₈ minus 9³/₄, or ⁵/₈, versus 1 for the 20 strike price call and 1¹⁵/₁₆ for the 25. This lower cost for the "pure option" is the only reason for buying the 15 strike price call.

If the stock goes up, that portion of the premium that pays for the present stock value will not increase. There is absolutely no leverage in the portion of the option representing the existing value of a stock.

On the other hand, if the stock goes down, the call buyer loses a large portion or even all of the money that he had to pay for the present value of the stock.

Thus, his gain is sharply limited by the fact that the calls are so expensive. For a given amount of money he can buy only a relatively small number of calls, thus greatly reducing his chance to make a large amount of money on the upside. Also, since he has paid so much to offset the fact that the stock was already above the strike price when he bought it, he stands to lose a great deal. This disadvantage of the lower strike price call can be better illustrated by Table 2.4, showing the effects of varying prices of the stock upon 100 calls of the 15 strike price, costing $1,038, versus 300 of the 25, costing $581. I am doing this to show that even the one supposed advantage of buying a call with a low strike price, namely that you will lose less if the price stays where it is or goes down, is largely unfounded.

The better way to accomplish this objective of minimizing loss is simply to buy fewer calls at a strike price closer to the current price of the stock, as this table clearly shows. And to maximize gain, for every additional dollar that the stock climbs in price, the purchaser of the 15 call makes an additional $100, while the purchaser of the 25 call makes an additional $300.

I hope this makes clear that the purchaser of the call with the low strike price is a real loser. Looking at the table, we can see that if the stock falls below 20, the buyer of the 15 call loses more money than the 25, until at 15 or under he has lost twice as much. Furthermore, on the upside, the purchaser of the 15 call doesn't do as well once the stock gets up to 28, which isn't an impossible gain from its current $24^3/_4$. And over 28 the difference is quite marked, with the 25 call outgaining the other by three to one.

TABLE 2.4 Effect of Stock Price

| | Profit (or Loss) on Calls | |
Price of Stock at Expiration	100 Calls at 15 Strike Price	300 Calls at 25 Strike Price
$15 or under	$(1,038)	$(581)
20	(538)	(581)
25	(378)	(581)
27	163	19
28	263	300
29	363	600
30	463	900

Only when the stock is between 20 and about 28 does the 15 strike price call come out ahead, and even in this range the difference is not usually very much. At 21, for example, the 15 call loses $437 versus $581 for the 25. And the fact that the purchaser of the 25 call in this example is risking a total of only $581 as opposed to the $1,038 risked by the purchaser of the 15 call is another important factor favoring the 25.

In summary, the reason for Strategy Rule Number 2 of never buying a call when the strike price is far below the price of the stock is that you really get stuck when the price of the stock goes down. Even when the price of the stock goes up, you have paid so much for each call that your leverage and profit potential are severely limited. Considering the risk that you will lose all or a large part of your investment, there just isn't enough upward leverage to make it an attractive speculation.

Strategy Rule Number 3: Before Buying a Call, Carefully Compare All Durations for the Most Favorable One

This seems like an easy thing to do, indeed an obvious one, but oddly enough it is one to which very few call buyers seem to pay any attention.

If you will compare the trading volume of the various expirations of a call, you will invariably find that the highest volume is in the current (shortest-term) call. This is usually true right up to the end of the current call's duration. The reason for this is, I believe, that the short-term call is faster and more exciting. It is also a great deal cheaper, and thus has much more leverage. If the call has only a very short term left, and the stock is above the strike price, then its entire premium reflects the current value of the option. Then a change of 1 point upward in the price of the stock will result in a full point upward rise in the price of the call. If the stock is selling below the strike price, the premium will be very cheap, so that a rise in the stock's price of just a few points would cause an enormous percentage increase in the price of the call.

Yes, there is a lot of action in short-term calls, but the purpose of this book is not to advise the reader how to get a lot of action, or how to gain thrills and excitement from puts and calls. We assume that that is not the purpose for which a person invests in stock options. If anyone wants excitement, there are many commercial gambling games that provide more action than stock options, not to mention other legitimate investments such as commodities, for example. We are assuming that the reader is interested in making money. And making money is often not synonymous with excitement.

In addition to the fast pace, one might be tempted to buy a short-term call because one is pretty certain the stock will move up a few points within the next few days or weeks, but is not at all certain what it is going to do over the next few months.

There may be many reasons for this belief. Perhaps an investor's reading of certain technical indicators has shown him that the stock is ready to break through a resistance level. Perhaps he believes that a certain industry is about to experience higher profits than had been anticipated. Perhaps he senses a trend in the market that will soon transfer itself to this stock.

In any event, it is quite common for a person to feel certain that a stock will move up perhaps 5 points within the next few weeks, and therefore to be interested only in a call that will cover the next few weeks. Why pay more money for a longer-term call than one needs?

The answer is one that unfortunately is apt to be demoralizing and ego shattering and therefore not listened to. But I present it anyway, for those who have the detachment to profit by it. The reason for not looking solely at the short-term option is that neither you nor anyone else can be certain of correctly predicting what a stock will do within the next few weeks or days.

The reason is that the short-term trend of a stock depends on almost everything except the fundamentals. The fundamentals of a company, industry, or the market as a whole don't normally change very much, if at all, within a period of weeks. There might be a company interim earnings report, but it would be the height of foolishness to think that you can be more accurate in predicting what it will report than the many Wall Street professionals who follow the stock.

You may in fact turn out to be more accurate than they were, but this I submit is due not to your really being any better able to predict the earnings than others are, but simply to your good luck. If you don't believe me, just keep track of how accurate you are over a period of time with various stocks.

Rather than fundamentals, the short-term fluctuations of stocks are caused by the feelings of the investor community, and these feelings are a mixture of thousands or millions of different inputs, ranging from the price of wheat on the Chicago Board of Trade to the current interbank interest rate in Zurich, to the spot price of crude oil in Libya, to the health of the United States president, to the latest figures on the number of new housing construction starts, to the value of the euro currency in the world market, to the number of automobiles produced in Detroit last week, to this morning's statement on taxes by the House Ways and Means Committee chairman, and so forth indefinitely.

If you will consider it, I think you will agree that no one can correctly predict what the investment community will be thinking in four weeks, because no one can predict what all these inputs will be in four weeks. And even if you could do this in a general way, how in the world could you translate this general mood into what the investment community will be thinking about a particular stock?

If the investment community believes that a stock is worth $55 today on the basis of everything that is known about the stock at this moment, this price evaluation includes the community's assessment of what is likely to happen within the next few weeks to change that evaluation. So, if you believe you can predict the future price of a stock, you must believe that you have greater knowledge than the investment community or that you have superior methods for evaluating that knowledge. But the probability is that you, like everyone else, have neither. If you had either one, you would not be reading this book. Instead you would be quite wealthy from all the money you would have made in the past from your short-term trading of common stocks. Look back over your past transactions. Were you always right in the past? If not, then what makes you think that you are going to be right this time? My point here is not that anyone is always going to be wrong, but that you cannot be sure that this time you are going to be correct about the short-term movements of any one stock.

Now that we have concluded that you will not necessarily be correct in predicting the short-term movement of a stock, we can go to the next step. There are two ways in which you could be wrong in your belief that the price of a given stock will go up within the next few weeks. The first is that it might not go up at all. The second is that it might indeed go up, but not within the time you had anticipated; it does so after your option has expired.

Let's see what you can do to select calls that will reduce your risk of loss. If you are wrong in the first way mentioned and the stock goes down, then there is no method of buying a call that is going to eliminate a loss. If, however, you are wrong in the second way, so that the price of the stock goes up later than you thought, you can protect yourself by buying an option for a term longer than you believe you need.

Now let us look at the rights that a call confers in a different light—namely, that a call has value because for a certain amount of time you can profit by any increase in the price of a stock. Therefore, one of the most important factors in determining the value of a call from your viewpoint is this: How much is it costing me to have this privilege for a given length of time? In other words, what does it cost me per week to have the privilege of making money from this stock?

Therefore, before buying any call you should compute the cost of the different expiration date options available on a cost-per-week basis.

You will find that the most popular call, which is usually the shortest-term call, is also usually the most expensive on a per-week basis.

Let's take an actual example. The prices given here were closing prices on a Friday five weeks before the expiration of the October calls. In this illustration the stock closed at $25^1/_4$ with a strike price of 25, so that the premium represents almost the pure option value of the call. The October call was $1^3/_4$, the January call was $3^1/_2$, and the April call was $4^1/_8$. This comes out to a per-week cost of $0.35 for the October call, $0.19^1/_2$ for the January call, and $0.13 for the April call. In other words, the person who bought the shortest-term call was paying twice as much per week as the purchaser of the January call, and three times as much per week as the purchaser of the April call, for the privilege of making money on a rise in the price of the stock. To put the figures another way, the market evaluated a call for the first five weeks of the option at $1.75, but the final entire quarter consisting of 13 weeks cost only $0.62^1/_2$. Yet statistically the chances of a price rise in the final quarter are just as great as the chances of a price rise in the first. Thus this exercise should lead one to purchase the longest-term option in order to get the lowest cost per week.

The shortest term is not always the most expensive. Sometimes the investment community apparently thinks that the chances for a near-term rise in a stock are small, while the probability of a rise over a period of a few months is greater. This is particularly common for far-out-of-the-money options. In this case it might be prudent to buy the shortest call.

As a general rule, the various options are most nearly equal in cost per week during the beginning of a quarter. At this time the current option has about half as long a term as the following one, and premiums usually have a ratio close to 1 to 2. As the current option period comes to an end, its future life rapidly decreases, whereas the next option period still has a full 13 weeks, plus whatever is left in the current period.

When there is just one week left in the current option, the next-period calls have a life span 14 times as long as the current calls, but it is very rare to find such a disparity in the premiums. The result is that as the current period draws to its close, the current calls are greatly overpriced on a per-day basis. You'll be wise to pass them by and invest in the better per-day bargain.

Carrying this logic to its extreme, be sure to consider the LEAPS (long-term equity anticipation securities) that are available. They may have the lowest cost per week of all. In fact, one of the most successful options buyers I know based his entire strategy on purchasing LEAPS. His theory was that they last for such a long time that if you trade out of them in a year or so, there is only a very small loss of future time value, and this makes it possible to produce a profit from being long on these options. He traded LEAPS just as many people would trade stocks—buying on dips and then selling when the price of the LEAPS had risen to about five times what he bought it for. He had limitations on what percentage of the stock's price he was willing to pay for the LEAPS.

Because he was trading LEAPS instead of stocks, he averaged a beta of about three times that of the stock market. For a period of four years from 1996 through 1998 he made a profit each year of about 90%. His original stake of $700,000 became something like $7 million. Of course, those were years when the stock market did quite well. Nevertheless, this is one of the very few cases I know of where a person was able to make money on a consistent basis by buying calls, and he did it with LEAPS.

Strategy Rule Number 3 for buying a call is to carefully compute the cost of the call per week or day, and compare it with all the other calls available in that stock at the strike price you select. Then carefully evaluate the results in making your final selection. Generally it will pay you to pick the longer-term option.

Strategy Rule Number 4: Annualize the Premium in Order to Appreciate the Cost You Are Paying for the Call

By annualizing the premium I mean simply to multiply it by the proper amount so that you can determine the premium you would be paying if you were to buy a one-year call at the same rate per day or week.

For example, if there are seven weeks left in the life of a call and you are paying $2^1/_{16}$ for it, then the annualized cost of the call would be determined as follows: Divide the number of weeks in the year by the number of weeks left in the life of the option—52 divided by 7 is 7.4. Multiplying the premium of $2^1/_{16}$ by 7.4 we obtain an annualized premium of 15.26. This is the amount your premium would be if you were to buy a 12-month option at the same rate per week as you are now paying.

To utilize this figure more fully, compute it as a percentage of the underlying stock. The figure $2^1/_{16}$ used in the example actually came from the premium for a strike price of 50 call when the stock was selling at $48^1/_4$. Doing the arithmetic, we find that the annualized premium of 15.26 comes out to be 31% of the price of the stock. What is the significance of this to a person who is planning to pay only $206 ($2^1/_{16}$ times 100 shares) for a call? The answer is that if we accept the premise stated earlier in this chapter that it is impossible to know just when a stock will go up, then we face the possibility that it might be necessary to buy another call if the first expires without being profitable. This could be repeated. It then becomes important to know the amount we are paying per unit of time—the rate.

The most meaningful rate is the annual one, because investors are accustomed to determining stock gains on an annual basis. If you don't think that the stock will go up by the amount of the annualized premium in the course of the next year, then think twice before buying the call.

Of course it is true that the stock has to go up only $3^{13}/_{16}$ points (the $2^1/_{16}$ you paid for the call plus $1^3/_4$ to the strike price) for you to get back the entire amount of your investment, and that seems like a relatively minor amount of gain. But, you must realize that you are expecting this to happen in just seven weeks. While the chances of this happening are greater than the chances that the stock will go up 15.26 points during the year, just keep in mind that on a per-day basis this is exactly what you are expecting.

Mathematically, if the stock went up $3^5/_{16}$ every seven weeks, it would go up 24.6 points in a year. So, you are betting that at least for the next seven weeks, it will go up at the rate of 50% a year. And that is a pretty darn high rate, although it is certainly possible.

Another way of using the annualizing concept is to consider whether there might be better methods for achieving your goal. For instance, if you buy the call now and the stock does not go up, do you intend to purchase the call again during the next quarter? And if so, at the same rate for the premium? If you don't purchase the second call, then you have thrown away 100% of your investment.

If you do buy another call, then you make it just twice as hard to come out a winner, because the profit from your second call must now pay not only for its own premium but also for the premium that you lost on the first call. Of course, if you follow this reasoning out to the third quarter, it becomes almost absurd. Remember that, unlike the money that one pays for a stock itself, the money spent for an option is not an investment in anything tangible unless the stock is above the strike price by the expiration date.

The moral of this story is that if the annualized premium is as high as 50%, an investor might do far better to buy the underlying stock on margin. To buy on margin under current regulations, the purchaser need only put up cash equal to 50% of the price. The other 50% of the cost is borrowed from your brokerage firm, which charges interest on the amount. Thus, for approximately the same cost as the annualized premium of a call, a person could actually obtain the same leverage power by buying the stock itself—and could be much better off, for the money would actually have bought an asset with lasting value. The stock owner would also get any dividends on the stock.

Whether the stock goes up, stands still, or goes down, the purchaser of the stock will own something at the end of the year. It may be worth more than he paid for it, or it may be worth less. In extreme cases, where the stock declines drastically in value, the purchaser might have to put up more money for margin or lose some of the stock. But under normal circumstances, the purchaser of the stock on margin will continue to own the stock.

If the purchaser of the call, on the other hand, repurchases a similar call each quarter and the price of the stock remains unchanged or goes down, he has paid out $24.60 per share, for which he has obtained absolutely nothing. And even if the price of the stock were to go up a very dramatic 24.6 points, or 50%, during the year, the purchaser of the calls has probably only recovered his cost. He has not made a single dime!

The purchaser of the stock would have the 50% profit on the stock, and if he had bought on margin, the gain on his cash investment would be 100% (less his interest costs but plus any dividends). So, there would be no question that a one-year call at the rate of the seven-week option would be completely absurd. If this is the case over a one-year period, why is the call any more of a bargain over a period of only seven weeks? Thus, Strategy Rule Number 4 is to annualize the call's premium and consider the value of the call accordingly.

Strategy Rule Number 5: Sell One-Half Your Calls When They Have Doubled in Price

Most people buy calls when they expect that a stock has the potential to move up by a really substantial amount. When the stock does start moving up, this serves to confirm their view that it is going to go much higher. The natural tendency is to hang on to your options, or even to roll them up, rather than get out of half your position. And certainly, if the stock continues to go up, you might be sorry that you did sell half your position. And yet, in suggesting this rule to my clients, I do not know of a single one who regretted having applied it. Although it is the arch example of an arbitrary rule that can easily be ridiculed by mathematicians and stock traders, who will say that if you like a stock you hold on to a call, and if you don't you sell it. And I am also certain that I will get many comments from people who will say that they never could have made the money they did in options if they had ever followed this rule. It has nevertheless served me well, and here is why.

We start with the principle that buying options is extremely risky. As pointed out often in this book, your entire cost is constantly at risk of going to zero in a matter of weeks. Let's assume that you originally decided to buy 10 calls at $1\frac{1}{2}$ on your favorite stock. This means that you wanted to have $1,500 at risk in options on that stock. Now the option goes up to 3, and your investment becomes worth $3,000. That's wonderful, but let's not lose sight of the fact that you now have at risk exactly twice as much as you originally intended. You have $3,000 on paper, and that is how much you stand to lose. This rule of strategy says that you should now sell out half your position so that you will bring the amount of money at risk back to your original commitment. In other words, why should you let the action of the marketplace force you to have twice as much at risk as you originally planned?

Another major benefit of this rule is that once you have sold half your position at twice the original cost, you have recovered your entire original investment, less commissions. Incidentally, commissions can easily be covered by selling for twice your *net* cost of the options. The beauty of recovering your entire original investment is that the entire cost of your remaining position has been paid for by the market increase. You have gotten back your cost, and now the entire psychology of owning the calls is different, because now no matter what happens, you can never lose anything. So you can decide to hold them until the last day and be completely free of worry, because no matter what happens you can only be a winner.

A final reason for this rule is that in a trading market that is characterized by short-term stock price moves up and down, it is surprising how often an option will double in price and then drop down again to where it was. With hindsight it would have been better to sell out your entire position, but the big advantage of this rule is that it lets you get back your entire cost and permits you to continue being in the position of making more money if the stock resumes its rise.

Strategy Rule Number 6: Know and Understand the Beta/Volatility of the Stock Underlying Your Call

The *beta* of a stock is the propensity of the stock to move with the market. The market as a whole is assigned a beta of 1. If when the stock market went up 10% a particular stock would usually go up 20%, then it would have a beta of 2. If another stock would usually go up only 5% on a 10% market rally, its beta would be 0.5.

While beta measures how much a stock is likely to move relative to a move of the entire stock market, volatility is a measure of how much an individual stock moves up or down independently of the rest of the stock market. It is therefore nondirectional and has come to be the pre-ferred characteristic for options traders. A stock which has an average volatility is said to have a volatility or "vol" of 50. If a stock has been gyrating violently its volatility could be up to 200 or more and a half-dead stock could have a volatility as low as 20. Historical volatilities of stocks can be found on the Internet at www.cboe.com, under the head-ing Snapshot, Historical Volatilities, and at www.optionstrategist.com where you will find a weekly update of 20, 50, and 100 day historical volatility plus the latest implied volatility of the options.

The philosophy of this book is that it is impossible, at least for the short duration of a stock option, for anyone to predict accurately the direction and price movement of the stock. But I do believe it is possible to know whether a particular stock is likely to have large price movements based on its historical performance. With respect to volatility of movement, as distinct from direction of movement, I be-lieve that historical performance has a great deal of validity in pre-dicting the amount of future action of a stock.

Note that I do not say that past history can predict whether a stock is likely to go up or down, only that it usually can quite accu-rately tell us to what extent a stock is likely to move if the market as a whole moves. Certain stocks, throughout many years, have always moved up sharply when the market as a whole moved up, and these stocks are very likely to do so again. And of course they are likely to fall a large amount when the market falls.

Typical stocks that have large swings are Internet, high-technol-ogy, airline, and auto companies; stock brokerage firms; anything connected with housing, building, or real estate and resort busi-nesses; and stocks that have a high price/earnings ratio. On the other end of the scale, stocks that are apt to move only slightly include util-ities; companies supplying basic commodities for which demand re-mains fairly constant, such as tires, canned foods, and soaps; supermarket chains; and life insurance companies.

The importance of the beta and volatility of a stock to successful option trading cannot be overemphasized. It is the sine qua non of successful option buying. The reason is quite simple, as the following comparison with the purchase of a stock shows.

Stock Purchaser versus Option Buyer. The purchaser of a stock typically buys the stock for many reasons. He hopes that the price of the stock will go up in the next three or six months, but this is far from the only reason why an investor buys a common stock. He may be perfectly will-ing to have no price increase in the next few months, feeling confident that the next few years will amply reward him with a slow but steady growth. He may not be looking for any increase in price at all, having bought the stock because it pays a good dividend, and he is quite content to realize a high rate of return on his investment exclusively via dividends. Or he may have selected a certain stock because he believes that it represents a secure, safe investment, which may eventually go up, which pays some dividends, and which he feels quite certain will not decline in value very much if at all.

Thus, to the stock purchaser, the short-range price movement is only one of many factors that may have influenced his decision and that will eventually determine whether he made a successful investment.

The contrast with the call buyer is startling. The call buyer is interested in one thing and one thing only: that is, how much the stock is going to go up within the highly limited duration of the option. This is all that matters to him. He will not share in the dividend, so he couldn't care less about its rate. He will not be around next year to realize the gains from an increase of price then (at least not unless he constantly buys one call after another, at great cost to himself, or has bought a LEAPS). If the price of the stock stays the same or goes down just a little bit, this is of little solace to the option buyer, who usually can then say good-bye to 100% of his investment. Every other consideration that enters into the decision of the stock buyer is obviated for the call buyer. For him the only questions of any interest, the only points that make any difference to him at all, are whether this stock will go up during the period of his call, and if it does, by how much.

In determining the answers, the behavior of the stock price movement in the past is invaluable. And the stock with the greatest movement has the highest volatility. Therefore, the call buyer should seek a stock with as high volatility as possible. A high beta and high volatility do not indicate that the stock will necessarily go up. Alas, it could go down, but presumably our call buyer has satisfied himself that the stock should go up within the duration of the call or he would not be considering the call in the first place. Having made that judgment, he then must determine how high it is likely to go.

In order to be successful, the call buyer needs to find stocks that have the potential of going up at least enough so that he can double his money. And if the typical premium for a three-month call with a strike price close to the price of the stock is 3% to 8%, this means that the stock must be capable of going up 6% to 16% within the three-month period, plus an amount to compensate for commissions. This requires a stock with high volatility.

On the other side of the equation, it is no coincidence that the calls on stocks with the highest betas and volatility are the ones that command the highest premiums, and that stocks with low betas have low premiums. For example, when General Electric closed at 134, the one-year 140 call was bid at 18⅝ or 14% of the price of the stock. By way of comparison, when Yahoo! closed at 313, the premium for its one-year 320 call was 83⅝ or 27% of the stock price, or almost twice as much as the similar option for GE.

Thus, because GE has a historic volatility of 30, its premium was substantially less than Yahoo!'s, which had a historic volatility of 119.79. Call buyers knew that GE would probably not go up a great deal higher but they believed that Yahoo! certainly had the potential to shoot up like a rocket.

In the final analysis it comes down to a matter of judgment. Is the high premium made worthwhile by the greater probability that the stock with a higher volatility or beta is going to go up faster and further than one with a low beta? My answer is that in almost all cases it is worthwhile.

Take the example of GE and Yahoo! GE has a wonderful record, but it is one of the largest capitalized stocks and for this reason it is simply not likely to have an unusually large move. Furthermore, its earnings are growing at a good but predictable rate. Yahoo!, on the other hand, is a fast mover. Its high in early 2000 was 500, up dramatically from its low of 110 just five months earlier on August 5, 1999, so there was no doubt about its ability to move upward fast. For just twice as much in the price of the premium per share, the buyer gets a much better chance of receiving a really good return on his money. Remember, the call buyer is not looking for a nice little increment. By the very nature of his investment, he must be seeking a big increase in a relatively short time.

If you have to pay a little more in the cost of the premium, or even substantially more, it is usually money well spent. Don't forget that a low beta is no assurance of safety, either. In this example GE could easily stay below 140 and the call buyer would then lose his entire investment regardless of how safe the GE common stock is.

Strategy Rule Number 6 may be summarized by saying that the buyer of a call wants to be certain that the stock is one that has a good probability of going up enough so that the premium for the call will at least double. This means that it must be a stock that can move fast, and the measurement of that movement is the beta and volatility of the stock. Although stocks with higher betas have calls with higher premiums, their extra performance potential is usually well worth the extra cost. In short, buy calls on stocks with high betas and volatility.

Strategy Rule Number 7: Never Buy a Call Unless
You Have Checked the Stock's Chart for at Least 10 Years

Before you buy a call you will naturally ask yourself how high the stock must go in order to realize your investment goal. Assuming that your investment goal is to at least double your money, you will calculate how high the stock must go by the call's expiration date in order for you to double your money and cover two commissions. Once you have that answer, check it against a 10-year or longer chart of your stock to find out how many times the stock has gone up by that much in the period of time left in the option.

For example, if you find that your stock must go up 6 points, and there are three months left in the option period, look at the chart to find out how many times in the past the stock has gone up by 6 points or more in any three-month period.

A fairly easy way to check the chart for this is by means of a simple indicator that you can make by taking the lower right-hand corner of a piece of paper and measuring off on the vertical scale along the right edge the distance representing the number of points the stock must rise. Then make a horizontal measurement for the period of time that the option is in effect along the bottom edge. When you have this right angle you can cut the paper into a triangle. Move the indicator along the chart, keeping the bottom line horizontal. (See Figure 2.6.) Note how many times the upper right-hand corner meets the price line on the chart. If the stock did not go up a full 6 points in any three months during the entire 10-year period, this would clearly be an indication that it is not very likely to do so during the next three months. Obviously, even if in the 10 years it had often gone up the required points in three months, that is no guarantee that it will do so in the future, but it shows you have a fighting chance.

It is possible that the next three months will see a rise in the price of the stock that exceeds any in its past 10-year history—but the odds against it are overwhelming, and you're not getting those odds when you buy a call. The odds you are getting may be the chance to double, triple, or quadruple your investment.

But what are the odds that the market is taking from you? If a stock didn't go up the amount you wish in any three-month period in the past 10 years, that means that it failed to do so a single time out of 117 chances. And now you are betting your money that it will go up that much on the 118th chance? I don't know what the odds are against you, but my guess is that 118 to 1 is an understatement. Just compare that to the odds that the market is giving you. Yes, I'm sure we'll both agree that there must be a better way to invest your money.

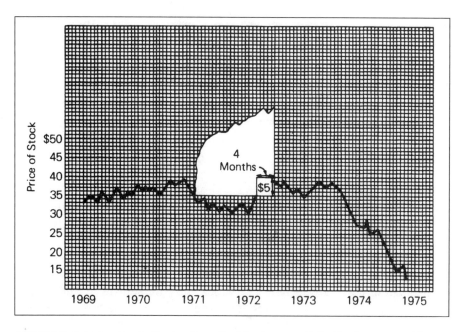

FIGURE 2.6 Using the Indicator Described in Strategy Rule Number 7 on a Five-Year Chart of the Underlying Stock's Performance

Suppose you discover that in the past 10 years there have been 33 three-month periods during which the stock has gone up by an amount that would be enough to let you double your cost. What does this indicate for you? As every brokerage report states, past performance is no guarantee of future performance. But when you are trying to forecast the possibility of certain short-term movements, it does give an indication of the range of future conduct.

If your stock went up the right amount in 33 three-month periods out of a total of 117 three-month periods, it did this 28.2% of the time. Subject to all the qualifications given earlier, the chances of it going up the required amount in the next three months are just about 28.2%. And that is probably too low for a bet that will get you only 2 to 1. You might find, however, that in most of those 33 three-month periods, the stock had gone up much more than the amount needed for you to double your investment. It may be that in 30 of those times it went up enough for you to quadruple your investment. Now you are talking about something that gives you fair odds, namely, a 30 out of 117, or 25.6%, chance to quadruple your money. This is worth considering.

Strategy Rule Number 7 is therefore to check a long-term chart for the stock whose call you are considering buying. Make certain that in the past it has gone up by the amount needed to achieve your investment goal enough times to give you odds equal to what you expect to get from your call.

Strategy Rule Number 8: Never Put All Your Eggs in One Basket

The experienced call buyer expects to lose on half the calls, and perhaps more. He does not expect to lose money on the calls as a whole because he expects to win far more than 100% on the calls that are successful. Nevertheless, this type of strategy requires as wide a diversification as possible. And even the small investor can easily scatter his purchases over at least five different calls.

But you must first overcome the temptation to concentrate on one or two stocks. You may think that a certain call is far more likely to be profitable than any other. The stock may be selling at the strike price, the premium may be modest, the beta may be fabulous, and the charts may show that it has made the gain you need to double your investment at least 40 times in the past 10 years. And in addition to the statistical indicators, you may have an inner feeling that the stock is poised on the brink of a tremendous price breakthrough.

The temptation will be almost overpowering to put all your eggs in one basket. My advice is simple: Resist the temptation.

Anyone experienced in buying calls will tell you that you can never tell in advance which calls are going to work out and which are not. All you know is that, based on past performance, half of them are not going to work out. So don't risk your entire investment on one call, when that may turn out to be the one that goes down.

Always keep in mind that when you buy a call, there is no tomorrow. The stock buyer who sees his stock go down can decide to hang on to it anyhow because he is convinced that eventually it will get back up to where it belongs. But for a call buyer who sees the stock go down, or even just stay still—when the final gavel falls above the trading floor on the last business day before the option expires, that's the end of the ball game. And mighty Casey has struck out. Finally and permanently. Your call is worthless—absolutely, irrevocably, and forever.

There is no reason why you shouldn't diversify. In the stock market anyone buying less than 100 shares pays slightly more for the stock than the 100-lot purchaser pays. This is not true for options. The price per option (on 100 shares of stock) is the same whether you buy 1 or 1,000. Only the commission cost per option is less as the volume goes up.

The only point to watch for is that the minimum commission at most brokerage firms for any option of over $1 is $25. Therefore, if you are buying one option and your actual commission should be less than $25, you will be paying excess commissions. But two will get you up over the minimum. The actual number of different calls to buy is a matter of judgment, but since you want to purchase only those that are the very best for you, I would suggest restricting yourself to between 5 and 10 stocks.

Strategy Rule Number 8 may be summarized very easily. Since most calls turn out to be losses to the purchaser, you must be willing to lose your investment on some calls because you expect to more than make it up on the ones that are winners. But since you cannot predict with any degree of accuracy which calls will be the winners, it is necessary to give yourself protection by diversifying your purchases among a number of different calls. Far better to win some and lose some than to have one great big loser.

SUMMARY

Now you know the eight rules of strategy for buying calls to make you as successful a call buyer as the experts. This chapter on buying calls may be summarized by stating that the purchasers of calls will lose their money much of the time. The general purpose of these rules is to reduce those losses to a minimum while making certain that you actually get to keep as much of the profits as possible.

Rule 1. Never buy a call when the stock is more than slightly below the strike price, or in other words when the strike price is too far above the price of the stock. The premium of the call may be low and it may look like a bargain, but it's not nearly enough of a bargain. The odds are against any call buyer, and when you expect the price of the stock to go up before it can even begin to cut into your loss, you're really stacking the deck against yourself. Get a fair deal; buy a call when the stock is not too far below the strike price.

Rule 2. Don't buy a call when the stock is more than slightly above the strike price. This is simply making you underwrite an insurance policy for the owner of the stock. You are paying so much for the present value of the stock that is above the strike price, you won't have enough money to buy many options. Because of the huge cost of these calls, your upside leverage is slight—too slight. And the downside risk is still there. It may be small, but it is there, and the fact that it is small is no consolation if you are one of the unlucky ones who has to watch that stock fall and fall. True, this may be a more conservative investment than others, but if you want conservative investments you don't want to buy calls in the first place. Calls are for swingers. If you want a safe investment, ask your stockbroker for a recommendation. It won't be calls.

Rule 3. Check all the option durations on a cost-per-week basis. If there is a large discrepancy, it would be well worth your while to buy the more economical one, even if the premium costs more because it is for the longer term.

Rule 4. To fully comprehend the cost of your call, annualize the premium. Although your stock doesn't have to go up nearly as much as if the call actually were for a year, this exercise will give you a clearer understanding of the rate at which the stock will have to climb before you can make any money. And if it turns out that the annual rate of gain is staggering, ask yourself why the stock should climb at such a high rate in the next three months, if you will concede that it wouldn't do so for an entire year.

Rule 5. Stocks go up, and stocks go down—a statement so obvious that one sometimes forgets its everlasting truth. But if you have bought an option and watched it double in price, only to have the stock fall back down again leaving you holding a worthless option, you will not forget this statement quickly. The solution is to sell out half your position when the option price doubles. Other advantages are that you are maintaining the amount of money at risk at your original level, and you are now free of any psychological worries because no matter what happens, you will no longer be able to lose any (of your original investment) from this position.

Rule 6. Before you buy a call, know the beta volatility for the underlying stock. This is a number that tells you whether a stock is likely to make price swings which are larger, smaller, or about equal to the price movements of the market as a whole. Since you are not going to make any money on your call unless the price of the stock goes up substantially in a relatively short period of time, it is important to select a stock with a high enough volatility to do the job.

Rule 7. Check the 10-year record of the stock before you buy a call. While the future is never going to repeat the past exactly, it is also true that the past is prologue to the future. To gain the most from the past record of your stock, compute how much the stock would have to increase in order to double your investment in the call. Then go over a 10-year chart of the stock to learn how many times in the past the stock has gone up that much in the period of time left on the option you are considering. If the stock has risen that amount only a few times, the odds are sadly against you, and another call would be indicated.

Rule 8. Diversify your investment by buying at least 5 different calls, and perhaps as many as 10. The experienced call buyer expects to lose money on many of his call purchases. Therefore, it makes good sense to be sure that you don't invest all your money in one of those that turns out to be worthless. Play the percentages and you'll do better.

These are the eight rules for sensible call buying. They have been developed from experience, and will stand you in good stead.

3

SELLING COVERED CA~~LLS~~
A Conservative Method fo~~r~~
Increasing the Return on Stocks

Option trading is generally recommended only for investors who have money they can spare for speculative investment. If an investor would suffer financial hardship from losing his entire investment, then he should neither buy nor sell naked options or engage in option *spreads*. There is, however, one method of taking advantage of options that is recommended for investors who are not willing to assume the high risks associated with the methods described elsewhere in this book, and this is to sell covered calls. A call is covered when its seller owns the underlying stock. For example, if a person sold a call option on IBM when he owned 100 shares of IBM common stock, he would have sold a "covered IBM call."

Covered call writing has now become so established as a prudent, conservative method of investing that it has received official recognition by almost every regulatory body that has control over investments. The Comptroller of the Currency, who regulates the national banks, has ruled that covered option writing is appropriate for use by bank trust departments in investing their trust funds. The insurance commissioners of most of the states have now ruled that insurance companies may use covered option writing on a portion of their own investments, and various officials charged with seeing that pension plans are properly administered have given their blessings to the use of covered option writing for pension plans. In addition, an enormous number of conservative, professionally managed investment groups have begun to use covered option writing, including church, university, and college endowment funds and union welfare plans. Clearly, the time has now come when the speculative stigma of options should be completely and irrevocably removed from the concept of writing covered options.

Perhaps nothing can explain so well why covered option writing is appropriate for the conservative investor as to note that it is more conservative than simply owning stock. By its very definition, in this context the word "conservative" means to be more concerned with protecting what one has than with increasing it through possible changes in market prices. Covered option writing by definition protects the investor from declines in the price of the stock up to the amount of the premium received from the sale of the option. Thus, covered call writing is conservative in that one of its basic effects is to protect against a downside move in the price of the stock. Its other purpose is to make money on the future time value of the option price. As we shall see in this chapter, these benefits are bought with the cost of giving up some or all of the chance to make a greater profit from an upward movement in the price of the stock. Thus, covered option writing perfectly matches the concept of the conservative investor, that is, one who is interested in protecting capital first and, second, in making a modest return on an investment while forgoing potentially large profits from changes in the price of the stock.

There are two other reasons for the popularity of covered option writing. The first is that covered option writing from the viewpoint of economic participation is at least 90% about owning common stock, and less than 10% about options. Since investors already have a very good concept of what it means to own stock, it is a relatively easy matter for them to learn about writing options against stock that they will continue to own. It is not like asking an investor to write two-on-one option spreads, where he is starting out with a totally foreign concept. Here the concept is to continue owning common stock, but to give oneself some downside protection and to take in some profit if the stock stays still or moves up.

The second reason that covered call writing has become so popular is that it is one of the few forms of investing where one can compute exactly what the return on investment will be if the position is successful. When one buys a stock one can compute the dividend, but the result of that investment a year from the date of purchase is going to be determined mostly by what has happened to the price of the stock, and only to a minor degree by the amount of the dividend. Similarly, when one buys an option, there is no way to calculate in advance how much profit one can expect to make. And many serious investors like to go into a situation where they can calculate in advance that they should be able to make an annualized profit of, let's say, 27% on their investment. It gives a degree of certainty to the investment that is very comforting. As we will see, there is no guarantee that the investor will actually make the expected profit, but at least there is a wide parameter of stock prices at which he will be able to make that expected profit, and in a world of unknowns, it is worth something to have a precise figure that one can lean on.

DISAPPOINTMENTS

Perhaps no other concept in the investment world has been so thoroughly sold by so many brokers who sincerely believed in it as that of covered option writing. And it is also unfortunately true that many of those who have undertaken covered writing have been disappointed with the results. There are a number of reasons for this, and after you have read this chapter, hopefully you will be able to avoid some of the pitfalls that can lead to this disappointment. Perhaps the original cause of the disappointment was that some brokers oversold the idea. Some almost put it in terms of "How can you lose? If the stock stays where it is or goes up, you will make 18% in six months, and even if the stock goes down, you have the income from the option to offset the loss."

The problem arises when some of the stocks under the option are more volatile than one would have expected. To use a simple example, suppose that two stocks are both 100, and both have 100 strike price options at $10. An investor buys 100 shares of each, and sells one option on each. Stock #1 goes up to 150, and the investor has the $10 per share that he received from selling the option. This is fine because he has made his 10% profit in six months, just as promised. Stock #2 is not so fortunate, and declines by 50% to $50 a share. The investor has received $10 per share from the sale of the option, so that his loss is cut from $50 to $40 a share. Combining his loss of $40 on stock #2 with his profit of $10 on stock #1, we come up with a loss of $30. Not so good. If he had just bought the two stocks and not written options, his $50 loss on the one would have been completely offset by the $50 gain on the other. So the first cause for disappointment comes when some of the stocks in an option-writing portfolio decline steeply in value.

The second disappointment with covered option writing has been that the level of option premiums has dropped significantly in recent years. There are many reasons for this. Perhaps the most important is that, by and large, option buyers have not made money. In fact, they have lost large amounts of money, despite the fact that there have been exceptions during brief periods of bull markets and for certain stocks that produced enormous profits. But on the whole, option buyers have lost money, and when you have lost a large amount of money buying options, you don't feel like buying them again, even if you can still afford to. Thus, the demand for options has decreased.

Another reason for the drop in premiums is that many institutions are beginning to get interested in writing options on their vast stock portfolios. This has greatly increased the supply of options. Applying fundamental principles of economics to option prices, we find that when demand falls and supply rises, the price of the commodity must go down. And basically that is what has happened. So that a person who acquired a stock for the purpose of writing an on-the-money option for six months for 15% found that six months later he might be able to get 10% for a six-month option, and that next time he was able to get only 7.5%. Each time, he is giving up the same upside potential profit, and he is assuming the same downside risk on the stock.

In summary, selling covered options has become a much tougher strategy to make money on, and thus it is more important than ever that anyone who wants to embark on such a course be fully familiar with the potential, the risk, and all the rules of strategy that can possibly help him. That is what this chapter will try to do.

LIMITED RISK

The covered call technique does not involve any risk if the price of the stock soars upward. In that case, a covered option seller loses money on his call when the stock goes up but he offsets the loss by gaining an even greater amount on his stock. Thus, he cannot lose money by the stock's rise. In effect, he has perfectly hedged the risk incurred by being short the call, by being long the stock.

As an example let us assume you sell a call with a $25 strike for a $2 premium when the stock is at $25. If the price of the stock rises to $26, let's assume that the premium on the call will go up to $3. Although you have now lost $1 on the sale of this call, you have made $1 on the increase in value of your stock. If the price of the stock now advances another $3 to $29, the price of the call may go up by $2. Thus, every step of the way, the loss on your call is either exactly offset by the gain on your common stock or more than offset by it when the stock goes up by more than the option and the future time value of the option shrinks.

Finally, when the expiration date of the call arrives, there is no need for you to produce any money to cover. You simply sit back, and your shares of stock are called away from you.

What is the advantage to the seller of the covered call? The advantage is that he gets to keep the entire future time value of the premium, and this can add up to a very hefty percentage of the value of the common stock, considering that there is no risk of loss when the stock goes up. The gains measured as percent return on investment are not usually as attractive as for a naked seller who does not have to cover, but then the risk simply isn't anywhere near as great.

The owner of 100 shares of common stock who decides to sell a call on his shares does so because he has made a decision that he would rather take a limited but certain gain on the decline in the future time value of the option than take the risk that his stock will perhaps go up much more, but perhaps will not go up at all. If the stock goes down, the decline in the option will offset the stock price decline by the original price of the option.

To continue with the example, when we started out, our investor owned stock with a value of $25. At the end of the example he had received a premium of $2 and he had tendered his stock for $25, so that he had a total of $27 for a profit of $2. This is a gain of about 8.5%, which is nothing to sneeze at, especially if we assume that the call was for the current quarter so that the annualized return is 34%, excluding commission (but see later in this chapter for an explanation of how important commissions are). This profit was made without taking the big risk of losing money if the price of the stock was to go sky-high. Why doesn't everyone sell calls on their stocks all the time? There are reasons for not doing so.

Profit-Limiting Decisions

The seller of a covered call must make two decisions before he sells a call. I would not say they are risk-taking decisions, but rather profit-limiting decisions, because they create two disadvantages concerning potential future profits.

The first limitation that a covered call seller must accept is that he is giving up possible large future appreciation of the stock in exchange for a premium that rarely if ever will exceed 10% for a three-month period. (An exception to this would be the case in which the price of the stock is above the strike price, but this is only because the premium for the option then represents a part of the present price of the stock.) By selling a call, the investor is giving someone else the chance to receive all the appreciation over the strike price (minus the future time value of the option).

If one thinks of a stock as a vertical bar graph, one could say that selling a call is like breaking the stock up into two portions, with the buyer of the call purchasing the top part of the bar. Therefore, if a person believes that his stock is grossly underpriced, that there is about to be a major market breakthrough, and that his stock could easily double in value within the next six months to a year—then under these circumstances he should not sell someone else the right to skim this cream off the top of his stock. So, disadvantage number one for a potential seller of a covered call is that he must be willing to give up the chance to make any gain over the strike price on his stock except for the premium he receives.

Disadvantage number two is that regardless of how badly his stock performs during the period when the call is outstanding, he will not be able to sell the stock unless he buys back the option he sold, or is willing to accept the great risk of being a naked call seller. This means that the covered call writer is subject to the risk of loss from a decline in the value of his stock, reduced by the amount of the premium received.

What kind of investor can best benefit from selling covered calls? The answer is anyone who wants to make a good annual return on his stock and who is (1) willing to give up the possibility of any spectacular gains if the stock suddenly takes off and (2) willing to absorb the risks of a downside turn in the price of the stock. But the rewards for making these two sacrifices can be meaningful, and they can come without any risks other than these two.

MAKING YOUR DECISION

So, if this concept appeals to you, here's how to do it. Buy 100 shares (or multiples of 100) of a good-quality stock that you are willing to own for the long haul, and for which calls are listed. It is important to select a solid stock that you are willing to stick with even if the price should go down substantially because, as pointed out earlier, even after you have sold a call, you continue to bear the risk of loss if the stock declines significantly in price. Then make up your mind that you are willing to part with the chance to make more than a limited return every three months. If you think that the stock will go up more than the possible return, then selling a call on it is not for you.

If you have made these two decisions, however, then you are ready to sit back and make a very reasonable annual return on your investment even if your stock does not go up and assuming that it does not decline by more than the option premium you have collected. There is a method for boosting your rate of return higher.

This strategy is made possible because when you sell a covered call, in the eyes of your broker you are selling a call short, but instead of the usual cash margin requirement, you are depositing the stock instead. It is not necessary to put up fully paid-for stock, however. The stock used to cover the call can be owned on margin. This greatly increases the return.

Taking a typical lively stock that is selling at the strike price, the return might be 10% for a six-month period. This works out to 20% a year if you have paid in full for the stock. But if you have bought the stock on full margin and put up only 50% of the price of the stock, your 10% premium now represents a return of 20% on your investment twice a year, or 40% annually.

Please note, however, that these are gross returns before commissions and interest expenses and that these costs have a surprisingly great impact on reducing actual returns. If you are buying 300 shares on margin of a $40 stock paying a 2% annual dividend, and you are selling a six-month on-the-money option for $4, then the return to you, excluding transaction costs, is actually 25%. You buy the stock for $40, paying 50% on margin ($20), and take in $4 from the option, leaving $16 as your cost. The $4 received from the option is 25% of this. If we deduct all transaction costs, including interest on your margin debit at 7%, the actual net return on your six-month investment (using standard full-service brokerage firm commissions and assuming the stock is called away) would not be 25%, but rather 15%. Even more dramatically, if the return without transaction costs had been 15%, the actual return less these transaction costs would be only 5%. So you can see what an enormous difference commissions make. Of course, if the price of the stock declines, it will not be possible to achieve the returns on your investment. See Appendix I for a worksheet showing exactly how to compute the annualized return on covered writes, whether purchased for cash or on margin.

It is worth noting that the seller of a covered call continues to receive the dividend on the stock. In some covered writing situations the yield from the dividend makes up a very large proportion of the total expected profit. This is particularly true in the case of utilities, where the dividend is large and the option premiums are very low.

Premature Assignments

One potential problem that all covered writers have is that their stock may be prematurely assigned (i.e., called away from them). If you made your original estimate of the return from your investment based on receiving two dividends, and the stock is assigned the day before the stock goes ex-dividend on the second dividend, your return could be substantially lower than you had expected. There is no way that you can prevent your stock from being assigned. The Options Clearing Corporation (OCC) makes assignments to various brokerage firms on a random basis, and then each brokerage firm allocates these assignments in accordance with a method it has previously elected. Each brokerage firm can decide to make its assignments on the basis of either (1) first in, first out—that is, the first person to write the option is the first one assigned—or (2) a random assignment to everyone who is short the option; and (3) certain large option writers, primarily institutions, at some firms can elect to have all or none of their options exercised to save them from the bother of being exercised on one option a day.

Premature exercise is particularly likely to happen to an in-the-money option on the day before it goes ex-dividend when there is only a short period of time remaining on the option. The reason for this is that some of the option owners may wish to exercise the options rather than sell them. By exercising the day before the stock goes ex-dividend, they receive the stock for the same cost as if they had waited until the expiration, but in addition to the stock they pick up a free dividend. The moral is that when you are computing your expected return from a covered option situation, perhaps you should not count on the final dividend if the stock goes ex-dividend just a week or two before expiration. Obviously, the larger the dividend the greater the chance of this happening.

"Getting a Cash Flow"

One claim that is sometimes made for covered option writing must be particularly well qualified if it is to be accurate. This is the claim that "We'll sell some options in order to get a cash flow." This presumably is being said to someone who is now getting an income from the dividends on the stock and would like to get a higher yield. The difficulty with this claim is that it will work only if the investor is willing to let the stock be called away when the option expires. If he is not, then the sale of covered calls may not produce cash, and could do just the opposite. For example, if your stock is now at $50, and you sell a $50 strike price option for $5, you certainly have created a cash flow, and you could have your brokerage firm send you a check for $500. But the story doesn't end here.

If the stock remains at $50 at the expiration of the option, all is fine and good. If, however, the stock rises to $60, and for reasons such as high capital gains tax exposure you do not want to part with that stock, you must now buy back the option for $10, for a cost of $1,000. Instead of creating $500 in cash, this maneuver has used up $500 in cash. So if someone tells you that he wants to create some cash flow on your portfolio, make sure that you realize this might not be the case unless you are willing to have the stock called away. It must be noted that in either case you are making a profit of $500; it is just that if the stock appreciates too much you are not doing the very thing you set out to do, namely creating a positive cash flow. Rather you are losing cash and retaining ownership in a stock which has appreciated in value.

IMPLEMENTING A COVERED CALL PROGRAM

So much for the theory of selling covered calls. If you're not convinced by now that this is for you, just skip the rest of this chapter and go on to the next. If you are interested, you probably have questions about the best way to go about selling covered calls. The next few pages will try to answer them.

If you already own 100 shares or more of a stock that has a call traded on an exchange, then your decision is which of the available options you should sell. Since there are always at least three durations available, your first question is probably whether you should sell the shortest-term call, the medium-term one, or the longest. The first step in answering this question is to get all the options on an equal basis so that you can compare them in a meaningful manner. The easiest way to do this is to compute what each call is paying in terms of weeks or months. Generally the shortest one should be paying the highest return on a per-week basis. Just remember that the longer-term options don't involve such frequent commissions and other transaction costs—mainly buying at the offering price and selling at the bid price—and this is a significant savings that should be taken into consideration.

Determining the Best Duration

If you want to let your theories on the market's future come into play and guide you, then you can make further refinements. If you believe there is a good chance your stock will decline in value during the current period, then, when the current call expires, you will not be able to get nearly as high a premium for the next term. In such a case you should sell the longer-term call, even if it does not pay the highest premium on a per-week basis, because over the full span of the longer call it will give a higher return per week.

To illustrate, let's assume you own a volatile stock with a current market price of 100. For the 100 strike price option, the shortest-duration call might be 6, the next one 10, and the longest one 13. Assuming that these prices are for the beginning of an option quarter, the per-month return on the calls is respectively 2, 1.67, and 1.44. Normally, of course, you would sell the shortest-term call, expecting that if the call is not exercised you will sell another short-term call for the same amount. You would continue until (assuming circumstances stay the same for purposes of this example, which in real life they will certainly not) you will have received a total of 3 times $6, or $18, over the nine-month period. Compare this with the $13 that you would have gotten if you had originally sold the long-term call. And thanks to the liquidity of the options exchanges you will always be able to sell a new call on your stock as soon as each old one expires.

If you are afraid that in three months the stock will be down 10 and selling at 90, you should sell the long-term call. The reason is that if you sell the short-term call for 6, and are correct that the stock will be 90 when the call expires, the premium on the next three-month 100 strike price call may have dropped to around 2. The same thing will be true in another three months if the stock stays at 90. Thus you will receive total premium income of $10 over a period of nine months, when you could have received $13 by selling the long-term call. And you will pay three sets of commissions instead of one.

If the price falls to 90, the directors of the options exchanges will start trading a call with a strike price of 90, and the premium at this strike price for a three-month call could well be $5\frac{1}{2}$ or 5. This is the call you could sell after your first three-month call expired. But the danger here is that if the price of your stock then goes up to 100, to buy back the option for $10 you incur a $5 loss, and in effect lock in a loss.

On the other hand, if you believe that your stock has a good probability of going up during the next three months, then you should sell the shortest-term call. The reason is that if your stock does indeed do as well as you expect it to, you will be free to cover the call and reinvest your money elsewhere. Perhaps you will decide to sell another call at a much higher premium. For example, if your stock has risen to 110, you could allow your stock to be called away and be left with the $100 you received for your stock (the strike price) and the $6 premium.

Using the perfect hindsight with which we are all gifted, you will realize that you made a mistake by selling a call on the stock. Remember, however, that we are playing the averages and you should expect to lose a few. Furthermore, you could well argue that getting a 6% return in three months, equaling 24% a year, is hardly losing. Getting back to our example, you now have $106 and you're a free person, able to do with it what you will. Had you sold the nine-month call you would be sitting with your capital tied up in the stock and with no chance of investing it in anything else, or of ever making more than the premium you already received.

Having sold the three-month option, you might even decide to scrape up $400, add it to your proceeds, and buy 100 shares again. You could, of course, at this point sell another call, and if there is now a call with a 110 strike price you will be receiving a premium of $6 or $7 again. At the end of six months you will have made a total profit from premiums of $12 to $13. And you can make another $6 or $7 in the third quarter. The fellow who sold the long-term call will just be sitting there waiting for the nine months to finally expire so that he can get out with his $100 and the $13 premium.

These examples show how you should plan your strategy concerning duration if you believe that the stock is going to go up, or if you believe that it is going to go down. But what if you really don't have any strong feelings? This, incidentally, is the best attitude to have, in my opinion. In that case you follow the general and simple rule of selling the call that gives you the highest return on a per-week basis.

Determining the Best Strike Price

Another major question you will face if you own a stock and are planning to sell a covered call is which strike to sell. There will probably be a large number of strike prices available. This occurs because when an option first comes out and a stock is selling at 102, the strike prices will be set at 100 and 105 or even 110. Then if the price of the stock declines to 95, a new option will be issued with the strike price at 90. If the stock price declines further, another call will be issued, and so on indefinitely. Thus, some stocks have had more than 10 different strike prices available. What are the consequences to the covered call seller of choosing a high strike price rather than a low one?

Obviously a low strike price gives a higher premium, but the amount of this premium that represents future time value will be relatively low. And it is only the future time value of the option that is the potential profit. The rest of the premium represents its current cash value and provides downside protection but does not represent an opportunity to make any money. A high strike price gives a much lower premium but the future time value of the option may be higher. In addition, if the option is out of the money, the call writer can make any profit caused by the stock rising up to the strike price.

To use an example (see Table 3.1 and Figure 3.1), when a typical stock was selling at 78 its five-month calls were priced as follows:

TABLE 3.1 Option Premiums for Various Strike Prices

Strike Price	Option Premium
70	11½
80	5¼
90	2

If we assume for purposes of this example that the stock remains at 78 until the expiration date of the option, the seller of the 70 call will realize 70 from the exercise of the stock plus the 11½ premium, making a total of 81½. The seller of the 80 strike price call will receive 78, if he chooses to sell it, for the stock plus the premium of 5¼, mak-

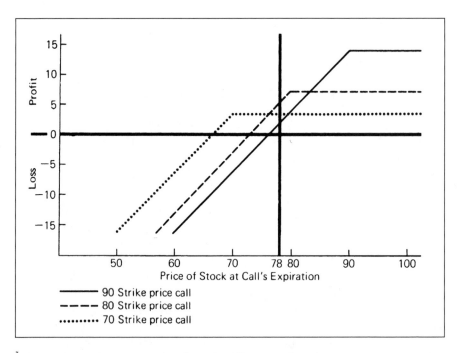

FIGURE 3.1 Writing Covered Calls with Different Strike Prices
The call with the highest strike price will be the most profitable if the stock goes up, but the call with the lowest strike price will perform the best if the stock goes down (price of stock when calls sold: 78). See text discussion for an answer to the quandary of which is preferable for the covered call writer.

ing a total of 83¼. The seller of the 90 will keep his stock, which we will value at 78, and will have the premium of 2, making a total of 80.

On the other hand, if the price of the stock had gone up to 90, the seller of the 90 call would be the clear winner. The seller of the 70 option would have the same amount as when the stock was 78, that is, 81½. The seller of the 80 option would receive 80 for his stock plus the 5¼ option premium, making a total of 85¼. The seller of the 90 call would have the value of his stock, 90, plus his premium of 2, giving a total of 92. Sounds as if the smart strategy is to sell the call with the highest strike price. But wait.

What if the price of the stock had gone down? Let us suppose that the price falls from 78 to 68. In that case, none of the options will be exercised and each seller will be left with the stock and his premium. So, each call seller has stock worth 68. The investor who sold the 70 call has a premium of 11½ in his bank account, the one who sold the 80 strike price call has 5¼ while the big winner in our previous example ends up with a measly 2. As a great commercial asked a few years ago, "What's a poor mother to do?"

To answer this question, one has to go back to an understanding of the basic reason for selling covered calls in the first place. The reason is that the sophisticated investor is willing to give up a large potential future gain, which may never materialize, in exchange for a certain gain in hand now, which is the amount of the premium. But how much of the premium is being paid for actual future time value and how much is just covering the present value of the stock?

At the 80 and 90 strike prices, the answer is clear. It is the full amount of the option. To determine how much is actually being paid for the option at the 70 strike price, as opposed to how much of the premium represents a payment for the current price of the stock, one has to find the difference between the strike price and the current price of the stock. Since the stock is now selling at 78 and the strike price is 70, for a difference of 8, we subtract 8 from the premium of 11½ to learn that the actual amount of the premium paid for the future time value of the option is 3½. Thus the amounts paid for the future time value of the option are 2 for the 90 strike price call, 5¼ for the 80, and 3½ for the 70.

Thus, the highest price for the future time value of the option is at the strike price closest to the price of the stock. This stands to reason, because the premium for the high 90 strike price call must reflect the fact that the stock is not very likely to rise 12 points to reach the strike price, and the premium for the future time value of the option at the low strike price of 70 is small because a large amount of the total premium represents a heavy insurance premium in case the price of the stock falls. Since the call buyer can only lose from this "insurance," he demands a reduction in the call premium as compensation.

Preference for Lower Strike Price. Now, back to our basic philosophy of selling a covered call, which is to get an assured income. The one big risk is that the price of the stock you hold will fall. Therefore, my general rule is that when selling a covered option you should give preference to the call with the lowest strike price. This affords you as much protection as you can get against the one Achilles' heel of selling a covered option. Of course, if the price of the stock goes up, you would have been better off selling at a higher strike price, but so what? You're still making a good profit with the lower strike price. The proper mental conditioning to have when you sell a covered call is that you are translating possible future windfalls into specific present gain. The moment you sell your call, you have accomplished this conversion.

In our example, the moment you sell the 70 strike price call you have made an extra $3\frac{1}{2}$ on your stock, which turns out to be 4.4%. Since this gain will be earned in five months, it means that you are earning an annual rate of 10%. This is not bad, especially when you consider that the buyer of your call is giving you free insurance for every single dollar that your stock could fall down to 70.

Obviously, if you strongly believe that your stock has a good chance of rising, you may wish to sell at the highest strike price. In a way you might think of a high strike price option as selling a partial option. You get to keep the benefit of a fairly good rise in the price of the stock, and have to turn over to the call buyer only the excess increase in your stock, which wouldn't bother you a bit. But, if the price goes down, you will be left with a loss on your stock and only the tiny premium to console you.

Selecting the Right Stock

If you do not already own any stock and would like to sell a covered call, you face the major decision of deciding which stock to purchase. Of course, you can select only a stock that has exchange-traded calls. First, you should check the quotations to find out what the premiums are for the various stocks. The amount of the premium varies greatly depending on many factors. For details on this see Chapter 1.

It is sufficient to note here that if you are buying stock for the specific purpose of selling calls on it, you should first select a stock whose call has a reasonably high premium. The stock mentioned in the previous example is a stock that carries an unusually large premium. Utilities usually have the smallest premiums. Generally the lower-priced stocks bear the higher percentage premiums. For a detailed discussion on the relationship between volatility and option premiums see Strategy Rule Number 3 later in this chapter. For sources of information that evaluate options in relation to the volatility of the underlying stocks and point out options that currently are overpriced, see Appendix A.

Second, you should select a stock that you personally will be happy to own and hold. For instance, if you feel that there will soon be a downturn in retail store profits and stock prices, there is no point in buying Kmart stock just because it may have a high premium or be attractive in other ways. Pick a stock that you would want to own, just as if you were not going to sell a call. Remember, if the price of the stock falls, you will be left holding the stock, and the only risk in selling calls is that the price of the stock may go down. Thus the major determinant of whether you will eventually make money from a covered call write is not the amount of premium you receive, but rather the subsequent price action of the stock.

Third, notice what the strike prices are for the stock you are considering. As suggested earlier in this chapter, the safest call to sell is the one with the lowest strike price. So if you are seeking safety, pick a stock that has a call with a strike price well below the current market price of the stock. On the other hand, if you are an optimist, you can pick a stock that has a strike price well above its current price, realizing, however, that this will reduce the amount of your premium and provide you with little downside protection.

While checking the strike prices available, it would be a good idea to check not only those for the current option period, but also those for the next three-month period, and the one after that, because not all strike prices may be available for future periods. If the price of the stock has declined substantially, then the highest strike price is not going to be offered for the longest-duration call.

Using Margin

One of the interesting aspects of covered call writing is that the use of margin can increase the percentage profit on your investment by a substantial amount. Investors in the stock market know that when the maximum margin is 50%, a brokerage firm will lend you one-half the money needed to purchase a stock, so that in order to buy a $50 stock you have to put up only $25. In regular stock trading this will double your leverage. But strangely enough, when it comes to covered writing, it is possible for margin to increase your return even more. The following example will show how. (See Table 3.2.) To simplify things I have excluded interest charges against the amount you are borrowing from the brokerage firm, so the results will be slightly overstated, but often the amount of dividends received from the additional stock you buy on margin can go a long way toward offsetting the interest cost.

TABLE 3.2 Cash versus Margin

Example 1: Stock Purchased for Cash	
Buy stock for 100	100
Sell 90 strike price option for 16	−16
Cash required	84
Potential profit (future time value of option)	6
Profit on investment	7.14%

Example 2: Stock Purchased on Margin	
Buy stock for 100; cash required = 50% of cost	50
Sell 90 strike price option for 16	−16
Cash required	34
Potential profit (future time value of option)	6
Profit on investment	17.64%

In this example, we can see that the use of margin did not just double the return, it actually increased it almost two and a half times. The reason that margin can increase the rate of return so dramatically is that while the investor pays for only half the stock, the entire premium is applied toward this half of the cost. Thus, every dollar of the option is paying for two dollars' worth of stock. Anyone who is legally able to purchase stock on margin (this excludes many trusts, pension funds, custodial accounts, and endowment funds) and is willing to accept the risks of owning stock on margin should seriously consider doing so. Some of the risk usually associated with a margin account is reduced provided that Strategy Rule Number 2 of this chapter is followed.

Once you have written your call, you could wait until it expires and then decide what to do next. But in most cases it will be to your advantage to monitor carefully the position to determine whether changes could be made before expiration to increase your profitability or decrease your downside risk or perhaps do both. If you are writing in-the-money options, you may wish to see all your stocks called away. In such a case, the only concern you have is if the stock should fall below the strike price. See Strategy Rule Number 2 later in this chapter for the correct procedures.

Two Times to Take Action. As in all option-writing programs, you should be watching your positions to see if you are earning the maximum amount from the future time value of the options you have sold. There are therefore two situations that should immediately alert you to the need for action. The first is if the current premium of any option you have sold declines to a small fraction. The exact amount depends on the price of the stock, but certainly if any of your outstanding options are selling for $1/4$ or less it is time to do something. The reason for this is twofold: (1) no matter what happens, the maximum profit you can make from that option is only 25 cents a share, and (2) your downside protection is now only 25 cents a share, which is almost meaningless. This reduction in the price of your outstanding option results from either the passing of time or a decline in the price of your underlying stock, or a combination of both.

The second situation that should alert you to immediate action is if the future time value of your outstanding in-the-money option has fallen to a small amount, such as $1/4$ on low-priced stocks and a relatively small amount on higher-priced stocks. As you may recall, the future time value of an in-the-money option is found by adding the price of the option to its strike price and subtracting the price of the stock, and represents the maximum profit you will be able to make from the option. When this amount begins to approach zero, there is no point in maintaining the position. You still have the chance of loss if the stock declines, but you no longer have the possibility of a meaningful profit, so you should take action at once to change this. An in-the-money option reaches a low future time value with the passage of time and with an increase in the price of the underlying stock.

MANAGING THE COVERED WRITING PROGRAM

There are four types of action you can take in managing a covered writing program: (1) rolling out your option, which means buying in the option you previously sold and selling another at the same strike price with a longer duration; (2) rolling up, which means buying in the option you previously sold and selling one with the same expiration date but a higher strike price, typically done when the stock has gone up in price; (3) rolling down, that is, buying in your existing option and selling one with the same expiration date at a lower strike price; and (4) buying in your existing option and not writing any other option, so that that you are out of the option writing program. This is typically done when there simply are no options available that meet your criteria for writing. You then should decide whether you want to hold the stock without writing any options on it or you want to sell the stock. Let us now look at each of these strategies in more detail.

Rolling Out

The big question in rolling out is when to do it. If the price of the stock were to stay constant, then you would be best off waiting until your current option expires, or shrinks to a small fraction, before writing the next one. But since your stock is probably going to fluctuate, you take the risk that by waiting too long the credit you might be able to get by rolling out now will be less. If your option is out of the money now and the stock goes down, you will be able to get less for the longer-duration option later. If your option is in the money now and it goes up, you will also get less of a credit for the spread if you wait. You should roll out when the future time value of your present option has declined to the point where the future profit potential no longer justifies the risk of holding the stock. The decision of which duration option to roll out to is made in exactly the same way as you decided which option to sell in the first place when you entered into the position.

Like the other strategies mentioned here, rolling out should be entered as a spread order. That is, rather than buying your existing option at a certain price and then trying to sell the longer one, the orders should be placed simultaneously for a net credit. If you were trying to buy back your April 45 for $1/4$ and sell the July 45 for $1^1/4$, you would enter the order as a spread order for a 1-point credit, since it makes little difference to you what the prices of the options are as long as you get 1 point more for the July option than you pay for the April.

Rolling Up

Rolling up is what you do when your stock has gone up in value, and should be done as soon as the future time value of your existing option declines due to an increase in the price of the stock. By then there will be an option trading at a higher strike price, and it will be offering more future time value. Another way of deciding when you should roll up is if doing so will result in your new option bearing the same relation to the stock price as the original option did to the stock price when you put it on. That is, if you originally decided to write an option 1 point out of the money, so that you wrote the 35 option when the stock was 34, and the stock is now 39, you would be keeping with your original plan by rolling up from the 35 to the 40 option.

Suppose that when you bought the stock for 34, the 35 option you sold was 2. Now, a few weeks later, with the stock at 39, the 35 option you sold might be selling for $4\frac{1}{2}$ and there would be a 40 option with the same expiration date that might be selling for 2. You could therefore buy back your 35 option and sell the 40 option for a combined cost of $2\frac{1}{2}$ points, which is to say that you are rolling up for a $2\frac{1}{2}$ debit. Normally in a covered writing program one likes to take in money, but in this instance you are paying out $250 for each 100 shares you own. The reason you do this is that for $250 you have increased the maximum value to you of each share on the expiration date of the option from $35 to $40. Whether you will actually be able to benefit from this rolling up will depend on how high the shares are selling at the option's expiration. If they are selling at 40 or better, your rolling up has been well worth your while, because for a cash expenditure of $2.50 a share you have increased their value to you by $5 each. If the stock stays at 39, you have increased their value to you by $4.

The danger in rolling up is that if the stock falls back to where it was, you have spent cash and received nothing of value in return. If the stock falls back down to 34, you are left with stock worth that much a share, and you are out the $2.50 a share it cost you to roll up. In short, your roll-up has been a complete failure. This kind of whipsaw will happen from time to time, but the law of averages says that the stock will continue on up at least as often as it falls down. And when it stays at 39 you will come out ahead by $1.50 ($4 minus $2.50). Thus rolling up does represent something of a risk, because you could lose the entire cost of the operation. But generally it is worth it, and when it works it results in making the covered program far more successful than you originally anticipated.

Let us assume that you sold your original 35 option in this example for $2. That, plus the possible $1 increase in price from 34 to 35, was all that you expected to make from this option expiration period. But by rolling up when the stock went to 39, you were able to squeeze out an additional $1.50 (assuming the stock stays at 39) or an additional $2.50 (if it goes above 40), which means that you will realize a 50% to 83% greater profit from this position than you had originally expected. And if the stock goes up to 44, there is no reason why you would not roll up again, with similar gains in potential profit. To conclude our discussion of rolling up, while it requires an expenditure of cash that could be a total loss if the stock comes back down, the roll-up requires taking no more risk than the original covered writing position and offers the opportunity to increase your profit from the position by a very substantial amount.

Rolling Down

Rolling down is the saddest of the strategies and the most difficult to do. It is sad because it is done only when the stock has depreciated substantially in price and the position is already a loser, and furthermore, rolling down will not transform a losing position into a winning position. On the contrary, it actually locks in a loss, which is what makes it so difficult to do. Let's use the same example we did for rolling up. You buy a stock for \$34 and sell the 35 option for \$2. Now let's assume that the stock declines to 29 and the 35 option is at $1/8$, and there is a 30 option worth $1^{1}/_{2}$. You have lost 5 points on your stock and made $1^{7}/_{8}$ on the 35 option, giving you a net loss of $3^{1}/_{8}$. What do you do?

The easiest answer is to do nothing and hope that the stock will return to 34 or better. This would mean that you would have the profit you wanted, but it depends on the stock going up 5 points, and the entire purpose in covered option writing is that you want to minimize your dependence on the price movement of stocks. Furthermore, the price of the stock could continue downward at a time when you have virtually no downside protection. The only alternative to doing nothing is to buy back the 35 option for $1/8$ and sell the 30 for $1^{1}/_{2}$, for a credit spread of $1^{3}/_{8}$. Adding this $1^{3}/_{8}$ to the 2 you originally took in means that you have taken in a total of $3^{3}/_{8}$ in option premiums, while losing 5 points on your stock. You have a net loss of $1^{5}/_{8}$, but note that if the stock now goes up over 30 you will get that additional point, meaning that you would have a loss of just $5/8$ point. While no one wants to take a loss, one can take comfort in the fact that a $5/8$ loss when a stock falls 4 points isn't really so terrible.

In short, what rolling down does is to increase the amount of option premium you take in to offset the loss in the price of the stock, and the price you pay for this additional income is a substantial reduction in exercise price. It is never a very appealing choice, and at times you will conclude that it is not worth doing. But it is the only way to get in more option income once your stock has gone down. And just as in rolling up, rolling down can be combined with rolling out.

In fact, it usually is, because the additional income to be derived from selling the longer option helps to make the roll-down more palatable.

Buying In

If rolling down is just too depressing for you, then you should consider the fourth alternative of closing out your positions in the stock and the option, and taking your loss. The virtue of this is that there may well be other covered writing positions available that offer better opportunities for profit and downside protection. If you do nothing, but just let your depressed stock stay in your possession, then you are not in an option writing program anymore, and you are not getting any of its advantages. It's a free world, and you can do that if you want, but you owe it to yourself to make an objective decision as to whether this is what you want to do. There is no place in investing for taking action by default.

COVERED WRITING RULES OF STRATEGY

If you want to avoid disappointments and make money from your covered option writing program, here are some rules of strategy that I have developed from experience.

Strategy Rule Number 1: Calculate Your Anticipated Return on Investment

Figure out exactly what your anticipated return on investment will be. This probably seems like an obvious rule, but there are two reasons why it is specifically applicable to a covered write. In the first place, the maximum return on covered writing is fixed in advance, and no matter what happens after you have put on your position, your return can never be higher than was predictable from the minute that you put it on. This is quite unlike buying shares of stock, where the profit you could make is limited only by how high the price of the stock will go. When you buy shares of stock and sell options against them, you are automatically fixing the maximum return you can make, and you ought to know in advance what that maximum return can be. Once you put on the position things can only live up to that maximum return or they can get worse, and if you didn't do your homework properly beforehand, you are apt to be disappointed even if things work out as well as they possibly can.

The other reason why this rule is specifically appropriate to covered writing is that, since this is a conservative strategy, we are typically looking for a relatively low return over the life of the option. For example, if we sell a four-month option, we might be happy to get a net return on our investment of 8%. This is actually a very small amount of money in absolute terms, and a minor mistake in your calculations could reduce this to the point where you would not be interested in doing it. If you put up $10,000 in cash, you might be able to purchase $28,000 worth of stock on margin, and sell options worth $4,000. These are pretty big numbers to be throwing around when the maximum you expect to make on the options, if everything goes just as you planned, is only $800. It requires far more accuracy than doing out-of-the-money bull spreads (see Chapter 6 for a description), where the amount is also limited but you hope that an investment of $10,000 will bring you a profit of $30,000. If you're off by $800 on your calculations there it wouldn't even be noticed. Here it kills the entire profit of the transaction.

The method for figuring the return from a covered write is given in Appendix I. It should be easy to follow. The reason it is so important to actually go through the form and figure out the return is that if you try to eyeball the figures for the purchase of the stock and the sale of the option, you will invariably be too high in your estimation of the return. Commissions on the option, the purchase of the stock, and the sale of the stock when it is called away are extremely significant, and for the smaller investor who is buying a few hundred shares, the commissions can actually be so high that they will take all the profit out of some of the lower-yielding situations and will reduce some of the higher-yielding situations to returns so measly that it may not be worth the risk.

The individual investor needs to keep in mind that in writing covered calls he is competing with major institutions. These institutions can have three distinct advantages over the average individual investor: (1) They are satisfied with smaller returns than most individuals are looking for. Some are said to be looking for annual returns from writing covered calls that are just 2% better than the performance of the average stock. This may be less than the individual investor is looking for. (2) The institutions operate in such large volume that the commission they pay per share and per option may be only a small fraction of what the individual investor must pay. (3) The institutions may get help from brokerage block desks that will position covered writing trades for them. This means that instead of buying stock and then quickly trying to sell the option at a given price like most individuals must do, they can ask to put on the position as a unit. They would, say, buy 1,000 shares of Microsoft and sell the January 90 call for a net cost of $87^1/_8$.

All this points to the fact that when you are looking for covered writing positions you may be competing with an institution that is paying far less in commissions than you are and is willing to get a smaller annualized return. This means that when you find a situation you like, you had better examine it very closely to see that on a net basis it is really giving you the return you want.

Strategy Rule Number 2: Decide in Advance What You Are Going to Do If the Stock Falls

If there is one theme I would like to have permeating this book, it is this: Decide in advance exactly what you are going to do if the transaction goes sour. I know that this is difficult to do, because we buy options on a stock only when we "know" that it is going to go up, and we buy puts only when we "know" that it is going to go down, and we do covered writes only when we feel confident that this stock is not going to go very far below the strike price. But the difference between the dilettante on Wall Street and the professional investor is that the professional knows he can be wrong, and he is willing to admit it and to take whatever action he can to minimize his loss, while the amateur is so sure his original views were correct that instead of taking corrective action while he can, he sits back waiting for the gods to reverse the price action of the stock and bring him back into a profit position. When he finally concludes that maybe this time the gods are not going to save him, it is usually too late to take much in the way of constructive action.

This rule is particularly appropriate to covered option writing because the profit potential is limited, and the loss potential is far, far greater. It should be clear that if you can make $1 on a transaction, but you can lose $5, you had better do something to limit your chances of losing that $5, or you are not going to come out very much ahead. This is indeed the Achilles' heel of covered option writing, as we mentioned with our example of the two $100 stocks, one of which went up by $50 and one of which went down by $50. The way to overcome this is to limit the loss possible when the stock goes down.

Fortunately, there is a very simple and effective mechanism for doing this, and that is to enter a stop-loss order to sell the stock out when it declines to a certain price. As soon as the stop-loss order is executed you must be sure to buy in your options. The basic question is to determine what the price of the stop-loss order should be. If you are writing in-the-money options, then as long as the stock stays above the strike price, you will make your maximum anticipated profit. So there is certainly no point in getting out of the position as long as the stock is above the strike price. Once it starts to go below the strike price, you may still make money, if the stock does not go further below the strike price than the future time value of the option when you sold it (ignoring transaction costs). And of course, no matter how low the price of the stock goes during the life of the option, there is always the hope that the stock will come back up in price before the option expires, thus saving the position. But this is, alas, more wishful thinking than sound analytical reasoning. When faced with these conflicting forces, it sometimes pays to go back to the original theory behind the position to reach a solution.

Back to the Original Theory. You originally decided to do a covered write on this particular stock with this particular option because, while you weren't sure that the stock would go up, you felt pretty sure that it would not decline much below the strike price of the option. (If you didn't feel this way, one might wonder why you did the position in the first place.) Now that the stock has gone below the strike price, you have been proven wrong. Since you were wrong in the first place and it went well below the strike price, there is certainly a good chance that you will become even more wrong and the stock will move down even further. When you are wrong, it is often the best strategy to admit it, and then close out the position. Another way to look at a covered write is that you went into it because you did not want to have to worry about whether the stock went up or down, within certain limits. If you wanted to be concerned with the daily movements of the stock you would not have written an in-the-money option. Now that the stock has moved down below the strike price you no longer are accomplishing that objective. You now do have to worry about each move of the stock, because each move down of $1/8$ point is costing you $12.50 for every 100 shares you own—reason number two for closing out the position.

Therefore, the conclusion seems inescapable that in order to eliminate possible large losses that would wipe out the profits, you must have a program for automatically closing out potential large losers. Placing stop-loss orders is such a program. If you are writing in-the-money options, you can place these orders at a point or two below the strike price. Depending on how much time has elapsed, you might be able to get out of the position at a very small loss, no loss at all, or, if a great deal of time has passed, even at a small profit.

The disadvantage of closing out the position just below the strike price is that you may be taking a loss when the stock is at its low, and it may soon go back up to a profitable point. In other words, by closing out the position before expiration when the stock is down, you are virtually guaranteeing yourself a loss, whereas if you did nothing there is a fair possibility that the stock will go back up and you will end up with the very profit that you originally intended to get.

Is it really, therefore, a good idea to close out the position prematurely? The answer lies in the basic philosophy of the covered option writer. This is that he is someone who wishes to make a profit primarily from receipt of option premiums and not from the movement of stock prices. The amount of income that can be received is therefore fixed and limited. If you are not willing to close out a position when the stock is falling, then you are taking a chance that you will lose an enormous amount of money, and, as we noted, a large loss on one stock position is not going to be offset by a large gain on another position, because your maximum gain is limited by your sale of the option.

This method of making money is completely different from buying a selection of stocks, and a different method of monitoring must be used. The conclusion to reach when faced with the quandary of taking a certain loss now versus hoping that the stock will go back up is that you must take a certain loss now, because it is a small loss and there is no way that you can afford to take a large loss. If you do nothing now, that small loss might snowball into a large loss, and that would be disastrous.

Other Stop-Loss Strategies. Incidentally, closing out the position is not the only action that can be taken when the stock goes down, and I would certainly not preclude taking other actions. Sometimes it might be possible to roll down to the next lower option, or to sell an additional option at the lower strike price if you don't mind changing your position into a two-to-one ratio. (See Chapter 6 for details.) The important rule being stated here is that you must decide in advance exactly at what point you will take action and exactly what action you will take. If you do not, then you are probably playing a losing game, in which the option buyer gets to make all the abnormally large profits, and you get to suffer all the abnormally large losses. When you look at it this way, you realize that there really is no choice.

One example will demonstrate what I mean. It would be difficult to think of a better stock to write covered calls on than American Home Products, a consumer products giant that is also active in pharmaceuticals, agriculture, animal health, and even, for a little glamour, biotechnology. It's always taken a backseat when it comes to publicity, but this cost-conscious powerhouse makes many of the brand-name products you see advertised: Advil, Anacin, Centrum, Dimetapp, Dristan, Robitussin, and Solgar. With annual sales of $12 billion, and with products in areas that are not sensitive to interest rate changes or recession, plus paying a nice dividend, it definitely fits the parameters for a good covered-call-writing stock. In fact, it has done so well that a few years ago *Fortune* magazine named it the stock of the decade. On April 12, 1999, it closed at $69^3/_4$. Let's say you decided to buy 300 shares for $21,000 and sell the September 70 call for $8^7/_8$. Sounds like a good trade, and if the stock just stays where it is you'll make a very nice return.

Unfortunately, despite a neutral stock market in general, there was bad news from AHP. The stock quickly gave up 10 points, then held at 60 for a few weeks before falling down to 50, where it held until early August when it suddenly plunged down to 42. So here we have a conservative, blue chip stock that in just four months dropped by 28 points for a loss of 40%. Against this, what good is your 70 call with what now appears to be its pitifully small premium of $8^7/_8$?

This example is, fortunately, unusual, but by no means unique. Gillette with its dominant share of the shaving blade market giving it marketing power and almost guaranteed high profits, went from 64 in March 1999 to 33 just seven months later. Even Coca-Cola, owner of the most valuable trademark in the entire world, went from 88 in July 1998 to a low of 48 in October 1999. And remember, we're not talking about speculative stocks but rather the most solid, largest, time-proven blue chips. You can just imagine the kind of collapses that have happened to lesser-quality stocks.

Take the Small Loss. These are just some examples of stocks that had terrifying drops in price. There are too many other stocks to mention here that have had similar drops. And there will be many others in the future that will plummet in what will appear to the people holding the stocks to be a totally unjustified and irrational manner. The adjectives one applies to such declines are, unfortunately, immaterial. It is the fact of the decline that will affect your profit and loss columns at the end of the year, not your or someone else's opinion that the stock shouldn't have gone down. Therefore, you should take a small loss in order to prevent a potentially much larger loss.

If it helps, you can think of yourself as a forest warden who deliberately burns down a section of timberland in order to stop the spread of a raging forest fire, or as the captain of a freighter besieged by raging seas who throws part of the cargo overboard in order to save the ship, the lives of the crew, and the remaining cargo. Or the doctor who amputates a patient's leg in order to save his life. In each case, the common thread is this: There has been a serious occurrence that threatens to become disastrous and perhaps fatal. By taking prompt action, which action admittedly has unfortunate consequences and will obviate the possibility of success in that venture forever, the really serious disaster can be avoided. So, if you want to run your investing program like a professional, take some free tips from some other professionals.

I should point out, furthermore, that a stock's falling further than you had anticipated is actually to be expected and you must prepare for it. In developing your overall investment goals and anticipated returns you should factor in a portion of covered writes that will not work, and you deduct a reasonable loss on these from the others that you expect will work.

The good thing about covered option writing is that at least when premiums are at their normal levels, there is a generous enough return available so that you can absorb the losses from positions that do not work out and still achieve a satisfactory return from the overall portfolio. To do this one cannot seek too high a return. Remember, the average total return to stockholders over the past five decades has been about 12%. So whatever you can do above that is a plus.

Strategy Rule Number 3: Weigh the Stock's Volatility against the Option Premium

In selecting the stock you wish to write against, carefully weigh the stock's volatility against the premium of the option. This rule is where the entire skill of option writing comes into play, and it is here that the option writer finds his greatest challenge. When options first were introduced, brokerage firms started making up lists showing the highest-priced options and how high a return one would receive if one wrote these. Unfortunately, it turned out that the stocks that had the highest-priced options were also the stocks that many people would not want to own if they were the last stocks in the world. The ones with the highest option premiums were always the stocks with the highest price/earnings ratios, the lowest dividends, and the shakiest companies behind them. That is the way it always will be, for the very simple reason that when a stock is so speculative that no careful investor wants to own it, there will be a low supply of options available for purchase. Conversely, when a stock is stable, pays a high dividend, carries a low price/earnings ratio, and is one that the conservative institutions would be willing to own, it is easy to find plenty of option sellers, and the price of the option will fall. But this does not mean that that particular option is underpriced, any more than the fact that the option on the opposite type of stock is very high means that it is overpriced.

Over the years that options have been traded on exchanges a great deal of thought has gone into what the theoretical value of an option ought to be. Myron Scholes and Robert Merton gained worldwide recognition in 1997 when they won the Nobel prize in economics for their work on a formula for determining the correct price of options. Nevertheless there are still a number of different formulas in use by various institutional option traders. All these formulas have two things in common: They all relate option prices to (1) the volatility of the stock and (2) the dividend it pays. The more volatile the stock, the higher the price the option buyer is willing to pay, and the higher the price the option seller demands in return for giving up the upside potential and keeping the downside risk. A dividend reduces the price of the option, because if the stock pays a large dividend, then option writers are more willing to own the stock, reasoning that (1) the return on the dividend itself will help to make money for them as covered writers, and (2) the size of the dividend will give some downside protection, since there is a point below which the stock is not likely to fall because at that level it would be attractive on a yield basis alone.

The question of whether an option is overpriced or underpriced is not as important to a covered writer as the annualized return you are aiming for, as discussed in Strategy Rule Number 1. The purpose of this rule is to point out that whenever your stock declines to the point where you are going to take some action in accordance with Strategy Rule Number 2, you have a loss on your hands. You therefore must try to avoid stocks that have a probability of falling to that point. And the more volatile a stock is, the better chance it has of falling to that point. So your specific concerns as a covered option writer, in order of importance, are: (1) Determine what the maximum annualized return will be, (2) figure out what your action level is on the downside movement of the stock price, and (3) look at the volatility of the stock and perhaps at its recent price action to estimate what its chances are of falling to that action point.

It is practically a truism that the most volatile stocks are not always the best writing candidates. If you happen to believe in a stock for reasons other than its volatility, then you might be very comfortable in using that stock, even if a straight theoretical evaluation would show that the option is actually underpriced. And the more you believe in a stock, the lower you would be able to put the price at which you would take action in accordance with Strategy Rule Number 1. And the lower you put the action point, the less probability there is that you will ever reach that point and be forced to take a loss.

To summarize this rule, it is not enough for the option writer to look at the annualized rates of return that he can get from various stocks. He must carefully weigh the rate of return against the possibility of the stock going down below a break-even point. Unfortunately, there is no simple guide that can be presented in a book to make this weighing any easier. The various formulas that have been developed to determine whether options are overvalued or undervalued are of only limited assistance, because they are usually on a relative basis (i.e., in relation to what the option usually sells for when the stock is at this price).

But your decision must be made on an absolute basis (i.e., for this particular stock am I willing to take on the risk of its declining to my downside action point in exchange for the return I am going to get?). The only help it would be to know that an option was overpriced, would be that if you had to buy back the option later when the stock went down to your action point, you could expect that the option would return to its normal price and thus would be relatively cheaper, thereby decreasing your loss. So, basically, in making the decision of what options to write you are on your own, and certainly a subjective view of the underlying stock can be of great value in helping you.

Strategy Rule Number 4: Don't Wait Until the Options Expire to Write the Next Options

Some option writing programs are based on buying stocks for the purpose of writing a specific in-the-money option and then holding on to the position until the stock is called away. But if you are in a continuous option writing program against some stock that you want to hold for a longer period, then it is important not to wait until the options expire before you write the next series. If you are writing in-the-money options and you wait until they are about to expire, there is a very good chance that you will be prematurely exercised in the final weeks. This happens when the options are selling at around their actual cash value, and is especially prevalent the day before the stock goes ex-dividend. The result is that you lose your stock and have to pay a commission on selling it at the strike price. If you were planning to write another option against the stock, you now have to buy the stock in again. Result: two commissions on the underlying stock that were totally unnecessary, plus usually buying the stock at the offering price for an additional $\frac{1}{8}$ or more.

If you are writing out-of-the-money options, you do not have to be concerned with premature exercises, but there is another reason for not just waiting until the option expires. This is that you originally went into an option writing program with the idea that the option you had written gave you a certain amount of downside protection against an adverse move in the price of the stock. If you bought the stock for 40 and sold a 40 strike price option for 4, you knew that if when the option expired the stock was at 36, you would break even (disregarding commissions). And you did not mind owning the stock with this kind of protection from the option. If there had been a 45 option available with a price of $\frac{1}{4}$, you probably would have rejected it because it did not offer the downside protection you wanted.

Now let us assume that you put on this position, and the option is in its final week. The stock is at 39, the option you originally wrote for 4 has dropped to $\frac{1}{4}$, and you are happily waiting for the option to expire so that you can sell the next one and take in more money. What I am suggesting in this rule is that you have already strayed from your original philosophy. When you started out you wanted 4 points of downside protection, and now that you have only $\frac{1}{4}$ point, you are waiting for that entirely to disappear! How much downside protection will you have the day before the option is to expire? Absolutely none, for all practical purposes.

Let's further analyze the position of a person who owns stock and has an option written that is worth $\frac{1}{4}$ point. He is still giving up all profit over the strike price, just as if the option were worth 8 points. So the fact that the option is cheap does not decrease what he is giving up. But it certainly does take away any downside protection. So the conclusion is that you should not wait until the last minute to trade in your old option for a new one. One must concede that if the stock stays in the same place, or moves up to the strike price, the maximum return to the covered writer would be achieved by holding on to the option until expiration and then rewriting. But in the real world there is the strong chance that the stock will go down instead of up, and then the urge to squeeze the extra $\frac{1}{4}$ point out of the old option could have grave consequences. Because if the stock goes down, then the price you will be able to receive for writing the new option could be several dollars less.

Just when should you roll out your old options? There can be no hard-and-fast rule, since this, like everything else in options, is a trade-off. You are trading off a higher possible return if you wait against a more certain and even return by rolling over. Probably the best method is to decide what you consider a realistic annual return, which should be less than the theoretical return achieved by selling the option and waiting for its expiration. When the option you wrote has declined enough in value over the period of time to give you this annualized rate of return, then you should consider rolling the option out. Your maximum profit may be less, but conversely it could easily be a great deal more. The decision is not unlike that which car owners must face on when to trade in their old tires. Sure, there may be a few thousand more miles on those treads you're driving now, and trading them in today means that you are losing out on all those miles. But if you should have a blowout next week, the cost could be many times that of getting the new tires a few weeks earlier.

One of the recurring themes of this book is that when you are faced with a question of what to do, go back to your original purpose in taking the position. If your original purpose in covered writing was to get meaningful downside protection, then you've got to roll out when your existing option is priced so low that it is no longer giving you that protection.

Strategy Rule Number 5: Maximize Your Return by Rolling Up Your Options at the Proper Occasion

Just as you must expect there are going to be stocks that will decline so fast that you will take a loss on the position, so on the bright side there will be some occasions when you will be able to make more money than you anticipated because you will be able to roll up your options. In deciding when you should roll up, you must take the following into consideration:

1. *Will your downside protection be the same?* You should try to maintain at least the same downside protection that you had when you first went into the position. Thus, if you initially sold a 40 strike price option for 3 when the stock was 40, and the stock is now 45 with the 45 option at 2, you would not be getting the same downside protection. The big danger in rolling up is always that the stock will fall back down to where it was, and you will be left with a losing position rather than a winner. At least when you go into a roll-up be sure that you are getting the same protection.

2. *What proportion of the increase in strike price are you paying to do the roll-up?* In the example where you roll up from the 40 to 45 options, you are gaining 5 points in the value of your stock, assuming

that the stock is over 45 when you do the roll-up. Since a roll-up is done for a debit, it is easy to compare the amount of the debit with the increase in strike price. If the 40 option were 6 and the 45 option were 2, the debit to do the roll-up would be the difference between the two, or 4 points. To pay out 4 points, with the greatly increased risk in case the stock goes down, for the sake of increasing the value of your stock by 5 points is not a particularly appealing move. It is frequently possible to pay out only 60% of the increase in strike price. For instance, if here the 45 option were 3, then the cost of rolling would be only 3 points, and dividing this by the 5-point increase would give you a cost of 60%.

3. *Can you combine rolling up with rolling out?* Rolling up is often combined with rolling out in order to reduce the cost of the move and to obtain more downside protection. So, in this example, if the 45 option with the same duration as the one originally written is 3, the next longer duration might be 5. Rolling up and out to this option would cost only 1 point, which means that the cost would be reduced to just 20% of the increase in the value of the stock, remembering, of course, that we are now also including another three months.

Strategy Rule Number 6: Get Out of a Stock
When It No Longer Offers Attractive Writing Opportunities

Professional options managers have no loyalties to any stock. And neither should you. A stock is valuable to you only when it can provide you with option-writing opportunities that fit your criteria. When the stock can no longer do so, your response should be to get out of the stock and into something else. A resistance to getting out of one stock and into another is often a habit of people who are used to trading or investing in stocks, where there may be a virtue in staying with a stock over a period of time. But in a covered options program, you set your sights at the outset on trying to make money by capturing the future time value of options that you sell. You may also set a goal of obtaining a certain amount of downside protection or the possibility of getting a certain percentage increase in the value of the stock if you are writing out-of-the-money options. But the most important criterion of all is the first covered writing strategy rule discussed here, that you be able to obtain a certain annualized rate of return from option income.

It happens frequently that a stock that is just beautiful for your option writing program when you first sell an option will simply not be appropriate later when the option expires. The most common reason is that the stock moves into a range where there just isn't any option around offering what you want. For example, say you like to write options that give at least 20% downside protection and offer an annualized rate of return of 25% when you buy the stock on margin. Let's say stock XYZ is selling for 11, and the six-month option at the 10 strike price is 2, which nicely fits your criteria. You write the option, and six months later, when the option is about to expire, the stock is at 13.

Now the 10 option with six months to go is selling at $3\frac{1}{2}$, which has far from enough future time value (only $\frac{1}{2}$ point) to give you your desired annualized rate of return. On the other hand, the 15 option is selling for $\frac{3}{8}$, which doesn't give either the downside protection you want or the annualized return. What do you do? Many people would buy in the old 10 option and sell the 15 option hoping that the stock will continue to go up. But that is clearly not within the bounds of your original goals. You have now let circumstances convert you from someone who demanded a 20% downside protection to someone who is accepting a downside protection of only 7% because it was the convenient thing to do. Don't be lazy. If a stock doesn't give you what you want anymore, simply get out of it.

When the Stock Goes Down. Another common example occurs when the stock goes down. Let's say you get into a stock when it is 30 and you write the 30 six-month option for 3. That's a gross potential profit of 11% in six months on your cash investment (30 minus 3 equals 27; 3 divided by 27 equals 11%). The six months pass and the stock is now 26. You have lost money on the transaction and now you are wondering what to do to get even. The 25 option with six months to go is selling for $2\frac{1}{2}$ and the 30 option is now selling for 1. If you sell the 25 option for $1\frac{1}{2}$ points of future time value you have locked in a loss on your overall position, but more important for this discussion is that you can make only $1\frac{1}{2}$ points of future time value on your investment, which comes out to a potential gross profit of only 6.5% for six months (26 minus 3 gives you your investment of 23; future time value of 1.5 divided by 23 equals 6.5%). If you sell the 30 option for 1 point, you are getting only 4% in option income, although you have the possibility of making more if the stock goes up.

The conclusion is that neither of these alternatives should be acceptable to you, unless something drastic has happened to premiums of all optionable stocks, which is usually not the case. The problem here is that a stock which was in a good position for option writing when you bought it has now become unacceptable, because the stock is simply not in a good price range vis-à-vis the option strike prices, and because as the price of the stock has dropped in the past six months the premiums for the options have also fallen. The undisciplined option writer would pick either the 25 option, saying that he will get his 6.5% return with less downside protection because he doesn't expect the stock to drop below 25, while others will choose the 30 option with the wishful thinking that the stock will go back up to 30 and everything will come out all right in the end, just as in fairy tales.

But neither of these "solutions" is bucking up to the hard realities of the situation, which are that the stock just isn't right for you anymore as an option-writing situation. If you wanted to get only 6.5% for a six-month option you could probably find a better stock, and if you wanted to write options that were so far out of the money that they gave only a 4% return you wouldn't have gone into this writing program in the first place, when it yielded 11%. So the conclusion is to stick to your original guidelines. Get out of the stock. Get into another one that has downside protection and annualized yields closer to what you are looking for. With hundreds of optionable stocks it is sometimes remarkable how many good writing situations there are at any one time. There will almost always be one stock that is just at the strike price, or just 1 point above it, or whatever you are looking for. But it obviously won't always be the same stock. So don't be reluctant to get out of one and into another when the prices so dictate.

Strategy Rule Number 7: When Initiating Positions, Buy the Stock and Sell the Option Simultaneously

When you buy a stock you know exactly what you are able to sell each of its options for, and you can calculate what your downside protection is and what your potential annualized rate of return will be. That is the time to decide which option to write, and to write it. If you are not satisfied with the rates of return, then don't go into that stock. Wait until the premiums get better, or the stock gets nearer a strike price so that the annualized rate of return gets better.

Unfortunately, many people buy the stock now with the thought that after it goes up by a few points, they will then sell the option for a higher price, having the best of all possible worlds (i.e., a low-cost stock and a high-priced option). On Wall Street this is known as *legging*, as in putting on one's pants one leg at a time. The only trouble with legging into a position is that it has little to do with covered option writing. What these investors are doing is simply buying a stock with the idea that it will go up in price. There is certainly nothing wrong with this, and thousands of people do it every day, but it is not a way of rationally writing covered options. Because if these investors are right and the stock does go up, then they don't need to sell an option; they could just as well sell the stock and be out of it completely with a good profit. If the stock goes down, then they have missed out completely on the chance to get the downside protection that selling an option provides, and if the stock stays still, they will never sell the option at the price they could have gotten originally.

What often happens is that if the stock does go up, the investor decides that it is going to go up even further and sees no point in selling an option right now, with the result that he never does sell the option. If the stock keeps going right up, he will be glad that he didn't, but if it turns around he will be very sorry. In any case, he is not in a covered-option-writing program.

So let's analyze things as they are. If you want to trade stocks by buying stocks that you think will go up, that's fine. But don't delude yourself into thinking that you are in a covered-option-writing program. You are simply trading stocks and using options as a supplement.

Strategy Rule Number 8: Formulate Your Objectives and Then Adhere to Them

Formulate your objectives when you start your covered writing program and then stick to those objectives. This is a general rule that applies to every covered writing situation. This rule has two parts, and the second is much more difficult than the first, but also far more important. The first is that you should try to quantify your goals when you start your program. It is not sufficient just to decide that you want to make about 20% annualized by buying stocks on margin and writing covered options. That is not specific enough to be of much help. The specific questions you must answer are: Just how volatile a stock am I willing to buy? With tighter downside cutoffs (e.g., a stop-loss order on the stock) am I willing to buy a more volatile stock? How much downside protection do I want from the options I am selling? How low a rate of annualized return am I willing to accept? Do I want to write out-of-the-money options or do I want the downside protection that only in-the-money options can provide? How little future time value will I accept in an option before I buy it back to roll out, roll up, or close out the position? How low am I willing to let a stock get before I take action, either closing out the position or selling another option at a lower strike price or longer duration? These questions should be carefully thought out before you get into a writing program, and their answers should be written down, so that you can review them from month to month as the program continues.

The second part of the rule is then to follow these guidelines and actually use them as directives for running your program. You will be fighting a constant battle against inaction and wishful thinking. The best example of this is when your stock starts sinking. The normal reaction is to hope that it will move back up. Unfortunately, this is the most dangerous single circumstance in writing covered options, and the one that can destroy the profitability of an entire covered-option-writing portfolio. So, as difficult as it is, it is imperative to adhere to the rule that it is always better to lose a small amount of money now than to risk losing a larger amount later. Those people who bought American Home Products at 70 to write covered options either took prompt, vigorous action when it started going down or saw their positions get killed.

Similarly, when stocks have gone up, the covered writers either rolled their options up or missed out on what could have been one of the most profitable investments they will ever make. American Express went from 70 in October 1998 to 140 in six months. Anyone who had written the 65 or 70 options and decided to "wait a while and see whether it's going to keep on going up or whether it will come down" missed out on a one-in-a-hundred opportunity to make an enormous return in a short time.

Develop Your Own Rule. No matter how long or how detailed a book like this is, it cannot answer all the questions that will arise from the actions of hundreds of stocks interacting with thousands of options. The intelligent way of solving problems has always been not to memorize hundreds of little rules, but to understand the general principles and then apply those principles to each situation. That's all that this rule of strategy is saying. First, develop your own general rule of conduct. Then whenever you have a question, go back to that rule. For example, if you are a conservative investor who originally decided not to write out-of-the-money options, then if you had bought American Home Products at 69, you would have sold the 65 options as soon as they became available, and you would have been selling each new option as the stock went down, at an enormous savings to you. If you were more risk oriented and said that you did not want ever to write in-the-money options, but wanted to write only options that were 2 points or less out of the money, then if you had written options on Amazon.com you would have known exactly what to do and when to do it as the stock went up.

No plan will provide the right answers all the time. Sometimes it is going to happen that just after you have rolled up an option at considerable cost to you, the stock will immediately begin to fall back. With hindsight it will be obvious that you have done exactly the wrong thing. But you are going to do the wrong thing a certain percentage of the time no matter what method you follow. By following a consistent procedure you ensure your being right at least half the time, which may not sound like much but is much better than asking yourself, "Why do I always do everything wrong?"

My point here is that with a rational, well-thought-out set of criteria to guide you, you will have a much better chance of fashioning a program for yourself that will fit your objectives, and ultimately be profitable, than with a hit-or-miss approach, where every single decision is based on the typical question, "Do I think that the stock is going to go up or down from here?" An option-writing program is designed to replace that question with "What action should I take now so that this position will meet my original criteria for downside protection and annualized return on investment?"

Covered option writing should be an intellectual, rational pursuit of return on investment, and by applying this rule you will be making it as close to that ideal as is possible.

4
SELLING NAKED CALLS

A Highly Speculative
Method for Making Money

This is the most important chapter in this book in my opinion, for two reasons: first, because it describes a method that is usually overlooked or actually discouraged, and second, because I believe so strongly in its potential for being profitable that it is the only strategy I use to manage my clients' money.

The method I am referring to is selling calls on stock that the call writer does not own. This is usually referred to as writing *uncovered* calls or writing naked calls. Before we get into the details of uncovered call writing, I would like to explain how I became such a believer in the potential profit of this strategy.

I was a stock broker at a major firm for 20 years before starting my own investment management firm. When I began my stock broker career the first edition of this book had just been published. Due to my authorship of this book a large number of options traders started using me as their broker, and during those 20 years I had ample time to observe and actually execute all types of options strategies. From these years of hands-on experience I concluded that virtually all options buyers, no matter how successful they were at any one time in their trading, invariably ended up losing all of their money. Initially my only conclusion from that insight was that I did not want to be an option buyer.

Then as I thought about this longer, I realized that each option trade is a closed circle with a buyer on one side and a seller on the other. It is a zero sum transaction (less transaction costs) because what one side wins, must be a loss to the other. (In covered call writing when the stock rallies the loss to the writer is made up by his gain on the stock. If you just look at the option alone he is also a loser.) So it occurred to me that if option buyers usually turn out to be big losers, then the option sellers must turn out to be big winners. Since uncovered option writing is the purest form of selling options, this is one reason I am such a big proponent of its use by those for whom it is suitable.

In the previous chapter we discussed selling covered calls. These are calls on stocks that the call seller owns. This was described as a rather conservative transaction, because if the price of the stock goes down, the shareholder is better off than if he had never sold the call since he has the premium from its sale to offset the loss. If, instead, the price of the stock goes up, any loss from the sale of the call would be more than offset by the increase in the price of the stock owned by the call seller. Thus, the seller or writer of a covered call makes money if the stock goes up or stands still and loses less than other shareholders when the price goes down. The main negative is that if the stock goes up a large amount, he will make less money than if he had not sold the call.

In contrast to this, selling a call without owning the underlying stock—a naked call—is extremely risky and speculative. To understand why, let us take a simple example.

Suppose XYZ stock is selling for $50, and the writer sells a three-month call for $5 with a strike price of $50. If the stock goes up to $60, at the expiration of the call the writer must go out into the open market and purchase the shares of XYZ for $60 and deliver them to the call purchaser for $50. He has a $10 loss on this transaction (in addition to the cost of the commissions on the sale of the call and on the purchase and delivery of the stock), which loss is, however, offset by the $5 premium he received from the sale of the call. He thus has a net loss of $5 plus commissions. If, however, the price of the stock goes up to $70, he has a loss of $20 on the sale of the stock, and a net loss of $15. That's a rather steep price to pay for the gain he had hoped to make, which at the very most would have been just $5. But what if the stock goes above $70 and the naked call writer does nothing? In theory at least it could have gone right on up to $80, $90, or $100. If it did go all the way up to $100 (and more amazing things than that have certainly happened in the past) and the writer of the naked option did nothing, he would be out a net loss of $45 on each call he had sold. Again, this is the loss he would suffer for the sake of taking in a measly $5 on the sale of the call.

One can also write uncovered calls on a stock index such as the

Standard & Poor's 100 index (OEX), the Standard & Poor's 500 (SPX), the Dow Jones Industrial Average, or the Nasdaq Composite. The index that is preferable normally for writing equity options is the OEX because it has the most liquidity, which means that you will be paying less for the spread between the bid and asked prices. Particularly in violent markets it is very helpful to have good liquidity. The basic principles of writing calls on stock indexes are very similar to writing them on individual stocks except that the settlement is in cash instead of any delivery of actual shares of stock. One advantage of an index is that many of the unusually large moves of individual stocks are canceled out by the large number of stocks in the indexes. If you write a call on a stock that goes down, on that same day it might be canceled out in a stock index by another stock that goes up. Furthermore, there is far more liquidity in the stock index options than there is in the individual stocks. For anyone who is a frequent trader this is a particularly important point. It is for these reasons that for my clients I write uncovered options only on a stock index.

POTENTIAL LIABILITY

In short, while the maximum profit that could be realized from the sale of a naked call is fixed at the relatively modest premium received, the potential liability is theoretically unlimited. For an illustration of this see Figure 4.1. There is no way that the writer of a naked call who does not take defensive action can predict what the total potential loss could be. Fortunately, if the price of the underlying stock advances too far it is possible to cover by buying the call back, albeit at a much higher cost, thus closing out the position.

You may have heard the story of the man who bought some stock from his broker and was told a week later that the stock had gone up and he should buy some more. He did. A week later the broker informed the customer that the stock had gone up again and that he should buy some more. The investor did. The third week the same scene was repeated. Finally, when the fourth week came and the broker said that the price of the stock had gone still higher and suggested further purchases, the customer said, "No. The price is high enough now; I want you to sell all the stock."

"Sell?" asked the incredulous broker.

"Yes, sell," said the customer.

"But," asked the broker, "to whom?"

And this can be almost the case with respect to puts and calls. As the price of the stock goes up, and the writer wants to get out of the

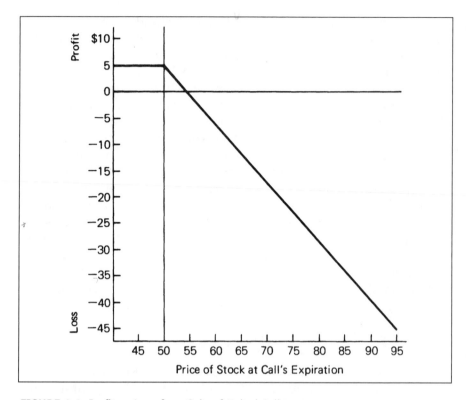

FIGURE 4.1 Profit or Loss from Sale of Naked Call
Call strike price: $50; premium received for writing call: $5
This chart shows the limited maximum profit and tremendous potential loss inherent in selling naked options; thus the imperative importance of Strategy Rule Number 1—plan what action to take if the stock goes up.

deal by buying in the call, it won't be hard to find a buyer of the call, but it could be only at a ruinously high price.

The picture is actually not quite that bleak. The writer of a call normally can find out at any minute exactly how much money he will make or lose if he wants to get out of the deal. The point is to get out while it can still be done at a reasonable cost.

But it is obvious that, if due to a news event the stock will open much higher, the loss one will suffer depends completely on how high the stock will be. Figure 4.1 stops at $95, but it could have been extended to higher stock prices with commensurately larger losses. In this chapter we discuss ways in which naked call writers can greatly reduce the possibility of large losses.

The real significance of the exchange-listed options that were created in 1973 (what we now trade) is that for the first time in history the writers of naked calls gained the liquidity that greatly increases their ability to control their potential losses. With this liquidity, a person can strive to achieve the advantages that astute traders have always realized could come from selling naked calls, and can also come close to solving the problem of unlimited potential losses.

Suitability Requirements

Nevertheless, because naked call selling is highly speculative, brokerage firms are reluctant to allow anyone to engage in naked call writing that they do not believe can satisfactorily sustain a large loss. Therefore, in addition to the margin requirements discussed in Chapter 7, each firm has its own suitability requirements for naked option writing. Unfortunately, in some firms the requirements are very substantial, such as a net worth of $250,000 plus annual income of $100,000 and at least $100,000 in the brokerage account.

If the requirements at your firm are so high as to prohibit you from writing naked call options, and if after reading this chapter you conclude that you do want to write naked options, then there is no reason why you should not open an option account with a firm that is more reasonable. Don't be afraid to call up the other stockbrokers in your area or out-of-town firms and check the Internet. There is a wide variation among firms in this regard.

Limiting Loss

There are three methods of reducing the possible loss from writing naked options. The first is to buy in the option when the price of the option gets up to a certain point. If you sold an option at 2, and you do not want to lose more than 2 points under any circumstances, you would carefully watch the price of the option, and buy it back as soon as it traded at 4. You could ask your broker to watch the price for you and leave him instructions to buy it in if it ever traded at 4, but he cannot guarantee to do this for you. If he should be away from his desk when it happens to trade at 4, you will simply miss out. Fortunately, there is a way of accomplishing this objective that does not rely on one human being's infallibility. This is to give your broker a *good till canceled (GTC)* stop-loss order. Your broker places this order on the floor of the exchange. It requires the floor brokers to purchase your option when the price gets up to 4.

You tell your broker to enter a stop-loss order to "Buy the option at 4 stop." Technically what this means is that as soon as the option trades at 4, your order becomes an order to buy the option at the current market price. In some cases, if the bid price gets up to 4, that may trigger the stop-loss order. This is a great way to control risk, but it has one major inherent flaw. That is that there is absolutely no guarantee that the order will be executed at 4, and in fact most of the time it will be executed slightly above that price. All you are doing is placing a market order after the option trades at 4.

Here is the big problem. Let's assume that the call is trading at $3^7/8$ at the market's close. At 4:30 news comes out that is sensational. You can imagine what it might be—perhaps a merger offer at a 40% premium to the stock's current price. In any event, the next morning the stock opens at a much higher price and the first trade of the option is at 12. Your stop-loss order is now triggered, and you buy the option at 12 on a 4 stop. Not a lot of fun, but that is the way it works.

This is an extreme case and happens rarely; nevertheless, events like this can and do occur. Despite these possibilities, I believe it is so important to have risk controls in place that I use a stop-loss order on every single option I sell for my clients. We'll discuss this in more detail in the strategy section.

The second method of limiting your loss is to buy in the option when the underlying stock reaches a certain price. For example, if you have sold 40 strike price options when the stock was at 37, you might decide that you want to get out of the position when the stock reaches 41. You could do this yourself by watching the stock continuously, or you could instruct your broker to buy back the option when the stock hit 41. This is known as a "basis" order, because you are buying one security based on the price of another security. Many brokerages will not accept this type of order, and some may do it only on large orders.

The third way of cutting your losses on a naked option is by placing a stop-loss order to purchase the underlying stock when the stock reaches a certain point, such as 41. When your order goes off, you have converted your high-risk naked option sale into a conservative covered write. You now have no risk on the upside, but have to worry about a loss in the stock if the price goes back down. This type of order is subject to the same risks as a stop-loss order on the option, namely that if there is a big gap move against you, you will buy the stock at a price that gives you a large loss.

The uncovered option writer must carefully weigh the advantages and disadvantages of the three means of getting out of an uncovered option position when it becomes untenable. One thing is absolutely certain: You must choose a method and implement it. Warning: Not to do so could be perilous to your financial health.

RETURNS ON WRITING NAKED CALLS

Let's compare the potential returns possible from writing uncovered calls with the possible returns from covered calls. If, as was recently the case, the price of a certain stock is 60 and that is also the call's strike price, the premium for a six-month option might be $4^{1}/_{4}$. If one buys the stock, even by doing so with the minimum margin requirement, that means a cash outlay of $30 per share. If we sell the call for $4^{1}/_{4}$, we subtract that from the $30 cash requirement for a net cash investment of $25.75 in order to earn a maximum income of $4.25, or 16.5%. This is not a bad return for six months, but it is the maximum possible return, and one must expect that in a certain number of cases the stock will go down to produce a loss so that the *average* return will be quite a bit less.

Now, look at what happens to the percentage return when naked options are used. Because one does not have to own the stock, it is possible to sell the call with a smaller investment. The current requirement is that the seller of a naked call must have a cash margin equal to 20% of the value of the underlying security, minus the amount the call is out of the money plus the current value of the option. Here the stock price is $60, and 20% of that is $12. Since it is exactly on the money we make no change for the amount that the call is in or out of the money. Finally we add in the price of the option, here $4.25, to give us a total requirement of $16.25. But don't forget we took in $4.25 on the sale of the call, which we can apply to the margin requirement. Thus the net requirement is actually $12.

Additionally, regardless of how far out of the money an option is, there is a minimum margin requirement, which cannot be less than 10% of the value of the underlying security plus the current price of the option. With respect to puts that are *deep out of the money*, this minimum requirement is that the margin must be at least 10% of the strike price of the option rather than 10% of the stock price. This exception was made to help option writers when the stock had soared up in price with the result that the minimum margin requirements were going up even as the put got further and further out of the money.

If you are writing options on a stock index, the value of the underlying index is multiplied by 15% before subtracting the amount it is out of the money and adding in the current option premium. The minimum margin requirement is 10% of the index, or 10% of the strike price in the case of puts.

Simply compare how much less this is than the $25.75 required to own the stock in our earlier example to see the great improvement that this brings about in profit potential. Since the margin requirement for the uncovered call is just $12 instead of $25.75, the return goes from 16.5% to 35.4%, which is 114% more than for the covered write. If the stock were selling below the strike price, the margin required for an uncovered call would be even less.

If you multiply this 35.4% return on a six-month option by 2 to get the annual earnings, you find that by maintaining the minimum margin you can earn up to 70% a year on your investment. But even this figure is too low, because if the investor wishes to maximize his profits, he will reinvest not only his original investment, but the earnings as well, thus compounding the rate of return, which gives a profit of 83%. On the other hand, in actual practice this figure would be much lower because we have not deducted commissions, which can be fairly high, and we are assuming that all the options expired unexercised. In actuality, of course, over the course of an entire year, many of the options will be exercised, or stopped out, resulting in substantial losses to the writer, so that the profit will be considerably smaller. But this shows that it is theoretically possible to make a large profit selling naked calls. Now, you can see why some people are so wrong when they look upon selling calls as a way to incur unlimited losses while getting the chance to make only a meager profit.

Margin and Returns

The low margin requirement is what makes this high profit possible. The effect of this margin requirement is even more striking when you use an out-of-the-money option. For example, let's take a stock priced at $38\frac{3}{8}$ near the end of August when the October 45 call had a premium or price of $\frac{3}{4}$. Using the formula for determining the minimum margin required to sell naked calls, we do the following: $38\frac{3}{8}$ times 20% equals $7.68. Subtract from this the amount by which the strike price is above the price of the stock. Since we are selling a 45 option, that minus $38\frac{3}{8}$ is $6.63, and subtracting this from $7.68 gives us a margin requirement of $1.05. To this we add the current premium of the call, which is $\frac{3}{4}$, giving us $1.80. The final step is that the minimum amount of margin for a call cannot be less than 10% of the value of the stock, here $38\frac{3}{8}$. That times 10% is $3.84. Adding the current option premium of $0.75 gives us $4.59. This then is the margin requirement. However, to determine the amount of money that must be sent in to fulfill the margin requirement, we are permitted to subtract the amount of money received from the sale of the option. Subtracting $0.75 from $4.59 gives us $3.84. This is the amount of money required to earn a possible $0.75, which would mean a return of 19.5% (if the price of the stock does not go up) in a two-month period. This annualizes out to a return of 117%. It must be emphasized that premiums of this magnitude are rare, but this shows what can be done with a stock that does possess such a high option premium.

Another aspect of margins that must be explained is that a naked call writer must mark to the market. This means that in addition to putting up the required margin on the day that you sell a call, you must meet the margin requirements at the close of each trading day. This can be very expensive, and it is another reason why selling naked calls is only for sophisticated investors who can readily afford to lose all the money that they put up, and also have additional funds they can apply to their option account in a hurry.

Let us assume that you sell a call with a strike price of 100 on a stock selling for 80. Your margin is 20% of 80, or 16, less the 20 difference between 100 and 80, leaving a margin requirement of minus $4 plus the option price. Of course the minimum requirement comes into play here. That is 10% of 80 plus the option price, giving you a requirement of 8 plus the premium. If the premium were 4, you would need $12 per share, or $1,200 per option, in your account after the trade for margin. Now, let's say the price of the stock goes up 10 points to 90. Your requirement is still the minimum, 10% of 90 for 9, but now let's assume the call has gone up from 4 to 6. Your requirement is now 9 plus 6, or $15.

If the stock goes up an additional 5 to 95, the regular requirement is now more than the minimum requirement, so we use the regular one. That requirement now becomes 20% of 95, which is 19, but this time you can only subtract the 5 points out of the money, to give you 14. That plus the premium, of perhaps 7 by now, will give you a requirement of $21. This is quite an increase from $12. Of course, if the stock gets up to 100, a level at which you would still make the entire premium as a profit at expiration, your margin requirement has increased substantially. It is 20% of 100 or 20, with no deduction for being out of the money. If the option has now risen to 8, that would make the requirement $28. Compare that to $12. This gets very expensive very fast in the case of a steadily rising stock.

The one encouraging thought is that you are only talking about margin. Anytime you do not have the funds to meet your margin needs, you can ask your broker to close you out. And if you don't come up with the requested funds, you will not even have to ask your broker to close you out. He will do so automatically, as he is required to. This may be the best thing for you if the price of the call continues to rise.

But in many cases, if the price of the stock is still well below the strike price, you will want to hang on to the call even though the premium has doubled in price. The reason is that if the price of the stock stops rising before it reaches the strike price, the call will be worthless upon its expiration. In such a situation, if you do not cover the margin call, you may lose money when you would have made a complete profit if you had covered the margin requirement and held on to the call.

We must state again that there is absolutely no guarantee that any results like the 117% annualized return mentioned earlier will be achieved. Even in a bad year when the market as a whole goes down, there are always certain stocks that rise, and if an option writer has been unfortunate enough to sell these particular calls, he can lose money. Or he may have a very bad quarter, and if the bad quarter is his first quarter selling options, this may wipe out much of his capital, so that he isn't able to continue and recoup his losses. Nevertheless, the purpose of the example and these paragraphs is to show why I believe that on average the seller of calls will make money over the long run. In my opinion, the odds are in his favor when option premiums are at their normal levels. You may wonder why this should be.

I think that it is true for the same reason that so many people buy stocks with great expectations, only to be disappointed with their performance later. People are naturally optimistic. And their optimism is fanned by the brokerage firms that are constantly churning out reports indicating that companies are about to enter a wonderful new period of rapid increases in profits, and that their stocks are now a real bargain. The function of brokerage houses is to sell stocks.

As Bernard Baruch said in his advice to investors, don't accept everything the brokerage firms say because they are in business to sell stocks. They sell stocks by telling the public how wonderful a stock is, just as any salesperson tries to sell any commodity. In the brokerage business, the way you sell a stock is to convince the customer that it is going to go up. And the brokerage firms succeed admirably, both in convincing people that the stocks are likely to go up by significant percentages and in selling stocks to the customers.

If they can sell stocks this way, imagine how much easier it is to sell a call! Who cares if the stock goes down? The buyer of a call is putting up only a small fraction of the cost of the stock, so if the stock goes down the clever broker tells the customer how smart he was to have bought only a call and not invested really big money in the stock. On the upside, it is so easy to tell a customer that you believe a stock will go up by at least a few points. If it does, the option buyer will not have just a small percentage gain, but may be able to double his money. It just all seems so wonderful. And it is—but for the person on the other side *who sells* the call. Because there is no such thing on Wall Street as a free lunch. The stock is no more likely to go up "a few points" in the next few weeks, than it is likely to go up by a much larger percentage over the course of the next year.

UNCOVERED WRITING RULES OF STRATEGY

Now, we'll get down to actual rules of strategy showing how you can greatly increase the odds in your favor when you sell uncovered calls.

Strategy Rule Number 1: Plan
What Action to Take If the Stock Rises

Immediately after you have sold the call, decide exactly what action you will take if the stock goes up. This is the most important rule of all. Chronologically, it should come after all the other rules that tell you which calls to sell. But I have deliberately placed it first, so that you will never forget it. Without a stop-loss decision you could lose your entire investment and more on one call that represents just a fraction of your total investment. Just reread the first few pages of Chapter 2 on the rise of Amazon.com, and you will know what I mean.

If you had sold 10 call contracts of Amazon.com on October 9, 1998, you would have received $15,000 and have had to have margin of $26,000 in your account. As the price of the stock began to rise, for every rise of $1 you would have been required to mark to the market with an additional $1,200. This is because you must add $1 per point ($1,000 on 10 calls) for the decrease in the amount by which the strike price is out of the money. Since you also take 20% of the current price of the stock, each point increase requires an additional 20 cents per share or $200 on 10 calls. In addition you have to add the increase in the market value of the calls.

For example, when Amazon.com reached 150 the margin requirement would have been 20% of 150, which equals 30, plus 50 for the fact that the call was now that much in the money, giving 80. In addition you had to add the current premium on the call, which was about $60. This makes a total margin requirement of $140 per share, or $140,000 on 10 calls. Perhaps your financial capacity would simply not have been large enough to keep on doing this, and your broker would have had to sell you out long before Amazon.com got to its high.

But once you have made an investment in selling a call, a strange but compelling psychology takes over. You begin to become convinced that the stock is overpriced. The fact that it has gone up so far so fast seems strong evidence to you that it is headed for a major fall, and headed there fast. Besides, the cost of the option is always going to be more than the amount by which the price of the stock exceeds the strike price, and you may believe that by hanging on to your call longer, you will at least be able to reduce that amount of extra loss.

My point is that sitting back now and knowing from hindsight what happened makes it very easy to think that if you had been so unfortunate as to sell Amazon.com calls then, you would certainly have gotten out as soon as it started going up in price. But don't be too sure. When it is happening, it is far easier to think that the price will go down tomorrow.

But as we know, it didn't. And if you had held on to your contracts until the expiration date of that option in January, you would have had a loss of $300,000. That's an unbearable loss to have when the most that you could have gained was a mere $15,000.

Fortunately, there is a way to protect yourself from this sort of fantastic loss. That is by instructing your broker what to do immediately upon receiving from him the confirmation that he has sold your calls. You would tell him to close out your position as soon as you sustain a certain loss in your investment. When that point is reached, your broker will buy as many calls for your account as you previously sold. He therefore cancels your short position, and you have closed out your position. You have thus cut your losses to what they were at that point, and no matter how much more the price of the stock goes up, your loss is fixed. Normally, your loss will be limited to far less than the amount of your original investment in margin, if you follow the guides in this chapter.

Since the margin requirement is far more than the current premium of the call, even though you may have suffered a large loss when you are closed out, you will usually nevertheless free up a substantial amount of your margin and be able to start again selling another call. For example, let us assume that you have sold a call for $1 and that this requires $5 margin from you. Unfortunately, the stock goes up and your broker executes your instructions, closing out your position by buying the call for $2. Your account was credited with the $100 received from the sale of the calls in the first place, so your loss is just $100. Since you had put up a margin of $500, your loss of $100 means that you still have $400 left in your margin account. If you want, you can now sell some calls using that as margin without putting up any additional money.

Stop-Loss Procedures. There are three kinds of stop-loss procedures, and there are advantages and disadvantages to each of them. The most common is to close out your position when the premium for the call reaches a certain point. For example, let us say you sell some calls for $5 each and you would like to limit your potential loss to that amount. As soon as your broker has sold the calls, you can instruct him to buy the same number of calls for you at the market price as soon as they sell for $10. Since the market might be rising, it may not be possible to buy the number of calls you need at $10, and the order may have to be executed at a fraction higher, such as $10\frac{1}{8}$ or $10\frac{1}{4}$ On a big gain by the stock on the morning opening, the price could be significantly higher.

The second method is to ask your broker to buy you out when the price of your underlying stock reaches a certain level. This method can be particularly useful when you are selling a call that has a strike price substantially above the current price of the stock. If you have plenty of reserve margin to cover your margin account in case the premium for the call goes up substantially, you don't have to worry as long as the price of the stock stays below the call strike price. When the expiration date arrives, your call will be worthless and you will make a profit on the entire premium you received for the call.

To illustrate: You sell a call at the 100 strike price when the stock is at 88. You receive $2\frac{1}{2}$ for your call. Now, if the stock suddenly shoots up by 10 points to 98, the price of the call would probably rise to 5. But you may conclude that the chances are still very slim that it will go up another 2 points to the level where the option will eventually become worth anything. So instead of closing out your position because the option has doubled, you rely on the stock price. You ask your broker to close out your position when the price of the underlying stock reaches 100—because until that happens, you will not be out any money, provided you hold the call until it expires.

The advantage of the first type of strategy, based on the amount of the premium, is that it is a much more precise method of limiting your losses. If you sell a call on a stock that is selling above its strike price, this is probably the kind of stop-loss order you will want to use, because otherwise you don't really know how much protection you are getting against a sudden loss. To illustrate, if you sell a 25 call on a stock selling for 27, you may receive a premium of $3\frac{5}{8}$. If you put in an order to cover your position when the stock reaches 30, you really have no idea what premium the call will be selling for when you have to buy it in.

If the stock jumps up that much in two days, the price of the call will not only increase by 3 points to reflect the rise in the price of the stock, but it may also increase an additional amount. Investors will naturally think that if the stock can move up so far so fast, it will be capable of moving up far more in the remaining period of the option. So, the option may increase to $6^5/_8$ or even 7. You would then find yourself losing more money than you had anticipated.

The big question is—at what price should you close out your position? If you choose a price that is too low, you will be fairly safe in never losing a large amount of money, but you might take many losses on calls that later turn out to be worthless. And sometimes this happens even when the price of the stock is higher than the strike price, because the stock will go up briefly and then drop down below the strike price.

On the other hand, if you decide to get out when the stock price is substantially higher than the strike price, you are really going to take a beating if you ever do get closed out. This practice should be used only when you have received a healthy premium for the sale of your calls. One fact always to keep in mind when deciding at what price to get out is that when the price of a stock is below the strike price, an increase in the price of the stock of 1 point results in an increase in the price of the call of only a small fraction of a point. And the further away from the strike price the stock price is, the smaller the fraction.

As the price of a stock approaches the strike price, on the other hand, it tends to move up faster for every point of the stock's rise. And, of course, once the price of the stock goes above the strike price, the premium for the call must go up virtually a whole point for every point increase in the price of the stock.

The third method of reducing your risk is to buy in the underlying stock when either the option you have written or the stock itself rises up to a certain price. What this does is to convert your strategy of being short an uncovered call, where you have a high risk and will lose more money if the stock continues up, into a conservative strategy, where you will make money if the stock keeps going up. The obvious negatives are that (1) it requires a lot more money to buy in the underlying stock than it does to buy in the option, and (2) you now have to worry about the possibility that the stock will go down, since that is where the loss possibility exists on a covered write. For these two reasons, this is the least popular means of controlling your risk.

Recommended Strategy. So here is the strategy I recommend to keep your losses down: If you receive a small premium for a call because the stock is far below the strike price, get out just a point or two below the strike price. In this way you will be getting out when the premium of the call should still be fairly small. The disadvantage is that if, for example, you have a call with a strike price of 40 and get out at 38, but then the stock never goes above 39, you will have suffered unnecessary losses. If you had decided to get out at 40 you would have made money.

But the alternative could have been very expensive, because if the stock did go up to 40 you would have to pay significantly more to buy back your calls. This is a crucial point in a successful uncovered call program, because each call on which you lose money is a double blow to your profits. It deprives you of the profit you had been hoping for on that particular call, and it incurs a loss that must then be offset by another profitable call. So, the procedure you choose for reducing losses is extremely significant.

Perhaps the best way to get an insight into this problem is to study the price action of a call as the price of the stock approaches and then climbs above the strike price. The example for October 30 calls shown in Table 4.1 occurred when premium levels were high, but this trait is even more pronounced when premiums are low.

Due to various trading factors, there is not a perfect correlation between the closing premium for a call and the closing price of the stock. Nevertheless, this table, as well as Figures 4.2 and 4.3, give clear evidence for my statement that changes in the price of the stock of about a point result in only small fractional changes in the premium of a call when the stock price is well below the strike price. When the price of the stock gets up to the area of the strike price, each increase of a point in the price of the stock is reflected in a much larger fraction of a point in the cost of a call. When the price of the stock gets more than a point above the strike price, every increase of

TABLE 4.1 Price Action for October 30 Call

Date	Stock Price	Premium of Call
September 5	26¼	$7/16$
September 6	27⅛	$9/16$
September 17	28	$11/16$
September 19	29	⅞
September 20	29⅞	1¼
September 21	30⅝	1¾
September 24	31¾	2⅛
September 25	32¾	3
September 26	33⅜	3¾

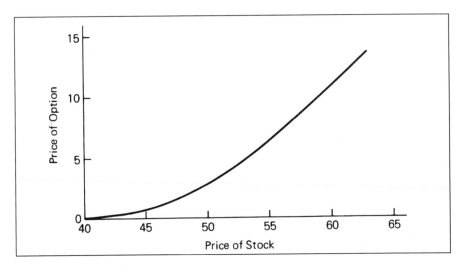

FIGURE 4.2 Effect of Stock Price Move on Call Price
Chart shows the price of a 50 strike price option with six-month duration. Between stock prices of 40 and 41 the option increases an almost imperceptible $\frac{1}{16}$ point, whereas between 59 and 60 it increases by almost 1 point. A more technical statement of this is that as the stock moves above the strike price, the hedge ratio approaches 1. Note that the percentage change in option prices, which are what really count to the option buyer, do not change at the same rate as the option price. Thus, between 40 and 45 the option increases by 1,100% while between 55 and 60 it increases by only 74%.

a point in the price of a stock is translated into an increase of almost a point in the premium for the call.

The moral is very simple, to the shrewd investor. Close out your position between a few points below the strike price and the strike price. You will take losses in a few instances where you would have made a profit if you had held on to the call, but you will take such a small loss when you do that you will come out ahead. In fact, you may find that in some cases, even where the price of the stock goes up substantially, the price of your call will be no higher when you close out your position than it was when you first sold your call.

The reason for this is that with the passage of time the value of the option automatically becomes worth less and less. To prove this point, let me refer to the stock in Table 4.1. On the first day of the quarter, August 1, the stock was selling at 27, but because the option had almost three months to go, the premium for the 30 call was $1\frac{3}{8}$. Thus, an investor who sold that call could have said to his broker that he wanted to close out his position when the price of the stock

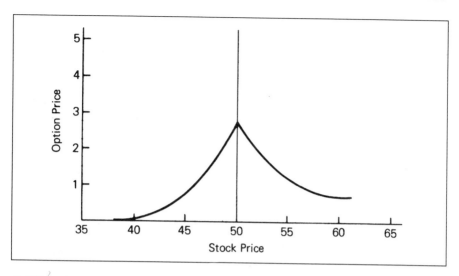

FIGURE 4.3 Effect of Stock Price Move on Future Time Value of Option
Chart shows future time value for a six-month option with a 50 strike price. With the stock price below 50, where there is no intrinsic cash value, this chart is identical to Figure 4.2 showing the effect of a stock price move on the option price. This chart is more important to covered call writers, because the only profit they can make is from the future time value shown here. This explains why as an option becomes deeper in the money, thus providing more downside protection, it also reduces the potential profit.

hit the strike price of 30. The table doesn't show the precise price of the call when the stock hit 30, but you can see that on September 20 the stock closed at 29⅞ and the call was only 1¼.

Reflect on that for a moment. Here we have a stock going up almost 3 points, or more than 10 percentage points, in a period of less than two months. This must be considered an outstanding performance because the stock was not a highflier but a blue chip industrial. Had an investor sold the stock short, he would be out $3 a share, which could be a lot of money. But if the investor sold a call, and bought it back with the stock at 29⅞, despite the fact that the stock had a gain of over 10% in just seven weeks, our investor actually would get out without losing a dime and would even be ahead by ⅛ of a point, which would cover a large portion of his commissions.

Be Wrong and Still Make Money. Herein is the real advantage of selling calls. Can you think of another form of investment involving a high degree of speculation where the investor can be dead wrong and still not lose any money? And let's admit it—anyone who sold the call when the stock was at 27 was dead wrong, because a rise of a full

10% in such a short time is very unusual for a conservative stock. What everyone should have been doing at that time, if they had had actual foresight, was to be buying the stock instead of selling a call on it. Nevertheless, the person who sold the call, being dead wrong, still could come out of the experience without losing a penny. That in a nutshell is what can make selling naked calls so profitable: when you decide in advance to close out at the right price. When you win, you can get up to a 25% return on your investment in three months or less, and sometimes even when you "lose" you can break even.

One must not conclude from this that it is possible to break even every time a stock goes up to the strike price—on the contrary, it usually is not. In this case two factors were at work that helped. One, the price of the stock went up gradually over a period of seven weeks. As time goes by, the value of an option automatically decreases, unless there is a large offsetting increase in the price of the stock. Had the price of the stock jumped up suddenly to $29^7/_8$ during the first week or two in August, you can be sure that the premium for the call would have been much higher than $1^3/_8$.

The second factor was that the particular stock in our example did not have a reputation on Wall Street for being a big mover. Therefore, even when it did go from 27 to 30, the Street was not inclined to think there was a big chance that it would suddenly spurt much higher. So the premium stayed at a fairly modest $1^1/_4$. If, on the other hand, this had been a wild action stock well known for its sudden jumps in price—like some of the Internet stocks, for instance—the premium would have been much larger when the stock got up to 30, and the call seller would have lost money.

In trading for my clients I have decided that the best stop-out procedure for me is to use a stop-loss order on the price of the option. Typically I will place the price of the stop-loss order at something like twice or three times the premium I received for the option I have just written. The disadvantage of this method is that because I usually write deep out of the money options, I am occasionally going to be stopped out of a call whose strike price is still far above the current price of the stock index. Who knows if it ever will get up to the strike price? If I had stayed with the option, it might have eventually expired worthless. But the risk I would have had to take is a big one. What if the stock did keep on going up to the strike price? If it did move up to the strike price quickly, there would have been a tremendous price to pay when I finally did buy in the option.

In an effort to keep my performance free from the large negative impact that such a trade would cause, I have made this decision to use a relatively tight stop-loss order. This means that I will have more and smaller losses, rather than fewer but often far larger ones. Perhaps you could consider this a moderating influence on a high-risk strategy.

If you, however, have adequate financing and are not opposed to taking higher risks in pursuit of higher returns, you can certainly use a stop based on the price of the index. One uncovered option trader I know is of this type. He has been very successful in writing options on stock indexes. He writes near-term deep-out-of-the-money options, and doesn't buy them in until the price of the stock index gets to within 2 points of his options' strike price. So far that has happened only on rare occasions, but once when it did he paid 26 to buy in some puts he had sold for 4. So this strategy is definitely not for everyone.

Your choice of a stop-loss method or price is never final, and shouldn't be considered so. For example, if a stock begins shooting up in price shortly after you have sold your call, you might very well want to lower the price of your close-out order—because a quick, high price rise means that when the price of the stock reaches a given level, the premium for the call will be higher than if the stock had slowly ambled up to the same price. Similarly, if you have asked your broker to close out your call when the stock rises by a small amount and the price of the stock stays where it is for a considerable period of time, you might well want to consider raising your stop-loss price on the stock—because as time goes on, if a stock does get up to a higher price, the call premium will be lower than it would have been earlier.

Similarly, when you place a stop-loss order to buy in your option at a certain price as soon you have written it, you should review that price frequently in light of the current premium of the option. If you wrote an option at 5 and put in your stop-loss order at 15, you wanted to buy it back if it got to three times your original price. You were willing to risk a loss equal to twice the premium you took in (15 minus the 5 you originally received is 10, which is twice your original premium). If the option subsequently shrinks down to $2\frac{1}{2}$, you should consider reducing the stop-loss order. If you are going to be consistent with your original ratios, you would now reduce your stop-loss order to three times $2\frac{1}{2}$, which is $7\frac{1}{2}$. As it continues to shrink, as we hope it will, you could continue to reduce your price.

This is the same principle as the ratchet on a fishing rod. You pull in on the line, and then the ratchet prevents the line from going back out. Here we hope that as the premium of our short option declines, we are reducing the stop-loss order so that our amount at risk is less and less. In this example, when our stop-loss order gets down to 5—which is the premium we originally received—we have greatly reduced our risk, and if the stop order works to buy in the option at the stop price, then we have locked in a no-risk position.

We can summarize Strategy Rule Number 1 for selling naked calls by saying that you *must* make a stop-loss decision as soon as you have sold your calls. You can do this by requesting your broker to buy you out either when the premium for the call reaches a certain amount or when the price of the underlying stock reaches a certain price. The former method provides more accuracy in limiting your potential losses, but it means that occasionally you will close out your position at a loss when the stock is well below the strike price. If you had held on to the call until its expiration you would have made a profit. The latter method avoids this problem, but you cannot know in advance exactly how high your losses might be.

The stop-loss price of the stock should never be appreciably higher than the strike price (assuming you are selling calls on stock that is below the strike price). When you receive a small premium from your call because the price of the stock is far below the strike price, your stop-loss order should be at a point well below the strike price so that when you buy back your calls they will be at low premiums. This simple rule will help to ensure that your losses are limited. You will then be able to enjoy the profits you will make from following the other rules in this chapter.

Strategy Rule Number 2: Sell Calls Only If the Price of the Stock Is Well Below the Call's Strike Price

The reason that this is a successful practice is based on a simple application of the law of probabilities to the stock market. The increases in stock prices over the long run are so small (about 12% a year) that in the short run, the three-month periods that we are talking about, they can practically be ignored. This means that at the end of any three months there is almost an equal chance that any stock will be down as there is that it will be up.

Furthermore, the odds are greatest that the price will be close to the price where it was at the beginning of the three-month period. This has been established by many serious and painstaking studies of the market. In statistical terms, the probability of any future price for a stock is shown by a bell curve with the current price of the stock at the center and highest point of the bell. (See Figure 4.4.) This means that in very few cases the stock will go down or go up by a rather large amount, as shown by the very small percentages for prices at the end of the period below 60 and above 140. In more cases the price of the stock will end up closer to the starting point, as indicated by the higher percentages in the 60 to 85 and 115 to 140 areas.

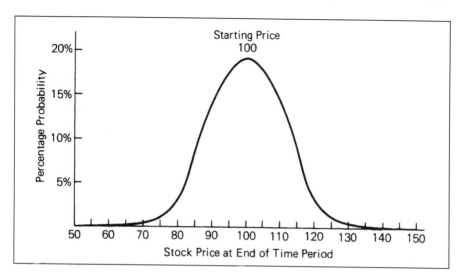

FIGURE 4.4 Probability of Price Swings in Stock Price When Option Expires
The probability that a stock will rise greatly during the option period is very small.
In this chart there is only a 3.8% chance that the stock will be over 120, thus il-
lustrating the theory behind Strategy Rule Number 2 for naked call selling. (*Note:*
Since actual probabilities differ with the length of the time period and the volatil-
ity of each stock, these figures cannot be applied in each specific situation.)

But the highest probability of all, as clearly illustrated by the chart,
is the probability that at the end of the period the price of the stock
will be in the 85 to 115 area. What this means for the practical investor is that by selling a call with a strike price at least 15% higher
than the price of the stock, the odds are enormously in his favor that
the stock will never reach the strike price.

Many years of experience with old-fashioned OTC call options indicated that about 60% of the options issued with the strike price at current market price were never exercised. This is because at the call's
expiration almost 50% of the stocks are at the strike price or lower,
and another 10% are above the strike price by such a small amount
that it would not even cover the costs of commissions to exercise them.

This statistic is derived from the old-fashioned options, which were
almost always issued at a strike price equal to the market price. Using
the knowledge we have about the probability of a price increase in any
stock, just imagine how many fewer stock options are exercised when
the stock is required to increase just 10% to reach the strike price. And
when the price of a stock must go up 15% or more to reach the strike
price, the odds that the call will ever be exercised go way down.

Of course, the argument against selling such calls is that the premiums for calls of stocks selling deeply below their strike prices are far less than for other calls. One thing is absolutely certain, and that is that the chances are no greater and no less that a stock selling below the strike price of a call is going to go up in the next three months than that a stock that is selling at or above the strike price of its call is going to go up.

Avoiding Loss on Small Stock Increases. Yet, if you sell a call on a stock that is selling at or above the strike price, the value of that call will increase by one dollar for every dollar increase of the price of the stock. This means that the call writer will suffer a direct one-dollar loss in his pocketbook for every dollar increase in the price of the stock. But when an option writer sells a call on a stock that is selling well below the strike price of the call, there is no such penalty for having picked a stock that goes up instead of down. Depending on the length of time left in the option and the distance from the strike price, the increase in the price of the call for each dollar increase in the price of the stock can range from about 50 cents when the price of the stock is close to the strike price to as little as $1/16$, or even nothing at all.

This often happens when a stock is hopelessly below the strike price and there are only a few weeks left in the option's life. Under these conditions, only a stock move upward of a large number of points can budge the call up from the basement where it is probably selling at a small fraction of a dollar. Therefore, when you are picking the type of call to sell, remember the risks you take if the stock moves against you.

Another good reason for selling calls with a strike price well above the price of the stock is related to the margin requirements. The margin formula permits you to deduct $1 from your margin requirements for each $1 that the stock price is below the strike price until you reach the minimum requirement. Therefore, it can be greatly to your advantage to pick a stock selling well below the strike price.

On the other hand, when you sell a call on a stock that is selling above the strike price, you receive a much larger premium, but the option will probably be exercised. More significantly, under the margin formula, your margin requirements go up by a full dollar for every dollar the stock exceeds the strike price. Let me illustrate with an example.

If you sell a call with a 40 strike price on XYZ stock, which is selling for $50, you may receive a premium of $15 for your call. Of this amount, $10 represents present cash value and only $5 is for future time value. This $5 might be said to be all you are receiving for the pure option aspects of the call.

The random walk theory holds that while it is not possible to predict the future price of a stock, the most probable future price is the present price. From this it follows that at the expiration date of the option the probability is that the stock will be selling at $50. You will then be able to buy back the option for $10, which when subtracted from the $15 you received on its sale gives a profit of $5. But note that in order to earn this $5, you had to provide margin of $20 (20% × $50 = $10 + $10 = $20). Putting up $20 to make a probable $5 means you will make a 20% profit on your investment.

But this discussion on margin is not at the heart of Strategy Rule Number 2, recommending calls with a strike price above the current stock price. The real reason is simply that most call buyers don't understand the law of probability as it applies to stock prices. They may believe that because the stock was much higher just a short time ago, it will probably go back up. Or they may believe for various reasons that it is an undervalued stock that will go up. In either case they can be wrong.

They are wrong in the first instance because the fact that a stock was selling at a higher price a few months ago has never been shown to have any bearing on the price it is going to be selling at in the future. They are wrong in the second instance because no one can predict what the future prices of stocks will be. So, they look at a call on a $45 stock and grab it as a real bargain if it is selling for only $1. My goodness, they say, that's only a cost of 2%, and the option still has a full two months to run. What a bargain.

No. It is not a bargain—because the strike price is $50. And the charts may show that never in the 60-year history of that company's stock has it ever gone up by 11% in just two months. And it probably never will, either.

So the fact that the premium is a small percentage of the price of the stock completely overlooks one of the essential elements of a call, its strike price. It is almost as if a person went out to buy a house and found a wonderful three-bedroom house at a very low price but didn't consider the fact that it abutted on a boiler factory. But let us not complain. Fortunately, a call on a $45 stock looks like a bargain to some people when it is only $1.

Call buyers typically are people who want to double or triple their money in a short time. They think that a $45 stock can easily go up 6 points, at which time they will break even on their investment. Every extra point from then on is money in the bank. And you know how quickly a stock like that can move once it gets going. At least this is the thinking of people who buy such calls. Their thinking is usually wrong, but we won't bother to tell them. The chances of the stock going up 11% in two months are very poor. Period, end of report. If it does go up that much, the shrewd option seller will, by following Strategy Rule Number 1, be out of his position before the stock ever gets that high. In short, Strategy Rule Number 2 is very simple. Sell calls with strike prices far above the current price of the stock. The reason for this rule is that the price of most stocks doesn't change very much in just three months or less, and the probability that it will change is inversely proportional to the amount of the change. By selecting a stock that must go up, let us say, 10% to 15% to reach the call's strike price, you are greatly increasing the odds that your option will never be exercised. The fact that you receive a smaller premium in relation to the price of the stock doesn't matter to you.

Unlike the seller of a covered call, your investment is not determined by the price of the stock, but by the margin formula. Your objective is to make as certain as possible that you make a profit of 100% of the premium you receive. You accomplish this by picking a stock selling far below the strike price of the call. By following this rule, your rate of unsuccessful options will be small, normally much less than 30%. Therefore, you will make the full profit most of the time, and on the options that are losers you will lose only a limited amount (following Strategy Rule Number 1), so your rate of overall profits should be good.

Strategy Rule Number 3: Maximize Your Profits by Constantly Reinvesting Your Principal

You might think that an option with a life of only three months is a very short-term investment. If you are used to buying and selling common stocks this may certainly be true. So, the usual reaction of someone new to options is to sell an option and stay with it until it either expires or goes up in value and his position is sold out. But this is not the way to make the biggest profits in the shortest time. How much can you make in a three-month period? The answer is not easy, since it is a function of the relationship of the premium you receive to the margin you must put up.

If you can sell a call for $5 and are required to put up margin of only $10, you can theoretically make a 50% profit in just three months. If, on the other hand, to sell a call for $5 you have to put up margin of $40, then obviously you are limited to a profit of 12.5%. Either one of these is very good, since with compounding, if you actually did make 50% every three months, you would have a 406% profit at the end of the year, and a 12.5% profit would become a 60% profit at the end of the year. But you can earn more than that by following the strategy of Rule 3.

Suppose that you sell 10 contracts at $4. This means that you receive premiums of $4,000, and let us assume that you are required to give your broker $16,000 in margin. Now let us further assume that the price of the underlying stock stays about the same for two months and that in accordance with Strategy Rule Number 2 you have selected a call with a strike price far above the price of the stock. By the end of six weeks or two months, the price of that call will probably have drifted down to $2 or less. This means that your call is now worth half of what you sold it for and that if you get out of your position by buying the 10 calls for $2 each you will have made a profit of $2,000. That is 12.5% of the amount that you invested and 50% of the value of the premium you received.

Well, you may ask, so what? You could have made a full 25% profit on your investment by letting it alone until the options expired unexercised. But the point is that you now are free to reinvest the entire $16,000 that you had originally invested. And in addition, you have made a profit of $2,000 that you can add to the $16,000 in your margin account, making a total of $18,000. If you can find another call that requires a margin of only four times the premium, you can now sell calls worth $4,500.

This means that if you hold them until the end of the quarter, and none of the stocks go over their strike price, you will have made $4,500 from those options, plus the $2,000 that you made from your earlier options, for a total of $6,500. Compare this to the $4,000 that you would have made had you not reinvested your winnings, and you will realize why this can be an important rule of strategy. Because, with it, you can actually increase your profit by 62% over what it would have been by just a straight investment. It also means that if you are successful in using this technique, you will have received a return on your total margin account of 40%. And that is just in one quarter of a year!

The strategy of not waiting for your successful calls to expire, but buying them out when they have declined by 50%, is not limited to one time in an option period. Especially in a falling market it can be done many times. In a declining market it is often remarkable how quickly the value of an option can go down by 50%. For example, the author once sold some calls for $1 when the underlying stock was $101\frac{1}{2}$. The next day the stock closed at 100 and the option went down to $\frac{3}{4}$. On the succeeding trading day the stock fell to 92 and the call closed at $\frac{5}{16}$. This represented 68% of the total possible profit in just two trading days. With this kind of luck, there is no reason why one should not close out the transaction right then and there, take one's profits, and reinvest them in something else.

An even more compelling argument can be made near the end of an option's life. Let's say you sell an option for $4 with five weeks to go before expiration. Everything works out well, and with a week and a half left before expiration the option is down to 25 cents. Should you squeeze out the last 25 cents and wait until it expires? Here's my thinking on this. You originally wanted to make 4 points over five weeks, which is making 80 cents a week. Now you have a week and a half left and you can make a maximum of 25 cents. That works out to 16.6 cents a week. And remember that those 16.6 cents are not a sure thing at all! Every naked position represents a real risk that something unexpected and potentially devastating can happen right up to the last day. Is it worth taking this real risk to make 25 cents? I think not. You entered this position to make 80 cents a week. Do you want to stay in to make 16.6 cents a week? I say no way. Close it down by buying in the option at 25 cents, and free up your margin so you can quickly get into the next opportunity to make 80 cents a week.

A vivid example of the danger inherent in cheap options occurred in my own personal account on Friday, October 13, 1989. I was short a large number of deep out-of-the-money stock index puts with one week to go. With so little time left and because they were so far out of the money I was trying to buy them back for a nickel. They were offered at 10 cents, which seemed ridiculous to me. I politely told the market makers on the exchange floor to take a flying leap. I could easily wait a week to make that dime, which was then $50 per option.

At 2:50 P.M. that day it was announced that the United Airlines leveraged buyout (LBO) deal could not be financed. UAL was to have been the biggest LBO deal, and ever since the 1987 crash the major factor holding up the market had been the hope that a stock would be the subject of an LBO. An LBO announcement had the same immediate effect on the stock as a takeover announcement, meaning that the stock price would shoot up by anything from 25% to 50%. With the announcement that the UAL deal was dead, everyone realized at once that there was very little left to hold up the market. The result was outright panic. The market did not decline so much as simply plummet straight down for the remaining minutes of the day.

There was so much fear and confusion that many options did not trade, and large numbers even of market orders could not be executed. Over the weekend people worried that the coming Monday would be a repetition of the 1987 crash known as Black Monday. The result was that the very puts I had disdained to pay 10 cents for on Friday morning I bought back on Monday morning for $11. The options I was short were then $500 a point. So because I wouldn't pay $50 a put I ended up paying $5,500 for each one. One remembers things like that.

Now I follow a general rule that I will usually buy back any option that has fallen to 25 cents. The principal exception is when there are only two or three days left before expiration, when it doesn't seem worthwhile.

When you do buy in an option before expiration, it can greatly speed up the amount of money you make in a fixed period of time. If this can be repeated a number of times during the option period, there is almost no limit to the amount of money that can be made. The reason is that each time you close out your position at a profit you can actually increase your future profits because the profit from the first sale has increased the amount of your margin account so that your next sale can be larger than the first.

Thus, toward the end of the option period you will have the accumulated cash profits that you made during the period, and the final amount you have invested will be far higher than the amount you started out with.

Strategy Rule Number 3 can then be summarized by saying that if you are in a profitable position from writing calls, don't just sit there and contemplate your profit. Consider closing out your position and then selling a different option. This operation can be repeated as many times as you wish as long as the market value of your option falls by 50% or more and as long as there are other options that you would like to sell. The potential for increasing your profit is almost limitless.

Strategy Rule Number 4: Avoid Disasters by Diversifying Your Call-Writing Portfolio

Strategy Rule Number 1 explained how to limit your potential loss. But when a stock does go up above its strike price, the chances are that in spite of that rule you will lose money. Frequently a call will double between when you sold it and when you are closed out. Your cash loss then might equal the amount of the premium at the time you wrote the call, but it could be much higher. Therefore, everyone who decides to go into a call-writing program must obey Strategy Rule Number 4, which is to protect yourself to the greatest degree possible against major losses by diversifying your investment.

The temptation to ignore this rule can be very strong. Before selling any naked calls you will carefully examine the calls offered on the exchanges and subject them to the various tests outlined in these rules of strategy. After you have reached your conclusions on the probability of each call making money for you, you may wish to write down the calls in order of preference.

Very often, there will be one call that for various reasons will seem to stand out and be head and shoulders above all the others. The stock may be selling at 20% below its strike price, and the call may still be fetching a premium of 4% of the value of the underlying stock. The next best call may be a stock selling only 15% below its strike price and paying a 3% premium. You may conclude that your first choice is so much better a selection than even the second best that most, if not all, of your money should be invested in it. Don't do it.

No call looks so good as when its stock is down. Let the price of that stock go up about 5 points and it won't look quite so attractive. Let it go up another 10 points and you will be wishing that you had never sold it. And then if it should go over your closeout price, you will thank your stars that you did follow this rule.

Remember that there is absolutely no way to predict the future action of a stock price. All the rules that you can read or even imagine can do no more than tell you the probability of what might happen in the future. And the important thing about selling a call is not what it looks like when you sell it, but what happens to it when the expiration date comes or when you are forced to buy it back. When you sell your call you just don't know what is going to happen. The law of probability is only effective in telling you anything about the future if you can utilize it over a large number of different situations. The law of probability is of no value to a person who puts his entire savings into selling one call, if it happens that one call rises over its strike price, with resulting heavy losses to the call writer.

So, when you find your "perfect" call, the one that shouts out at you to sell it, the one that says this is a "can't lose" situation, remember that there is no such thing as a perfect uncovered option write. Only hindsight can tell you that. No past history can tell you what is going to happen in the future. Stocks have gone up by 15%, 20%, 30%, or more in a single day, and the prices of calls have a way of increasing at a greater rate than the price of a stock when it leaps up like that. When you sell calls, be sure that you diversify. I recommend that at the very minimum, no matter how little you invest in writing calls, no more than 20% be invested in any one call. For larger investors, 10% would be a better rule.

One exception to this rule would be when you are selling calls on a stock index. Since a stock index by definition is compiled from the prices of a large number of stocks, it already has built into it many of the advantages that come from selling calls on a number of different stocks. While stock indexes do have frequent and sharp movements, there is a tendency that on any given day an upward movement by one stock is canceled by a down move by another.

Diversification is a good rule for every kind of investment with high risk. Where the risk is as great as it is for selling naked calls, the need for diversification is imperative. But let me point out that even diversification cannot protect the call writer when the entire market begins to rise. What it will do, however, is to force him out of his positions at various times, so that if he senses disaster coming, he may have enough time to close out voluntarily his remaining positions before being forced out at more costly levels.

To summarize Strategy Rule Number 4: Selling naked calls is a risky business, and one way to make it slightly less so is to make sure that you never put all your eggs in one basket. Even though diversification cannot save you from heavy losses if the entire market advances, it will help a great deal. No investor, no matter how small, should ever have more than 20% of his funds invested in one call, and more substantial investors should make certain that no more than 10% of their money is invested in any one call. Remember, no matter how good a call looks when you sell, there is no guarantee that its stock won't suddenly go up. Don't trust any stock to stay down.

Strategy Rule Number 5: Learn All You Can about the Stock's Price History

You are making a big investment, and a very risky one. The buyer of a regular common stock will investigate carefully before he invests. You should investigate at least three times as hard, because you are taking at least three times as great a risk as the buyer of the common stock. Whereas a stock can only go down in price to a fraction of the original investment, so that the potential loss is limited to the investment, you as the seller of a naked call are risking perhaps many times your investment.

Furthermore, the purchaser of common stock can afford to be wrong, at least for a while, because if his stock goes down he can always make the decision to hold on to it and hope that it will go back up in the future.

You do not have the luxury of a second chance. You are betting that during the period of your call the stock will not go above a certain price. If it does, you are out—out of the game, out of the ballpark, finally and irrevocably out of business in that call. There is no extension possible. Thus it behooves you to study carefully the nature of the movement of the stock's price.

For purposes of selling a call your analysis of a stock should be somewhat different from that of the buyer of common stock. If the purchaser of common stock is buying the stock for investment purposes (as opposed to trading purposes), he is interested in the future action of the stock over a period of a year or longer. For this reason, he can consider future changes within the industry, the next recession, future progress of inflation, the likely political climate in the next few years, and many other long-range factors that may affect the stock in the future. You shouldn't be distracted by these factors.

If you are selling a call that has only three months to run, there probably won't be time for any long-range effects to make themselves felt on your stock. So, I would strongly urge you to minimize the consideration that you give to the fundamentals of a stock. Concentrate instead on its past price movement.

By this I do not mean whether it has been in an upward trend or in a downward trend. This doesn't indicate which way it will move in the future. Similarly, I am not impressed with the work of chartists who can discern "head and shoulders" patterns, "double lows," and so on— all of which prove, at least to the chartists, the likely resistance levels, expected breakout points, and probable highs and lows of a stock.

But there is something that I believe you can learn from the past, and that is the nature of its price movements. That is, is the stock volatile or not? Does its price fluctuate by large amounts quickly, or has it always changed just slightly, achieving large price changes only gradually over long periods of time? Utilities were always the classic example of stocks that never moved much in a single day. Over the course of a few weeks, like the giant tortoise, they may manage to lumber up an aggregate of a whole point. Over the space of a month they can on rare occasions actually move a few points, but normally they are quite happy to inch along a few eighths of a point one way or the other.

In general, you can apply the same methods of studying the movements of a stock for purposes of selling a call as one uses in buying one. Thus, the reader should review Strategy Rules Number 6 and 7, set forth in Chapter 2, "Buying Calls." The only difference is that, naturally, you must deduce exactly the opposite conclusion. For instance, while the chapter on buying calls says to check the beta factor to be certain that it is high, the call writer checks that it is low. The premiums received for selling a stock with a low beta will necessarily be much less than for a stock with a high beta, but the results to the call seller can be just as rewarding and less risky.

Stop-Loss Strategy. When selling a naked call, you must always ask what the consequence will be if you are wrong and the price of the stock goes up. Presumably you have decided on a stop-loss strategy. How much money will you lose when the stop-loss order goes off? In the case of a stop-loss order computed on a certain price per call you know exactly, but you don't know what the price of the stock will be.

With a stock of a low beta you have a better chance of not being forced out when the price of the stock is still low, because the premium for a call on a low-beta stock will tend to rise more slowly and more directly in proportion to the price of the stock. Since the investing community knows that the stock is a slow mover, a move up of a couple of points will not start a wave of wild optimism that in the next few days the stock can easily move another 4 points to get over the strike price.

Rather, investors will calmly reflect that since the stock is now 2 points higher, it has 2 points less to go to get over the strike price and therefore the call should be worth slightly more. Thus, a stop-loss strategy based on the price of a call will tend to work out better on a stock with a low beta.

A stop-loss order based on the price of the stock is also likely to cause smaller losses because, while even a stock with a low beta can rise over the strike price, it is probably going to take longer to do so. And time works in favor of the call seller. So, like the example of the stock given earlier in this chapter, if you can sell a call at the beginning of an option period for a premium of perhaps 2, when the low-beta stock finally climbs up to the strike price there may be little time left in the option period. Investors will realize that at its slow pace of increase it will not get too much further during the life of the option and therefore the premium will not be much more than you received upon the sale of the call.

Thus a low-beta stock is good for the call writer. The obvious disadvantage is that with the small premium, it is not practical to sell calls when these stocks are very far below the strike price, because the premium will be too low to make the sale profitable enough.

The call writer will carefully check the chart to see the stock's weekly performance over a long period. Just as the call buyer looks to make sure that many times in the past the stock has gone up enough to make his hoped-for gain a good possibility, the option writer checks to make sure that the opposite is true. Just one word of caution: When selling calls you must be more cautious than when buying them, because the potential risk is higher. Thus, the fact that a particular stock has never gone up 12% in a three-month period cannot be taken as any assurance that it will not do so this time.

If you were thinking of buying the call you would assume that a 12% rise in the stock price would be impossible and shun the call. But as a call seller you must be far more open to the unusual and unexpected, because in this case the premium is probably going to be very low, and you are therefore taking a large chance that a quick rise will produce a dramatic increase in the premium of the call. So, if a stock has never gone up the percentage required to get over the strike price, that is indeed a positive sign to the option writer, but it is far from any assurance of success.

The easiest facts to learn about a stock are its high and low points for the year, and for the past five years. Stock information booklets containing these facts are available from most brokers, and they are entitled to some consideration. But just as sports records are consistently broken, so too stocks climb over their previous highs with even more ease than a high jumper clears a bar higher than any person before him had ever cleared.

The price/earnings ratio is another factor that everyone takes into consideration, but it is difficult to place any real importance on it for the call writer. The fact that a stock has a high P/E means indeed that it can fall further than one with a low P/E, but as a call writer you are not really so interested in how far or fast the stock can fall. If it just stays where it is, that will be fine, thank you. What you are concerned with is whether it is likely to go up, and if so by how much.

Surprisingly, here it is, probably an advantage to be dealing with a low-P/E stock. The reason is that if investors already believe that a stock is worth a high multiple such as 40 times earnings and for various reasons the investing community comes to believe that the stock should be worth more, there is nothing to stop it from believing that it is worth 45 or 50 times earnings. Once a stock gets up into that rarefied atmosphere it is not judged by the usual rules of performance. It has become a full-fledged glamour stock and is rated more by emotion than by logic. It may well be a unique company for many reasons, such as a strong patent position or an unassailable market share in a very rapidly growing industry. Therefore, it cannot be compared directly with any other company, and no one can easily prove that its price/earnings ratio is too high.

A more mundane stock, such as a steel company for example, is simply one of a number of steel companies, and its P/E ratio is not going to get far above that of all the other steel companies. Therefore, the high price/earnings ratio is a double-edged factor for call writers, and in fact does not make as attractive a vehicle for the conservative uncovered writer (and that is not very conservative) as a stock with a low P/E ratio.

On the other hand, since most stocks with high P/E ratios are more volatile than others they tend to command a higher premium, which can more than offset the volatility.

So Strategy Rule Number 5 may be summarized by saying that since the call writer is taking a tremendous risk in the hope of a fairly large gain in a short time it is extremely important that he study the price movements of the stock carefully before investing in the writing of a call. The type of business, dividend rate on the stock, and other fundamentals of the stock are of little importance to the call writer because he is interested only in the probability of a large price increase in the next few months and not in any long-term trends. Therefore, he studies those things that tend to indicate how much the stock will be likely to move, including the beta of the stock, price history as shown on charts, its highs and lows for the year, and its price/earnings ratio.

In general, the less volatile and more stable the price movements of a stock are, the better the vehicle is for the sale of a naked call. The reason for this is that the naked option writer should not be interested so much in making a quick profit on a stock that will go down as in not losing money on a stock that will go up. What he wants is a stock that will stay just about where it is, or go up so slightly that it does not reach the strike price, or of course actually go down. With this kind of price action the call seller will earn a very handsome profit.

Strategy Rule Number 6: Never Leave Well Enough Alone

This is an overall procedural rule. It may be particularly difficult for investors who are used to buying stock to obey it. Good, conservative stockbrokers for generations have advised their clients to buy stocks in good companies and hold on to them. The thought was that if the company was solid, profitable, and growing, the stock would take care of itself, and only an impatient investor who sold too early would lose out on an almost inevitable profit. As subsequent events have shown, this concept of "one-decision stocks" often does not fit the realities of the market, but it was a highly respected position, espoused by many of the leading and most successful professional stock investors.

The stock option market is totally different. One might almost say that a stock option is the opposite of the one-decision stock. For whereas a person can buy a stock for long-term investment, there is no such thing as a really long-term stock option, since the longest option available is only three years, and most options that are traded are for much less time, usually measured in weeks rather than months. I recommend writing options that are two months or less in duration, preferably about five to four weeks or even less.

This means that the investor has great freedom of movement, because the hardest part of investing in stocks has always been the agonizing decision of when to sell. How many investors, amateur and professional alike, have said that they are good buyers, but bad sellers?

They know a good buy when they see one, but they can't decide when to sell. And logically so. When a stock goes down, it appears to be an even better value than when it was purchased, and it therefore seems that if only it is held for a while longer the market will surely recognize how badly underpriced it is. On the other hand, if the stock goes up, why then you certainly don't want to get out of it, because nothing succeeds like success, and as the Swiss bankers are quoted as saying, "Cut your losses short and let your winnings ride." No one wants to part with a winner, so the tendency is always to hold, with the expectation that it will increase even more in the future. So whether your stock goes up or down the temptation is to hang on to it.

The person who sells a naked call cannot fall victim to these fallacies and traps for two very good reasons. The first is that he is dealing in a speculation with an additional dimension, the dimension of time. An investor in a stock may have personal investment goals for his stock to achieve in a given time. But time itself is not a dimension of the stock. The stock is a permanent certificate representing a share in a corporation with a perpetual life.

On the contrary, a call exists only for a finite period of time. Since the seller of a call knows that his call is going to expire, it is much easier to decide to close out his position and move on to another investment. Instead of making the big decision whether to get out of the investment, as the owner of a share of stock must make, the seller of a call need only decide *when* to get out of the investment. By taking no action at all he will automatically get out on the expiration date of the call, and anything he does will change only the date, not the fact of getting out.

The other factor that makes it so much easier for the option writer to get out of his position is that he is dealing with a very limited potential gain. If he sold the call originally for $1\frac{1}{2}$, the highest possible gain that he can make is just that little $1\frac{1}{2}$. It matters not whether the stock ends up just $\frac{1}{8}$ below the strike price, or crashes to almost nothing. In either case, the maximum that the call seller can make is his original $1\frac{1}{2}$. Thus there is not the great temptation to hold on to a call through thick and thin. Whereas the person who has bought a stock may well believe that if he just holds on to it for a little while longer it could increase by 200%, our option seller knows that he can get only his little $1\frac{1}{2}$.

So, the result is that the option writer has great actual and psychological freedom to move fast. In Strategy Rule Number 3 I have already suggested that the option writer can make more money by not holding on to his options until they expire, but rather covering his positions when they decline to half their sale price. But this is just one example of the rule. The astute option seller will be constantly reassessing his position to determine whether he can make any trades now.

He should confer with his broker at least once a week to learn what his free margin balance is. He should decide what the maximum is that he wishes to invest, and if his total margin requirements go down he should immediately make a decision as to whether he should invest more.

What this rule is saying is that an option writer must be constantly flexible. He must be ready to cover his position at any time when he feels that his money can be better utilized in another call situation. Not only must he be constantly reassessing the positions he has taken, but he must constantly think of how much money he wants to have invested in selling calls in total.

For example, if a person has committed a certain amount to writing options, it might be that if all his calls are doing well, and there are still some good opportunities around near the end of an option period, he will decide that for the period of one month he will invest additional funds.

In summary, Strategy Rule Number 6 says: Realize that a call is a temporary, fleeting object that exists only to cease existing in a short time. Thus there is no loyalty to be expressed, no fixed position that must be adhered to. Calls are traded in a very fast moving market, where premiums can easily rise 100% or fall by over 50% in a day. Thus the person who wishes to trade in call options should keep a daily lookout, and he must evaluate his position at least once a week to know where he stands. He must be able to act decisively, closing out positions where he can take a good profit, plunging into positions that look promising. The sky is not the limit. But by moving in and out adroitly the call writer can make a very generous return on his money.

SUMMARY

Let us summarize the strategy principles that have been laid down in this chapter:

Rule 1. Selling naked calls is made possible for the average investor by the liquidity created by the options exchanges that permits an investor to take steps aimed at limiting his risk when he sells a call. But this risk limiting is not a guarantee and it is not automatic.

The only way that it can come into play is for you, the option writer, to tell your broker at the time you sell the call that you want to take stop-loss action. This may be to close out your position either when the underlying stock reaches a certain price, such as the strike price, or when the price of the call itself reaches a certain level. In either event, once the price you have selected is reached and your broker executes the order, you are out of the market. The importance of this rule cannot be overstated, because without it the seller of a call is at the mercy of the gods. Your risks are close to unlimited.

Rule 2. Sell only those calls where the stock is well below the strike price; the minimum would be where it is 5% below the strike price, but 10% or 15% is better. The reason for this is that the odds against a stock's going up to the strike price are much greater than the price of the premium usually implies. Furthermore, such a call offers a type of built-in hedge in case of an upward price movement, because the price of the call does not increase in proportion to the increase in the price of the stock. Although you will probably lose a substantial amount of money in those cases where the stock does go over the strike price, this should be more than offset by the other calls for which their underlying stock does not. Furthermore, this can be reduced by putting in stop-loss orders for prices well below the strike price.

Rule 3. You can greatly increase your profits by not waiting until your successful options expire. Take advantage of the fact that the premiums have gone down by buying the calls when the price declines to less than 50% of what you sold them for. This will increase your potential profits from the sale of calls. Since the very nature of calls limits your possible gain to the amount that you have received from the sale of the original call, this method is vital to the investor who really expects to do well. By closing out your position as soon as your net investment has gone down 50%, you will immediately increase your earnings potential.

And of course if this technique can be done twice in an option period, the profit will go up even more. This is not impossible, because if you follow Strategy Rule Number 2 and sell only calls on stocks that are below the strike price, the price of the call will fall even if the price of the stock rises slightly (not if the stock shoots up, though). Over halfway through the option period the price of the call will have fallen by about one-half if the stock price remains stable. You can then close out your position and sell options on another stock, which in turn could fall to one-half its value in about three or four weeks, thus enabling you to repeat the procedure.

Rule 4. To maximize your chances for making a profit, you must diversify. This is made imperative by the highly risky nature of option writing. The option that you think looks the most promising may turn out to be the biggest disaster. The stock may simply go up far faster and higher than the rules of probability ever said that it should. But that is no consolation when it happens.

No call writer should ever have more than 20% of his money tied up in one call except for calls on stock indexes. As the investor expands his account, the amount ideally should fall to no more than 10%. In selling a call, the profit is limited for each call. The only way to make money is to have enough calls so that if you do lose on a few, they will not be able to drag your overall profit down to a loss.

Rule 5. This is the most obvious one—learn all you can about the stock you are dealing in, especially with respect to its price movement. Since an option exists for only a short period, it is my belief that you can ignore the fundamentals in your determination. They won't be very likely to influence the movement of the stock price in the few months or weeks of interest to you.

Do concentrate on its past price habits as shown on 5-year charts. Find out its volatility to learn whether it is a fast mover. Look up the high for the year and the low. Analyze its price/earnings ratio. In general, the higher the P/E ratio the more movement there can be in a stock. And of course you are looking for the factors that indicate that the stock is not a fast mover. You are looking for a stock with a good premium, but even more importantly, for one that does not move fast. Because even if the premium is small, if the stock never gets to the strike price, your profit is still 100% of the premium you received.

Rule 6. To make the maximum profits at writing options you must be constantly on the alert. Option writing is not for the person who wants to make an investment and forget it. Due to the limited time period of options, they change constantly and rapidly. The successful option writer must be able to get out of positions fast when he has a profit and get into new ones, perhaps committing a bit more money in the final month of the option period, letting some options ride, and selling out others because he sees better alternative investment opportunities.

Writing options is a highly risky business. But unless the market as a whole rises by an unusually large amount, the option writer who follows these rules should come out ahead. He must, however, use all the rules given in this chapter. Because some options are bound to go sour and knock out two or three that are winners, you must seek to make the most out of the winners. But if the market does not rise spectacularly and if you keep reinvesting your winnings and cutting your possible losses by a consistent stop-loss program, you should come out a winner.

5

BUYING AND SELLING PUTS
Buying Them, Selling Them, and How to Make Money Doing It

As we have seen in the preceding chapters, a call is the option to *buy* a share of stock for a specified price (the strike price) within a given duration of time. It is purchased by a person who believes that the stock will rise in price, and that his right to purchase the stock for the strike price will become a valuable right as the market price of the stock moves up above the strike price.

A put is the option to *sell* a share of stock for a specified price within a given duration of time. It is purchased by an investor who believes that the stock will decline in price. If he is correct, and the stock has declined to a point far enough below the strike price of the put to cover the costs of commissions, the put owner will go into the market just before its expiration, purchase the stock at the low market price, and then immediately sell it to the put issuer for the strike price. Of course, the owner could simply sell the put instead, which is what option traders usually do.

Puts have all the characteristics of calls; that is, they have an expiration date and a strike price. For example, when you check the price of a typical put if a stock is selling for 47, you may see that the four-month put with a 50 strike price is selling for 4. The 50 put already has an intrinsic cash value of 3, because the put takes on value when the stock goes down below the strike price, and this stock is 3 points below the strike price. The extra point in the price of the put is the future time value of the put. If you look for the price of the 45 put it may be 1. Since the current price of the stock is above the strike price of this put, the put is out of the money and the 1 price of the put is therefore entirely future time value. If there is a 40 strike price option it might be selling for just $3/8$ point because it is far out of the money. A 60 strike price put would be selling at $13^{1}/_{4}$, because it is *deep in the money*.

The 13 points represent the large intrinsic value of the put, and put buyers are willing to pay only an additional $1/4$ point for the future time value of the put. As the price of the stock goes down, the price of the put increases. At 43, upon the expiration of the option, the 50 put will be worth 7. It will be worth more if the stock reaches that price before the expiration of the put. The 45 strike price put will be worth 2 upon the option's expiration at 43, and at 40, the 45 put will be worth 5. Since it could have been purchased for 1, it is clear that puts can be a very profitable speculation on a stock that declines.

FUNDAMENTALS OF PUTS

For those who are used to calls, the seemingly upside-down concepts of puts can be a bit confusing at first. Thus if a stock is selling for 57, a 60 put is 3 points in the money and if the put is worth 5, then it has 3 points of intrinsic cash value and 2 points of future time value. Similarly, when a stock is 63, the 60 put is 3 points out of the money and has no intrinsic value. As the price of a stock goes up, the value of any given put declines, and as the price of the stock goes down, the price of the put increases.

But, of course, puts are not the mirror images of calls. For instance, one cannot offset a call position with a put position. If one is short a call, being long a put is not going to cancel out the risk of that position. In fact, being long a put when one is short a call is only adding to the risk, because both positions are on the same side; that is, they will both make money when the stock goes down. If you are short a call and you want something that will counteract that with a put, then you must find a put position that will make money for you when the stock goes up. The proper position is to be short a put, because if you sell a put and the stock goes up, then the put will expire worthless and you will make a profit of the amount for which you originally sold the put.

But, please notice that even this is not a way to cancel your risk from selling the call. For example, if you are short a 50 call, which you had sold for $3, and the stock is now 47, you might decide you want to offset the risk on the call. You could sell a 50 put (remember, that's in the money) for $4. Does this now mean that you have no risk on the upside? Not at all. Let's see what happens if the stock goes up to 60 at expiration of the option. The put expires worthless, and you have that profit of $4. But what happened to the call? You must now buy it back for $10, and since you originally sold it for $3, this leaves you with a $7 loss on the call. Thus, the $4 profit on the put does not cancel out the loss on the call. If the stock had gone higher, the loss obviously would have been even greater. The moral of the story is that while a put increases in value when a stock goes down, and a call increases in value when a stock goes up, they are not exact opposites, and you cannot assume that a put has the reverse effect of a call.

Now let's discuss the basic uses that investors and traders can make of puts. The most obvious is to purchase a put as a speculation for making money when you think that a stock or stock index is going to go down. A second use is to purchase a put on stock you own, or buy simultaneously, because although you hope and expect that the stock will *not* go down, you want the put to protect yourself in case you are wrong. A third reason to purchase puts is simply as insurance in general in case there is a decline in the market. Selling, or writing, puts can be used in a manner similar to selling naked calls, except that writing puts will be profitable if the stock does *not* go below the strike price. There are also many combinations of puts with other puts and puts with calls that can be used, and these are discussed in Chapter 6 on spreads.

BUYING PUTS

Buying Puts as a Speculation

The easiest use of puts is to buy them on a stock that you believe is going to go down. Here there are similarities to buying a call on a stock when you think that it is going to go up in that the selection of the strike price depends on the same factors as in a call, except of course that everything is upside-down. The put most people will find the best to purchase is just slightly in the money or slightly out of the money, because you are looking for a put that will make a profit for you on a minimum downside movement in the stock. If you take a put that is already deep in the money (where the stock is substantially below the put strike price) you will be paying a lot of money for the put. Therefore, you will not be able to make a large percentage gain on the cash you put up unless the stock moves down by a very generous amount. On the other hand, if you buy a deep-out-of-the-money put (where the stock is far above the put strike price) you run the risk that even if the stock moves down it will not quite get to the strike price, and your put will expire worthless.

There is one basic difference in the pricing and profitability of puts as compared to calls. This is that the dividend is working with you, and the higher the anticipated dividend, the better off you are. The reason is that the amount and date of a dividend are usually well known on Wall Street weeks before the actual ex-dividend date. Therefore, the stock price already fully reflects the fact that everyone who purchases the stock before the ex-dividend date is entitled to the dividend, and anyone who purchases the stock after it has gone ex-dividend will not get that dividend. The result is that stocks normally open on the day that they go ex-dividend at a price that is reduced from the previous closing price by the amount of the dividend. For example, if a company pays a dividend of 50 cents a share and the stock closes at $47^{1}/_{4}$ the day before it goes ex-dividend, it will normally open the next morning at $46^{3}/_{4}$. In the case of certain dividends, this change can be quite significant. For instance, in the past one company often declared special year-end dividends of $3 a share. What this means is that any in-the-money put should start appreciating in value before the ex-dividend date, and the day before the stock goes ex-dividend, the in-the-money puts ought to be selling at almost $3 more than their normal value.

When you are buying puts you certainly are going to take a close look at the price of the put. All the factors that influence the pricing of a call will have the same effect on the price of a put, so that volatile stocks with high betas, high P/E ratios, and low dividends will command the highest-priced puts, while low prices will prevail for puts on stocks with the opposite characteristics. The ease of making a *conversion* of an on-the-money option from a put to a call and back means that, at least for on-the-money options, there must be comparability of the prices of puts and calls in any stock. The reasons that the price of an out-of-the-money put is not the exact equivalent of the price of the call is due to the dividend, the cost of money, and public demand for either the put or the call.

Since there is such ease in converting calls into puts, it is axiomatic that the pricing will be comparable, and that is why it is so easy to apply the rules of strategy for buying calls to buying puts. The future time value will be greatest for those puts that are at the strike price, and will decrease as the stock moves away from the strike price in either direction. The longer-duration options will have higher premiums, but be less expensive on a per-unit-of-time basis.

Buying Puts to Protect a Stock Investment

If you own stock there may be many reasons why you are afraid of the downside risk but do not wish to give up ownership of the stock.

One frequent problem is that you have owned the stock for so long, or perhaps you have even inherited it, that its tax basis is so low that a sale would result in a very large capital gains tax. So you are in practice prevented from selling the stock, and yet you may have serious grounds for believing that the stock may decline precipitously. Or you may want to hold on to a stock because you believe in it for the long haul and do not want to sell the stock now, incur commission costs, and then buy it back later, also paying commission costs. In any situation where you do not want to sell your stock for some reason such as these, but do want to get absolute protection against a decline in the price of the stock, the purchase of a put is the perfect solution.

Before we discuss this in more length, let's look at some instances where buying a put is not necessarily the right answer. If you are going to sell the stock at some future date in any event and are holding on to it now because you believe the stock still could go up, but you do want that downside protection, then buying a put is an answer, but it may not be the best answer. The reason for this is that an equivalent of being long stock and long a put is to be long a call. Strange as this seems, in both cases on the downside all that you can lose is the premium on the option, whether it be the put or the call, and on the upside there is unlimited potential. Being long a call instead of being long the stock and a put has one big advantage, namely that you have freed up all the cash you had invested in the stock. So if you can have exactly the same position by being long a call, you should carefully consider selling your stock and buying a call. That way you can then invest the money from the stock in something that can be of more potential profit to you than simply substituting for a call.

But if there is a legitimate reason for not selling the stock, then the purchase of a put will provide you with absolute protection against a significant downside move. In fact, it is no exaggeration at all to say that the purchase of a put in this case provides insurance against any price decline, because no matter how low the price of the stock goes, down to and including zero, the put will give you absolute and complete protection against loss. The only catch is that you will be out by the part of the put's price that was its future time value plus the amount by which the put is out of the money. The future time value will be a direct cost to you no matter what happens to the price of the stock. So when you buy the put, you must realize that the future time value of the put will never be recovered, whether the stock goes up or down—that it is simply a loss like the premium on a fire insurance policy. It may save you many times its cost, but it is still a cost. For example, if you own a stock that is at 63 and you buy a 70 put for $9, you are paying $2 for its future time value and this money will never be recovered. The other $7 represents the intrinsic cash value of the put, and will be recovered when you sell the put, regardless of what happens to the stock. If the stock ends up at 53 when the put expires, your stock is down $10 and the put is worth $17, meaning that you have a profit of $17 minus $9, which equals $8 on the put, offset by the $10 loss on the stock, giving a net loss of $2. This is the future time value of the original put.

If the Stock Goes Up. Let's see what happens if the stock goes up. Remember that your put gives you protection up to the strike price, and not beyond. So, if the stock goes up $10 to 73, you should be making a profit of the amount by which the stock goes up over the strike price of the option, which would be $3. But you have a profit of $10 on the stock, while the put has become worthless with the stock above its strike price. Since it cost you $9, the loss on your put subtracted from the $10 profit on the stock gives you a net profit of just $1. This is the $3 profit you should have made minus the $2 originally paid for the future time value of the put. The moral of the story is that if you have the choice between two out-of-the-money puts to protect your stock position, you will wind up paying less if you get the one with the higher strike price (the one deeper in the money and hence with the lower cost for future time value). This must be carefully weighed, however, against the fact that once you buy a put on stock you own, you cannot make any money until the stock goes up above its strike price. So the higher-strike-price put will prevent you from making a profit until your stock goes above its strike price.

Tax Problem. One point to keep in mind in buying a put on stock you own is that if you have not held the stock long enough to qualify for long-term capital gains treatment (currently one year), then the purchase of the put will completely eliminate the holding period you already have and will stop the holding period from running until you have sold the put. For example, if you have owned some stock for 10 months and you then purchase a put on that stock to give you downside protection, then hold the put for five months, your holding period of the stock when you sell that put will be zero for purposes of computing whether the stock qualifies for long-term capital gain. You must therefore own the stock for an entire year after you have sold the put to qualify for long-term treatment. Thus, the time you held the stock before you bought the put and the time you owned the stock while you owned the put are completely lost.

Interestingly enough, once you have attained long-term status with your stock, then you can buy a put and it will have no effect on the status of the stock. So if you are considering buying a put to protect your stock, you ought to do it promptly after you have acquired the stock, or else wait for your year to run out, when it becomes long-term. Buying a put after you have owned a stock for 11 months could be a very expensive move in terms of taxes.

Puts versus Calls. After this long discussion, it might occur to you that another method of getting downside protection, without having to pay out any money but in fact getting money in, is to sell a call against the stock. This does take in money and can be profitable, but it is not insurance against a decline in the stock's price. It is protection merely to the extent of the money you take in from the sale of the call. If the stock goes down by more than that amount, you are on your own. If you are really worried about a stock falling out of bed, a call is not going to be a very good substitute, even though a deep-in-the-money call can give a great deal of protection. It is not the same as being insured.

An Expensive Practice. One further word should be said about the concept of buying puts on stocks you already own. It is the view of the author that this should be done only on a temporary basis. Even when premiums are low, the cost of continually buying puts on a stock one owns is very likely to drain out all the potential profit from owning the stock. Just as constantly buying calls on the same stock is unlikely to be profitable over an extended period of time, so buying puts on a stock is also likely to end up losing money. If you feel so uncomfortable owning a stock that you feel the need to constantly have the protection of a put, then perhaps you shouldn't own that stock at all.

A possible compromise would be to buy out-of-the-money puts. If these are available, they will be very cheap, because their strike prices are so far below the current price of the stock. They will not provide you any help if the price of the stock dips slightly, but in that infrequent time when the stock just crashes down, the put will be there to save you like the safety net under the trapeze artists at the circus. Perhaps such a program is worth its slight cost for the peace of mind it gives.

An alternative means for having some security in owning stocks has always been to put in a good till canceled stop-loss order at a price well below the current price of the stock. When the stock reaches the indicated price, the order automatically becomes a market order and the stock is sold. But there are two big differences and advantages that puts have over stop-loss orders. The first is that a put provides a continuous protection from the day the put is purchased until it expires. The bane of the stop-loss order is that the stock may go down to the level of the order, touch off the sale of all the stock, and then the price of the stock can soar back up to more than the purchase cost—without, of course, the person who was taken out of his position by the stop-loss order. This can happen no matter at what price you set the stop-loss order.

With a put working for you, you can simply wait until the put is about to expire and then cash it in. You will continue to own the stock for the entire period, and you cannot be faked out by a sudden dip in the stock. The stock can go up and down by any amount in any sequence, and you will come out owning the stock and making the profit if it is up while being fully protected against any loss (except for the put's future time value cost) if the stock is below the strike price of the put on the final day of the put's life.

The second big advantage of the put is that it is actually insurance, meaning that a put will give you the amount of money necessary to reimburse you for a loss on the stock. A stop-loss order gives you nothing. It simply is a means of limiting your loss. Thus, while a put is like a fire insurance policy, a stop-loss order is simply like a sprinkler system. It may limit the loss, but it doesn't pay the bills for you.

Buying Puts to Protect a Portfolio

We have already discussed buying a put to give you downside protection on a specific stock. Another very helpful use of puts can be as insurance against a decline in the value of your entire stock portfolio. Since puts may not be available on several of the stocks a person might have in his portfolio, it is invariably impossible to provide insurance against a decline in every one of the stocks a person owns. But, by carefully selecting puts on a representative list of stocks, or on a stock index, it will be possible to come up with puts that roughly resemble the securities in your own portfolio.

Since the typical portfolio is long stock, it makes a good hedge to own some puts in case the market goes down. If the market goes up, you could make so much money on the stocks you own that you shouldn't mind the loss of the money you spent for the puts. But if the market really goes down, the puts will produce many times their cost. For this type of scatter insurance, it might be wisest to use out-of-the-money puts, which are inexpensive. They will not become profitable until the market or the particular stocks you select have a substantial decline, but that is when you really need the help they can give. You are probably willing to wait out a small decrease in stock prices, or you wouldn't be in common stocks in the first place. So an out-of-the-money put could be just right; low cost in case the market goes up, but emergency insurance in case it drops severely. You could think of it as collision insurance with a large deductible. Unless there is a major accident, the puts aren't going to help you, but when you really need them in a disaster, they'll be there.

Some of the brightest money managers I know make extensive use of puts for just this purpose. Especially when combined with a covered call writing program they make sense. As one money manager who uses covered calls pointed out, "I can absorb a decline of about 10% with my calls, but beyond that any loss goes right down to the bottom line. That's why I need the protection of out-of-the-money puts." A comment well worth considering. One final note: The time to buy puts is always when the market is going up, everyone is bullish, and you are absolutely certain that you will not need them.

SELLING PUTS

When we discussed selling calls, we used two different chapters, selling covered calls and selling naked calls. We needed two different chapters because although both strategies involve the sale of calls, they are totally different in result and could not be discussed together. The interesting thing about puts is that there is literally no method of selling a covered put against stock.

At first glance one would think that selling a put against a short stock position would be the sale of a covered put, and I suppose theoretically that is correct. But although you may be protected on the downside from a loss on your naked put, you are totally exposed on the upside to a loss on your stock short position. And in any case, there are not many people who have large short positions. So, the Options Clearing Corporation (OCC) prospectus states quite clearly that the only way to sell a covered put is to be long a put on the same stock with a longer expiration period and with a lower or equal strike price. Thus, there is no put equivalent to selling a covered call. So this discussion is perforce limited to a consideration of naked put writing.

Fundamentally, selling uncovered puts is quite similar to selling uncovered calls. You take in the premium from the put, have on deposit the proper amount of margin, and the original price you received is your profit as long as the stock stays out of the money at the expiration date (i.e., above the strike price in the case of a put). A put seller is basically an optimist about the stock market, at least to the extent that he does not expect the stocks to go down below the strike price. As in selling naked calls, however, no matter how right he is and no matter how far up the stocks climb, he can make no more than the amount of the premium he originally received. His loss is limited to only how low the stock can go.

For example, if a stock is now 37, and you sell the 35 put for 2, you are betting that, upon the expiration of the put, the stock will be at 33 or better. At 33, the put will be 2 points in the money, and thus have a cash value of $2, so that if you buy it back for its cash value on the last day, you will break even. If the stock is at 34, the put will be worth $1 on the last day and anywhere at 35 or better it will be worthless, giving you a profit of $2.

Typically, the naked put seller will be selling out-of-the-money puts, and the amount by which they are out of the money will be determined by the amount of premium that can be obtained, and probably by the extent to which the put seller is bullish on the market.

Like his cousin, the naked call seller, a naked put seller will probably also be interested in maximizing his return on a per-week basis by selling only the shortest-term puts, almost never with more than three months of life left, and usually with about six to eight weeks left.

His selection of the proper stock will be determined by his quest for the highest premium possible and by his distaste for selling a put on a stock that could plunge rapidly in price. As is the case in every other aspect of options, so here too these two conflicting goals will result in a subjective decision that will not be the same for the many different naked put sellers. One factor that will undoubtedly influence decisions on which stock to write puts on is that premiums will tend to be higher on stocks that are moving down. This is because so many Wall Street aficionados are chart followers or technicians of one sort or another. Without trying to oversimplify a very complicated group of theories, it can be said that in general most chart watchers believe that if a stock is going down, it is likely to continue to go down, and if it is already reaching new lows, then it is even more likely to continue going down, because it has now passed its downside support area. Therefore, these true believers in the validity of technical analysis of stock prices will be rushing in to buy puts on stocks that are making new lows. The result is that these puts should be selling for more than their normal value given the volatility of the stock, the amount of time remaining in the life of the put, and the relationship of the price of the stock to the strike price of the option.

Finding the Overpriced Put

The true option believer, who is interested in whether an option is over- or underpriced and not in what some chart watchers say about the stock, will quickly spot such a situation as one that is made to order for him to sell the puts that the chart watchers are so eagerly seeking to buy. In fact, if the naked put seller partially believes stock prices move in an unpredictable manner (the position of the random walk believer, the purest form of option investor) but also looks at fundamental statistics of the stock such as price/earnings ratio and dividend yield, he might conclude that now that the stock is at a lower price level demand for the stock should increase, and it should be even less likely to fall in price than when it was higher in price. And so, one word of advice I can give the naked put seller is to look for those stocks that have been falling recently if you want to spot the overpriced put.

Computing the Margin Requirement

Just as in selling naked calls, the naked put seller needs to have on deposit the required amount of margin. This margin is computed in exactly the same manner as that required for calls. First, you must know what percentage your brokerage firm is requiring of you. The lowest percentage permitted now by federal regulations is 20%, but many firms require more; in many cases the requirement is 50%. Step one is to take that percentage of the current price of the stock. Step two is to subtract the amount by which the stock is out of the money (i.e., the amount by which the current price of the stock is above the strike price of the put) or add the amount by which the put is in the money (i.e., the amount by which the current price of the stock is lower than the strike price of the option). The minimum for out of the money options can not be less than 10% of the underlying security. Step three is to add the current premium of the put. Finally, to determine the amount of money you must deposit to do the naked sale, you can deduct the amount of the premium you take in.

For example, if a stock is currently selling for $66 and you think that it would be profitable to write the nearest-duration 60 strike price put for a premium of $2, the margin would be computed this way: (1) Assuming that you are required to use the rate of 30%, you would multiply the present price of the stock, $66, by 30%, which equals $19.80. (2) You next determine whether the put is in the money or out of the money. Here it is out of the money, so you can deduct the difference between the current price of the stock and the strike price. That difference is $6, and subtracting $6 from $19.80 leaves us $13.80. This is above the minimum 10% which would be $6.60. (3) You now add the current premium of the put which is $2.00 to give a margin requirement of $15.80. (4) Finally, to determine how much money you must add to your account to carry this position, you can deduct the full amount of the premiums you took in. Subtracting $2 from $15.80 brings us back to a total margin requirement of $13.80. Therefore, for the opportunity of making $2, you must invest $13.80, which means that your maximum return from this trade would be 14.5%.

If the option had two months to go you would multiply by six to get the annualized rate of return, which turns out be an 87% return on your money. Since that figure seems unusually high, remember that you will make that much money only if you can reinvest the entire amount at the same rate of return every other month, and only if all the trades you make during the year turn out to be completely successful. These are very large ifs indeed, and provide the basis for the SEC rule that annualized returns cannot be used by brokers to describe how profitable a particular trade is, but may be used only in a comparative sense so that equivalent option trades of different durations can be analyzed with a common standardized measurement.

But there is an even more important reason why that rate of return is highly questionable as a realistic measurement of rate of return. This is that just as in naked call selling, the amount of margin required for selling naked puts is marked to the market every day. This means that every time the price of the stock falls by 1 point, if you have only the minimum margin on deposit you will be required by your brokerage firm to come up with more margin money. The amount of money required for each decline of 1 point can be determined as follows: (1) Recompute the requirement for a percentage of the current price of the stock. Since the price of the stock is falling, this amount will be less. If you are on a 30% requirement, then each decline of a point will reduce this part of the margin requirement by $30 per put, and if you are on a 50% requirement, it will be reduced by $50 per put. (2) Add 1 point for each point decline to make up for the fact that as the stock gets closer to the put strike price the difference between the two, which you subtracted from the margin requirement, is reduced. (3) The result is that if you are on a 30% requirement, your margin requirement will increase by $70 per put, and if you are on a 50% requirement, then it will increase by $50 per put for each 1-point drop in stock. (4) As the price of the put increases, that increases the margin requirement by the amount of the increase.

When one originally sells a put it is impossible to tell whether the stock will go down, and therefore it is not possible to state that the original amount of margin is the amount that will be the maximum requirement later on. Therefore, if a person has $10,000 to use in writing naked puts, he cannot with any prudence write enough puts to use up his $10,000 in initial margin requirements, because if any of his stocks start to go down, he will get a margin call, which will result in some of his position being liquidated, probably at a loss. Anyone contemplating selling naked puts must have some additional capital in reserve with which to provide additional margin. Of course, it is possible that the stocks can go up. If this happens, exactly as much margin is released as was required when they went down (i.e., $70 per put if you are on 30% margin requirement, and $50 if you are on 50%).

Limiting Your Loss

One final similarity between writing naked puts and writing naked calls is that it is just as dangerous and speculative to write puts as it is calls. Stocks can fall even more rapidly than they rise and when they do it can mean quick losses for the put writer. In fact, since put premiums appear to be usually less than call premiums, the price of a put will increase proportionally even more rapidly than a call once the put becomes in the money. Thus, it is imperative to have a method of making sure that your loss is held to a reasonable limit. Otherwise you will be in the situation of trying to make money from a transaction with a very modest possible gain but an almost infinite loss. And you know that it is hard to make money from that kind of a game.

The best method of limiting your loss is to place a stop-loss order to buy in the put based on either the price of the option or the price of the stock. Usually one would place the stop-loss based on the price of the option. Typically you would decide on the stop loss-price either by adding a certain number of points to the premium you received or by multiplying the premium you received by a number such as 2 or 3. If you want to get stopped out on your put based on the price of the underlying stock or stock index, this would be called a basis order and you would have to check with your brokerage firm to see whether it accepts that type of order.

Please make sure that as soon as you have sold your naked put, you decide exactly when you are going to close out your position. If you do not, you are going to be tempted to fall into the treacherous trap of inaction. This means that when the stock falls by 3 points you may hesitate to close out your position because you will be creating an irrevocable loss. If you let things alone, the stock might go back up and you will have a wonderful profit, just as you had originally expected. Believe me, with this kind of thinking you can watch a stock go from 105 to 55 and without closing out your position. The resulting loss will be staggering. Of course you might be lucky and the stock could go back up. But don't bet on it. The entire purpose of this book is to suggest methods of substituting action that will give you the best probability of making money, lower the amount of likely losses, and reduce your dependence on luck. If you want to trust Lady Luck, don't be surprised if she turns out to be a fickle lady indeed, and you are later forced to close out your position by the ever-increasing margin requirement at a much larger loss than you would have had earlier.

Writing naked puts should be done only by someone who is willing to decide on his stop-loss limits before he writes the put and is then willing to stick to his decision exactly. It seems hard to do at the time, but life sometimes requires difficult actions. One way of making it easier is to have a number of partial limits. If you have written 10 puts, you might decide that you will buy back two when the stock gets to 45, two more at 44, another two at 43, and so on. This eliminates the terrible feeling when you buy in your puts that you are converting what might have been a handsome profit into a sure loss. By closing out only a portion of your position at a time you are never converting your entire position into a total loss at once.

WRITING PUTS AND/OR CALLS ON A STOCK INDEX

Since writing uncovered puts and calls seems to be such a likely way to make a profit, one might think that it is a great method of generating wealth on an almost continuous basis. Unfortunately, actual experience shows that it is anything but easy to generate profits consistently. One of the large problems is that stocks and stock indexes do not always behave as they should in theory. You may remember Figure 4.4 in Chapter 4, which showed a bell curve. That is the theoretical distribution curve that indicates what the probability is that a stock will have moved from its present price to a new price at some point in the future.

If this theoretical model worked well in practice, the preferred strategy would be to sell an equal number of puts and calls. This has the advantage that they help balance each other out, so that when there are losses on the calls, the puts will automatically be doing well. Also, with the high margin requirements on uncovered writes, it is good that the margin is computed only on the option that has the higher margin requirement. The margin departments also know that you cannot lose on both the puts and the calls at the same time. So you are making more efficient use of your capital. Now that we know the benefits of selling both puts and calls, we'll see why it isn't always the best course of action.

What makes it a bit of a challenge is that stocks don't always act the way they are supposed to. To give you a similar everyday situation, suppose you turn on the weather forecast and it says that tomorrow there's a 98% chance of pure blue sunny skies. You're going to an outdoor party, so you put on your finest clothes. Shortly after you arrive at the party, the sky suddenly turns dark and a heavy downpour comes out of nowhere, drenching you and everyone else present and ruining your clothes. In a fit of rage you phone the weather bureau, only to hear a voice saying that's why they told you there was a 2% chance that it would not be sunny. The problem is that you never know when the 2% is going to occur.

Like the weather, the movements of stocks and stock markets are largely unknowable to us humans. Yet, looking back one can see that there appear to have been major trends. For example, the S&P 500 had a number of years in a row when it made extraordinarily large gains. From the end of 1994 through 1999 it gained 220% which was an average gain per year of 26.32%. What this meant was that anyone who tried to run a balanced program of writing puts and calls would in all likelihood have lost so heavily on the call side that those losses would have more than offset the profits from the put side.

Is there anything that one can do? Maybe yes and maybe no. According to mathematicians, it would take about 30 years to actually demonstrate that any program of predicting what the market will do is really better than random luck, and most of us don't have quite that long to find out. Since I am running a program for my clients of selling puts and/or calls on a stock index it would be very valuable if I could figure out a way to minimize the number of times I am on the losing side of the trades. Sorry to write that I have not yet managed to come up with such a foolproof system, and I am quite sure that no one ever will. In lieu of that, I have come up with an approach that I use as a tentative guideline as to whether to write puts or calls or both.

THE ANSBACHER INDEX

My approach is in two parts. First, I examine the relative premium strength of short-term out-of-the-money OEX puts as compared to the comparable calls. The result of this calculation is called The Ansbacher Index and is detailed in Appendix D. Second, I take into consideration any major trend of the market. Of course, neither one of these can predict what the market will do, but it gives me a degree of comfort nevertheless for the reasons that follow.

The Ansbacher Index notes the price of a four-to-eight-week stock index put that is about 40 points out of the money. It then creates a theoretical call that is exactly as far out of the money as the put and has the same expiration date. We then divide the price of the call by the price of the put. The resulting number tells what percentage the call is of the put. If, for example, the number is 0.64 this means that the call premium is 64% of the put premium. Theoretically they should both be about the same price. The fact that the puts are so much higher priced than the calls tells me that the public is a strong buyer of the puts and is not a strong buyer of the calls.

This information is valuable in my opinion for two reasons. One, it tells you that if you are writing short-term out-of-the-money calls you will receive only 64% of the money you will receive from writing similar puts. If you are a random walk believer, meaning that we can't know what the market is going to do, then doesn't it make sense to sell the option that offers so much more money? So a reading of The Ansbacher Index of 0.64 would indicate that it would be better to be a writer of puts than of calls.

Another reason why The Ansbacher Index may be useful is as a sentiment indicator. It is well known on Wall Street that any consensus is usually wrong. If it is the consensus of the option-buying public that the market is likely to go down, then it would follow that the market is probably not going to go down. That is a second reason for preferring to sell the puts. Of course, if it showed that the public was a big buyer of calls, this would indicate that it probably was not going to go up and would be a further reason to write calls. Thus there are two reasons for taking the Index into consideration.

A word of explanation about The Ansbacher Index is required. The public is normally a heavier buyer of stock index puts than of calls because everyone who owns a stock or a stock portfolio is a natural buyer of a put as a hedge. There is virtually no counter party buying calls as a hedge. I believe that this is the reason that when it comes to stock index options, the puts are normally higher than the calls. Over the past 14 years the Index has gone from a reading of 0.30, showing extreme pessimism on the part of options buyers, to about 1.05, showing extreme bullishness. As you can see, these extremes are highly skewed to the side of puts being more expensive. I would estimate that the average reading during this entire time has been about 0.65. Whether this is truly normal or just reflects the fact that this has been mainly a bullish period for the market is still a question in my mind.

The fact that out-of-the-money stock index puts are generally more expensive than calls gives them another advantage over calls.

This is that as the market moves against them their premiums increase more slowly than they do for calls. This is an important distinction because once you have written an option and placed your stop-loss order, you hope that the option will not increase up to the level of the stop. With the puts there is generally quite a bit more room for the market to move adversely before touching off the stop-loss than there is with calls. If it does move, it is easier to rewrite the put at a much lower strike price and still get a good premium than it is to do the same thing with a call.

The other indication I use is a general sense of the market's direction. This is even less reliable than The Ansbacher Index, but the reason I take it into consideration is expressed in the old Wall Street axiom "Don't stand in front of a speeding freight train." If the market is moving down and has been doing so for a few weeks or months, it is just normal to extrapolate that trend and plan as if it were going to continue doing what it has been doing. The big question is whether it is the beginning of a major trend or just a minor reversal of the previous trend. You never know until it is over. So I leave to others the question of what is a major trend and how to best identify when it has begun.

Even when you are certain that a downtrend is in place, this still doesn't necessarily mean that you shouldn't sell any puts. It may be that the public is aware of the downtrend and is worried that it will even accelerate on the downside. This could cause the pricing of the puts to be excessively high. Perhaps you figure that even if the market does continue down, you can write a put that is so far out of the money that the odds are the market will not get that low before the put's expiration date.

SELLING PUTS AS A MEANS OF ACQUIRING STOCK

So far we have considered selling puts only as a means of making money on a margin balance. If the stock went down below the strike price, we assumed that the put writer would buy back the put before it was exercised. He obviously doesn't want it to be exercised and have to pay commissions on purchasing the high-priced stock upon the exercise of his put, and then pay another commission when he sells the stock out at the market price. But there is another type of put writer who would not complain if his put is exercised. This is the type of person who likes the underlying stock. He is not selling the put because it is necessarily overpriced and he feels confident that the stock will not get below the strike price. Rather, he likes the stock and would be happy to purchase it if he could get it at a discount from its current market price. He therefore sells a put, taking in premium income. If the put is exercised he has bought the stock at a price that is reduced from the price at the time he sold the put by the future time value in the put when he sold it plus any amount that the put was out of the money.

This type of put writer can write either in-the-money or out-of-the-money puts, depending on how badly he wants to own the stock and how he feels about making money simply by being a naked put writer. Let's take the same example we used before: The stock is now $66 and the nearest put at the $60 level is $2. Our put writer may decide to write this put, and if the price of the stock stays above $60, he is pleased to have made a good return on the sale of the naked put. He is not sorry that he didn't buy the stock, because he wanted to buy it at a price below $60. In this respect he is identical to our naked put seller described previously.

But if the price of the stock should drop to $55, he would behave differently. Unlike the regular naked put seller, who would set a level at which he would buy in the put, this put seller sets no such level. He doesn't care how low the stock goes, because he is quite willing to have the stock put to him at $60. With the premium of $2 he received for selling the put, his actual purchase cost for the stock is just $58—a large discount indeed from the cost of $66 that he would have had if he had purchased the stock in the open market originally.

This type of put seller could also sell an in-the-money put. Let us assume that there is a put with a 70 strike price and that it is selling for $6, consisting of $4 cash value and future time value of $2. If the put seller were more interested in acquiring the stock, this is the method he would use, because he is going to have to buy the stock unless it goes above $70 a share on the expiration date. If the stock goes up to $69, the put will be exercised and he will have to buy the stock for $70. Since he originally received $6 for the sale of the put, his actual cost for the stock is $64, which is a discount of $2 from the price of the stock on the day that he sold the put. Note that this in-the-money put seller is much more likely to end up as a buyer of the stock than the writer of the 60 strike price put. And if he does not end up buying the stock, it is only because it has gone up above the 70 strike price. The result of this is that the entire $6 he took in from the original sale of the put is his profit. So this person either gets the stock at $2 below the market price at the time he sold the put or he makes a whopping profit on his naked put. Either way he should be happy.

No Assurance of Actually Buying the Stock

A word of warning is in order here. Selling naked puts is not a way of acquiring stock if you really want to get the stock. If you really want to own some stock the only way to be sure of owning it is either to enter a market order to buy the shares or else to buy a call and exercise it at some future date. Selling a put gives you no assurance that you will own the stock, for the simple reason that if the price of the stock goes above the strike price it will not be put to you. And this is the very time you probably want to own the stock, when it is going up! So, don't think that selling puts is the miraculous method of always buying stock at a discount.

If you are right, and the stock goes up the way you think that it will, you will not buy it. But if you are wrong, and the stock goes down, then you will be forced to buy it, probably at a higher net price than it is currently selling for, all your kicking and screaming to the contrary notwithstanding! This is not following Will Rogers's advice on how to get rich on Wall Street. Said he, "It's very simple, you just buy a stock that's going to go up. And if it doesn't go up, then you don't buy it in the first place." A naked put seller is often doing just the opposite. But it is the perfect strategy for the person who would like either to get a stock at a low price or to make a good return on his money from the put premium.

6

SPREADS, STRADDLES, AND COMBINATIONS

A spread is a position that consists of being lon̴͟ ̴͟ ̴͟ ̴͟e options on a stock and short one or more options on the same stock, but of a different series (i.e., a different strike price or expiration date). Thus, if one is long five GE October 110 calls and is also at the same time short five GE July 110 calls, that is a spread. There are an enormous variety of spreads available, but they all have in common that one position is long and the other is short. Spreads can involve calls or puts but, where both puts and calls are involved in a single stock, that is a called a straddle or combination.

We have learned that one can make a great deal of money buying a call if the stock goes up, and a lot of money buying a put when the stock goes down. You might wonder why we have to fool around with a combination of being long and short the same options on the same stock at the same time. Isn't that contradictory and self-defeating? In a way yes, but in another way definitely no. Spreads are extremely popular because they serve a very useful purpose. If we have firm convictions that a stock is going to move a large amount in a specific direction, we will always be better off simply buying a call or a put as the price direction indicates.

But in the real world, clouded as it is in uncertainty, we often do not have a firm conviction as to what is going to happen, or we believe that a stock will make only a relatively modest move. It is in these circumstances that spreads are made to order. One can say that the purpose of a spread is to increase the range of prices under which a person can make money, but this is done at the cost of limiting the potential profit that can be made. In other words, there is a larger range of stock prices in which some profit will be made, but there is no longer the possibility of infinite riches as there is in simply buying an option.

An example would be a *bull spread*, which is a spread one uses when one is expecting a stock to go up. If a stock is now selling at 41, and the 40 strike price call is 4, the purchase of the call will not be profitable on expiration until the stock reaches 44. Of course it is profitable at any level above that, and if the stock really takes off, say to 55, there will be a profit of 11 on the 4 investment. On the other hand, a bull spread that consists in buying the 40 call and selling the 45 call, may cost as little as 2, which means that the position breaks even at just 42. Thus the break-even point has been reduced by 2 points, which is a substantial reduction. Unfortunately, the maximum profit is reached when the stock gets to 45, and no matter how much higher it goes above that level, it does not add one penny to the profit of the bull spread.

TYPES OF SPREADS

Vertical Spreads and Horizontal Spreads

Spreads are divided into two major groups. There are the vertical, or price, spreads, and the horizontal, or calendar, spreads. *Vertical spreads* consist of two options of the same expiration date with different strike prices. Since the options are listed in the newspaper columns with one strike price under the other of the same month, it is easy to see why these are called vertical spreads, and one can find them just by looking at the option above or below any other option. For example, a spread involving an October 25 and an October 30 option on the same stock is a vertical spread.

Another reason that this type of spread may be called a vertical spread is that the price of the stock must move vertically in order to make money, and hence they are also sometimes called price spreads.

In contrast to the vertical spreads, the *horizontal spreads* can be found in the newspaper columns by reading across a line. For example, a spread involving an October 25 and a January 25 option is a horizontal spread. Because these involve spreads of different expiration months, they are more frequently called *calendar spreads* or *time spreads*. Unlike vertical spreads, which make money primarily from the movement in the price of the stock, calendar spreads rely on the effect of time on the relationship of the option prices.

Volatility and Nonvolatility Spreads

Another classification of spreads that is useful is a volatility spread. This is a spread position in which one will make money if the stock moves in either direction, provided only that it moves far enough and soon enough. The opposite of this is a nonvolatility spread, in which one makes money when the stock stays right where it is now. An example of a volatility spread is being short an in-the-money 20 option for a price of perhaps 3, and then being long three 25 options at a price of perhaps $1/2$ each. In this case the spread is done for a credit of $1^1/2$. If the stock declines below 20, all the options become worthless and the spread is profitable. On the other hand, if the stock goes up far enough above 25, the three 25 options begin to make enough to offset the loss on the single 20 option.

The best example of a nonvolatility spread is an on-the-money calendar spread, because it is the most profitable when the stock ends up right at the strike price. Thus, if a stock is now 60, and you put on a calendar spread involving an April 60 and a July 60, you will make the most money when the stock stays just where it is, and hence this is called a nonvolatility spread.

Then there is also an almost infinite number of complex spreads, including the butterfly or sandwich spread, the *diagonal spread,* and the domino spread (see Figure 6.1). But one should remember, in options as in life in general, the theory of Ockham's razor applies. This theory holds that where there are two methods of accomplishing the same objective, the simpler method is preferred. This is especially true in options for three reasons. One, the amount of commissions and cost of the spreads between the bid and asked prices is greatly increased by using complex spreads. Two, complex spreads are much harder to execute and take off (get out of) than simpler spreads. Three, a complex spread will usually involve being short more options, and each option you are short may involve the danger of unwelcome exercise, which is the bane of the option trader's existence. So before you put on a complex spread, try hard to know whether it is possible to accomplish the same thing, or almost the same thing, with a much simpler spread. You don't want to be in the position of accidentally having done an alligator spread. What's that? That's the phrase brokers use for a spread in which the commissions eat you alive.

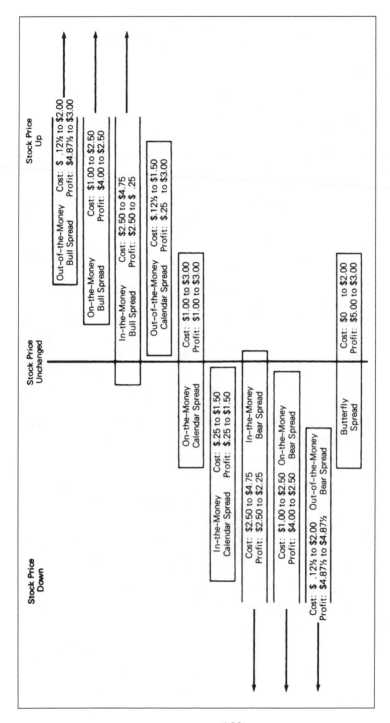

FIGURE 6.1 Profitability Range of Spreads

Area of box indicates profit zone. Figures, which are only approximate guidelines, are for spreads of options with strike prices $5 apart. Double figures if strike prices are $10 apart. Cost is also the amount of risk, all of which can be lost. Profit is the potential profit if stock ends up at proper price.

EXECUTING THE SPREAD ORDER

Now let's talk about how spreads are executed. When you intend to buy a share of stock, if you are a careful investor you may put in a limit order (e.g., to buy the stock at any price up to $25\frac{1}{2}$). With that type of order, you may never buy the stock, but if you do you will not pay any more for the stock than $25\frac{1}{2}$. The same thing is true when you buy options. Now, when it comes to doing a spread, where you are simultaneously buying one option and selling another, how can you be sure that they will both be done at prices that give you the spread you want at a price you are willing to pay? If you put in an order to buy an option for no more than 3, and then sell another for no less than 1 (if you are trying to do a spread at a cost of 2), you might find that the stock was going up, and you had no trouble in selling an option for 1, but you couldn't buy the other option for 3. So instead of having a spread, you are left being short a naked option, which is the last thing in the world you wanted to do.

The answer to this dilemma is resolved by the fact that you really do not care at what prices the individual options are bought or sold for; it is the net difference between the prices of the spread that you are interested in. And the exchanges all accept spread orders to be done at a certain difference between the two prices (e.g., for a debit of $3\frac{1}{2}$ or for a credit of 9). A *debit spread* means that you are going to pay to put on the spread, and a *credit spread* means that you will be receiving money when you do the spread. When you put in an order of this type, it may be possible to do the order at the limits you have placed on the spread. But if it is executed, it must be done either at the debit you request or lower, or for the credit you asked or higher or it will not be done at all.

This brings us to another point about spreads. You may think that if you are doing a bull spread you will make money from an increase in the price of the stock. And this may be correct. But the way option professionals describe making money on a spread is from a change in the spread. That is, they talk about a spread increasing or a spread decreasing. If you have put on a debit spread—that is, one that cost you money—you want that cost to increase so you can sell it for a profit. Thus, in a debit spread, you want to get in for a low debit and have the spread increase, so you can sell out for a high credit. A bull spread done with call options is a typical debit spread. You might go in with a debit of 2 (i.e., a cost of 2), and come out with a credit of 5.

A credit spread is where you take in money when you put on the spread. A *bear spread* done with calls is an example of such a spread. When you do a credit spread, you naturally want to take in as much money as possible when you do it, that is, to get as high a credit as you can. Then when you close out the spread, it is done at a debit and you have to put money in. Therefore, when you close out a credit spread you want to close it out for as small a debit as possible. For instance, if you are doing a bear spread with calls, you might put it on for a credit of $4\frac{1}{2}$. This means that you took in $450 per option when you did the spread. Now as time passes and the stock moves down, you might be able to close it out for a debit of only $100 and you have made money from a decrease in the spread.

In summary, a debit spread is closed out for a credit, and a credit spread is closed out for a debit. Both orders can be entered as spread limits. It is very easy to remember what you want the spread to do. If it cost you money originally, you want that cost to get higher, because you will be selling it out at the close and you want the spread to widen. If you took in money when you originally did the spread, you will have to buy it back for a debit at the close, and you want the spread to be as small as possible.

Think of it this way: In a call option spread, if it is a bear spread, you want to squeeze the spread in a bear hug down to as tiny an amount as possible. On the other hand, bulls are famous for pushing things over in wild charges, and so when you do a bull spread with calls you want to push the spread as far apart as possible.

CALL OPTION SPREADS

Bull Spreads

As we said, a spread is basically trying to accomplish what could be done by other means, but with an increase in the price range of the stock within which it is profitable. In a bull spread we are attempting to make money when a stock goes up or stays up. Thus, what we are trying to do is very similar to what one does when one buys a call option. And a bull spread is basically buying a call option. This is always the principal part of the bull spread, which means that you are always buying a relatively expensive call option. It is from the increase in price of this call option you have bought that you usually expect to make your profit.

So the first step in putting on a bull spread is buying an option, let's say at the 25 strike price. The second step is to reduce the cost of this call by selling a call of the same expiration date on the same stock, but with a higher strike price. The option you sell is always worth less than the one you buy because it is always at a higher strike price. So if you bought the January 25 option, you might sell the January 30 option.

In describing a bull spread we pointed out that you sold the option with the higher strike price. You might have remembered Chapter 4 on selling naked options and wondered whether you could sell an option without owning the underlying stock, as in covered writing, and without putting up the required margin, as is done in selling naked options. The answer is that when the price of the stock goes up, so that you might lose money on the January 30 option, you know that the January 25 option will also have to go up in price, and that, indeed, it will be worth 5 points more than the 30 option at expiration. Thus, you are always fully protected against any loss by reason of the stock going up too far. Therefore, the January 25 option serves as your margin here, just as owning the underlying stock itself serves as the margin in covered writing.

Margin Rule in Spreads. The rule in spreads is that the option you own provides the margin for the option you are short, provided that it is (1) of the same or longer duration *and* (2) of the same or lower strike price. Both of these requirements must be present, or the short option will be treated for margin purposes just as if it were a naked option (subject to a limitation we'll describe later if you own an option of the right duration but a higher strike price). So if you are long a January 25 option and short an April 35, the January option cannot provide margin for your short option because the January option is not of the same or longer duration. And there is no point in arguing that it is much more expensive and will certainly go up in value if the stock increases in price. The rules are the rules, and you do not have a spread in the margin sense of the word. To repeat, the option you own must be of the same or lower strike price *and* must be of the same or longer duration than the option you have sold. Thus if you are long the April 25 call, that would provide margin for being short the January 30 call, or the April 30 call, but not the July 30 or the April 20.

A bull spread requires buying an option with a low strike price, which is always the more expensive option, and selling an option with a higher strike price, which is always the cheaper option. Since you are buying something expensive and selling something cheap, this spread always ends up costing you money, and therefore it is also classed as a debit spread, since it results in a debit to your account. The general rule is that there is no margin requirement to a debit spread. You simply pay cash for the amount of the debit plus transaction costs. On the way out, whatever can be realized from the sale of the position is yours to keep, and if it brings in more than your original cost, you have a profit.

Now let's examine in detail a bull spread where you buy a January 25 option and sell a January 30 to see just what benefit you will derive from selling the 30 option. Assume that the stock is at 26, and that the January 25 is 3 and the January 30 is 1. If you buy the January 25 option for 3, it is obvious that the stock must increase to 28 before you can break even at expiration, and that in order for you to double your money it must go up to 31. As the stock goes up above that price, your option goes up point for point. The big disadvantage is that if the stock stays where it is, your call will be worth just 1 at expiration, and you will have lost 66% of your initial cost. Furthermore, an increase of 2 points just to break even isn't very tempting, and a 5-point increase, a 19% increase in the stock price, just to double your money is quite a bit to ask. The purpose of a bull spread is to make all three of these situations more favorable for you.

So you decide to use a bull spread, and at the same time that you buy the January 25 option for 3, you sell the January 30 call for 1. Immediately this does one thing. You take in $100, and reduce the cost of your position by exactly one-third, from $300 for one call to $200. The first thing you notice is that this reduction in cost is a great blessing if you are wrong and the stock goes down in price rather than goes up. As with buying a call, it is also true in a bull spread that you cannot lose more than you initially spend. Therefore, no matter how far down the stock goes, you will never lose more than $200, and that is just two-thirds of what you could have lost in buying the option. So the first benefit of a bull spread as opposed to just buying the call is greatly reduced losses in case the stock goes down.

Now let's see what happens as the stock goes up. If the stock is at 27 on the calls' expiration, the 30 call you sold will be worthless, and the 25 option you own will be worth 2. You could sell it and realize 2. Since the entire spread originally cost you 2, you have broken even, less transaction costs. Compare this with the purchase of the 25 call option alone. That would have cost you 3, and by selling it for 2 you would have lost 33% of your money. So, clearly, the second advantage is that at this price you are much better off with a bull spread because you have reduced the break-even level by a whole point.

Let's continue up the price scale at expiration. If the stock is 28 on expiration, the January 25 is worth 3 and the January 30 expires worthless. If you had put on the bull spread for 2, you would now sell out the 25 option for 3, and find yourself with a profit of 1, for a 33% profit. Very good. Now, let's see what would have happened if you had just bought the January 25 option without doing the bull spread. You would have paid 3 for it, and at its expiration, with the stock at 28, the option would have been worth 3, and you would have broken even, ignoring transaction costs. There is the big difference. Which would you rather have? A 33% profit or a mere breakeven?

If the Stock Goes Up. But the benefits of the bull spread do not stop here. Let's assume that the stock goes up to 30 at the options' expiration. Here again the January 30 option expires worthless. The January 25 option is worth 5, and if you have just bought the option for 3, you would have a profit of 2, which is a 66% profit. Not bad, but let's see what kind of a profit you would have with the bull spread. You originally bought the January 25 call and sold the January 30 for a cost of 2. Now with the stock at 30, and the January 30 expiring worthless, you sell the January 25 option for 5, giving you a profit of 3. But a profit of 3 on an investment of 2 comes out to be a profit of 150%. Just compare a profit of 66% with one of 150% and you will see that the benefits of the bull spread are way ahead of a straight option buy at this price.

But we can continue on further. As the stock goes higher and higher, the January 25 option purchased by itself will keep on advancing, point for point, with the stock. The higher the better. But the value of the bull spread cannot increase beyond the 5 points that the position has when the stock is at 30 on the options' expiration. To see why this is so, one must only consider that as the 25 option that one owns goes up point for point with the increase in the price of the stock, the 30 option that you are short is also increasing point for point with the stock's price rise. And since you are short the 30 option, you must buy it back when you close out the position. So each additional point in the price of the 30 option is costing you a point. Thus each point gain in the value of the 25 option is exactly offset by a point gain in the price of the 30 option once the stock gets above 30, and accordingly the value of the bull spread cannot increase once the stock gets above 30.

The maximum value that a bull spread can attain is the difference between the strike prices of the two options. Here the difference between the 25 and 30 strike prices is 5, and so the spread can never be worth more than 5. Of course, the profit on the spread is limited to the difference between the original cost, here 2, and the maximum value of the spread, here 5. Thus the maximum profit this spread can generate is 3. One of the nice things about a bull spread as compared to the outright purchase of an option is that you can have an idea of the maximum profit, so that you need not be disappointed by a failure to reach some exaggerated goal.

But back to our example. We left the bull spread when the stock was 30 and pointed out that at this point it had reached its maximum profit potential, whereas the option by itself would keep on becoming more and more profitable. Does this mean that at 31 the option is more profitable than the bull spread? Definitely no. Doing the arithmetic shows that the January 25 option is worth 6, with a cost of 3, giving a profit of 3 for a 100% profit. But as we already saw, the bull spread achieves a profit of 150%. So, even above the strike price of the short option, a bull spread can be more profitable than the outright purchase of an option. See Figure 6.2 for a complete comparison, including the purchase of the 30 option alone.

Just how high does the price of the stock have to go before the

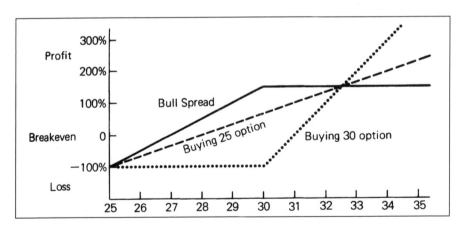

FIGURE 6.2 Profitability of Bull Spreads Compared to Buying Calls
Initial prices of options—January 25: $3; January 30: $1; initial stock price: 25
Note that at any price from 25 to 32 a bull spread is more profitable, but beyond 32 the purchase of either option makes more money, with the 30 option increasing the fastest.

option is the better investment? If we increase the stock price one more point to 32, we can get an idea. At 32, the January 25 would be worth 7 at its expiration. Since it cost 3, we have a profit of 4, which is 133%. And as we have previously seen, this is almost the profit on the bull spread. So the answer to our question is that in this case the stock had to rise more than 2 points above the strike price of the short option in order to become as profitable as the bull spread. And of course it would have to go higher before it became more profitable.

Incidentally, this is not a particularly exciting bull spread, but I used it as sort of a minimum. You may be able to find bull spreads that are much more advantageous—that is, where there is a much stronger ratio between the price of the higher option to the lower one. If, in our example, the January 30 option were priced at $1\frac{1}{2}$ instead of 1, it would greatly improve the performance of the spread. That would mean that the cost of the spread was $1\frac{1}{2}$ instead of 2, and the profit that could be achieved would be $3\frac{1}{2}$, or 233% rather than 150%. To equal the potential gain of the bull spread by buying the January 25 option alone, the stock would have to climb to 35 instead of 32. This means that it would have to advance by 9 points instead of just by 6 in order to make the same percentage profit. In other words, the stock would have to increase by 125% more just to make the same percentage return on your money, and at any point below that the bull spread would be more favorable. When premiums are high it is often possible to find bull spreads where the price of the upper strike price option is about one-half the price of the lower.

Here is the lesson of a bull spread. Under the right circumstances, it can clearly be the preferable investment. Consider our original case. Comparing percentages, and forgetting absolute amounts, we find that at 25 and below both strategies are equally bad (i.e., they both are worthless and we have a loss of 100%). But from 26 on up, the bull spread is clearly superior, and above 27 it begins making a profit while the option is still below breakeven. It is superior all the way up to 32, which means that at any price of the stock from 26 to 32, or any increase of from 0% to 23%, the bull spread is superior to the purchase of the option.

Buying an Option versus a Bull Spread. The next time you are tempted to purchase an option, work out the relative prices and profits of a bull spread versus the purchase of an option the way we did here. You may be surprised at how high the stock has to go before you make more money with the option by itself. And then there is always the psychological point that if you do make 150% or 233% profit on a bull spread, isn't this enough? Would you really be disappointed because you might have made even more by buying an option? Not me. If I made a profit of 233% on my investment in just a few months I would thank my lucky stars that I had done so well.

Three Types of Bull Spreads

Out-of-the-Money Bull Spreads. Bull spreads may be subdivided into three basic types, although there are no hard-and-fast categories. The first type could be called an out-of-the-money bull spread. This is when the price of the stock is below the strike price of the option you are buying. These spreads should cost very little, just a point or two, perhaps as much as 3 points when you are using strike prices 10 points apart. They are highly speculative and are the most similar of the three types of bull spreads to just buying options. They are speculative because even if the stock price goes up enough almost to reach the lower strike price call, the spread will still expire worthless. On the other hand, because of their small cost, the potential exists for quite a large percentage profit. Thus, if a spread between the 40 and 45 options costs $1, it could be worth $5 at expiration for a profit of 400%.

Since these are out-of-the-money bull spreads, in many cases the price of the call to be sold will seem quite insignificant, and the question will arise whether it is worth limiting the profit potential in order to take in the small amount realized from selling the higher strike price option. Typically one might be able to buy a 40 option for $1\frac{1}{2}$ and sell the 45 for $\frac{1}{2}$ or just $\frac{1}{4}$, or maybe $\frac{3}{8}$. Should one sell this higher strike price option for such a small amount and thus limit one's profit?

My personal conclusion is yes, and here's my thinking. While the money you take in is not a large amount, in terms of percentage cost of the spread it is substantial. If you can get only $\frac{1}{4}$ for the 45 option, you will be saving 16.6% of the cost of buying the 40 option. That may not seem like a lot, but in buying options or spreads you should be just as cost conscious as in any other purchase you make.

The Benefit of Selling the Higher Strike Price Option. Think of the last time you bought a new car. You may have trudged from dealer to dealer, getting the best deal you could on the car you wanted. It took a lot of work, discussing installment terms, trade-in allowance, cost of various options, and so on, but after spending a lot of time and effort you felt that it was all worthwhile because you were able to save $1,000 on your $25,000 car. And that certainly was a worthwhile saving. Yet it amounted to just 4%. Here you have a chance to save over four times that percentage without any work or time at all, and you can't decide whether it's worthwhile? The money you save on a bull spread will buy you the same things as the money you saved on your new car.

But what about the limitation you are putting on yourself in case the stock goes up above the higher strike price? Of course there is some price at which it might just be absurd to sell the higher option, but even if it were only $1/16$ you would probably be paying very little for the lower strike price option you bought, and it still might be a worthwhile percentage. But, in general, my way of looking at this is that if the stock should ever get up to the higher strike price, you have won a magnificent victory, and you should be pleased as can be. In over 80% of the cases this will not happen, and you will be better off having sold the other option. In the few cases where you are not, you still have a wonderful profit. So why not be happy?

You will note that in talking about profit, I have always described option prices at the expiration of the option. This is because when the options still have some time to run, both the option you are long and the one you are short will be worth more than their cash value, but it is not possible to know exactly how much more. As the price of the stock goes up and the option you are buying becomes deeper in the money, the option you are shorting will tend to have more future time value to it, whereas the one you are buying will tend to have less and will be selling for a price close to its intrinsic cash value. This situation is very good when you are putting on the spread, and it is why the two other types of bull spreads we are going to discuss are such favorable situations. The option you are buying represents solid cash value of the stock, but the one you are selling is the froth of future speculation. It's always good business to buy the solid and sell the problematical.

But there is a disadvantage to this when we come to close out the position. The problem is that the pricing of the options works exactly against us. Let's say we want to close out a 40 to 45 bull spread when the stock is at 45, and the options have about two months to run. You might think that with the stock at 45, you

could close out your spread for approximately 5 points, congratu-
late yourself for having made a super trade, and go on to the next
moneymaking opportunity. If you check the prices of the options,
you will find to your sorrow that the 40 option may be at $5^{1}/_{4}$ and
the 45 option may be at 2, which means that the spread you
thought would be worth 5 is worth only $3^{1}/_{4}$. This is the nature of
bull spreads, and there is nothing you can do. You must decide either to get out with whatever profit you will make from a $3^{1}/_{4}$
spread or wait until the expiration of the options. Then, if the stock
is still at 45 or higher, you will indeed get the approximately 5
points to which you are entitled.

On-the-Money Bull Spreads. This leads us directly into the second
type, which is an on-the-money bull spread. It occurs when the
stock is approximately at the midpoint between the two strike
prices of the options in the spread. We are now talking about a
spread that will cost you far more than an out-of-the-money
spread. Generally, depending on how high option prices are and
the volatility of the stock, as well as the time left for the options'
expiration, the cost of the spread will be approximately equal to
the cash value of the option you are buying. If it is less than the
cash value of the option you are buying, that is a favorable spread.
To illustrate with an example, let's assume that when a stock is
selling for 95, the October 90 option is 7 and the October 100 is 2.
The cost of the bull spread is 5, and this is exactly the actual cash
value of the 90 option.

The disadvantage of the on-the-money bull spread as compared
to the out-of-the money one is that the percentage return is necessarily much lower. In this example, where the cost of the spread is 5, the
most that the spread can be worth is the difference between 90 and
100, or 10. Thus, no matter how high the price of the stock goes, you
cannot make more than a 100% profit. And the risk of total loss is
still there, too. If the stock goes down below 90, you have lost every
penny you put into the spread.

The advantages are that you are getting into a position that is
quite rare in the world of options. That is, you are obtaining a situation where you make money as soon as the stock moves up by even
the smallest fraction, and you do so with limited risk. If you put on a
bull spread for a debit equal to the cash value of the lower strike
price option, you have in effect purchased an option for its actual
cash value. This is something we would all like to do and usually
can't. So this type of spread is ideal when you expect the price of the

stock to go up, but not necessarily by any large amount. If it goes up just 2 points by expiration our spread will be worth 7, giving you a profit of 2, which is a 40% profit. The out-of-the-money option spreads we discussed previously are almost always done at a debit above the current cash value of the lower strike price option, if indeed it has any cash value at all.

These on-the-money bull spreads are not quite as speculative as the out-of-the-money ones, because the stock can go down somewhat before you lose all your money, but make no mistake about it—they are still speculative on any absolute scale.

Another disadvantage of these on-the-money spreads is that since they cost you comparatively so much to put on, you will be even less inclined to take them off until the options are about to expire. So when you are deciding about which duration options to use, consider that you will probably be locked into the position until the expiration date of the option.

In-the-Money Bull Spreads. The third and final type of bull spread is the in-the-money spread. This spread is done when the stock is at or above the higher strike price. For example, the stock might be 47 and you are planning to buy the 40 strike option and sell the 45. The only reason that this type of spread can work at all is that the future time value of the higher strike option exceeds the future time value of the one you are buying. Unlike the out-of-the-money or on-the-money spreads, the movement of the price of the stock is not what makes this work. The stock has only to stay somewhere above the higher strike price. Rather, it is time that makes the spread work.

In this example, if the 40 option were selling for $7^{1}/_{4}$ and the 45 option were selling for $2^{1}/_{2}$, you would have a debit of $4^{3}/_{4}$. The most that the spread could be worth at expiration is 5, so your maximum potential profit would be just $^{1}/_{4}$. When you consider that you have two commissions in and two commissions out, it is easy to see that if you were to put on this spread it could only result in a certain loss, even under the most perfect conditions. And remember, too, if the stock goes down in price, you could lose your entire debit of $4^{3}/_{4}$. So, please avoid.

But, on the other hand, if this were a volatile stock, and options were selling at good prices, the 40 option might still be $7^{1}/_{4}$ but the 45 option might be $3^{1}/_{4}$. Now, the cost of putting this on is 4 points, and if you got out at 5 points you would have a 1 point profit, or 25% on your cost. This is the type of situation in which you could consider an in-the-money bull spread. You put on an in-the-money spread when you are quite sure that the stock will not fall below the upper strike price, when the debit to put it on can give you a fair profit, and when you are willing to hold the spread until almost the very last day of the options' duration, because unless you wait until then you will not be able to realize your anticipated profit.

To conclude our discussion on in-the-money bull spreads, remember they should be done only when option premiums are fairly high. If this is not the case, then the future time value of the upper strike price option will not be enough higher than the future time value of the option you are buying. And it is this disparity in future time value that makes the in-the-money bull spread possible. Second, these spreads are not a chance to strike it rich. Rather, they are a chance to make perhaps a 25% profit or less on a stock. On the other hand, the stock does not have to go up in order to realize that profit, and on the contrary there is even some downside protection because the stock can fall to the upper strike price and you will still realize the full profit.

These are the three types of bull spreads. They all have some things in common. In all of them, every penny that you put up is at total risk, and that is something of which you must never lose sight. It is especially dangerous in the in-the-money bull spreads because they cost you so much. Second, the potential profit is always limited to the difference between the debit you must originally pay and the difference between the two strike prices of the options you use. Third, you must usually stay with the bull spread until almost the last day of the options in order to realize this maximum profit. Therefore, if you are a quick trader who wants to be able to get in and out of a situation within days, you should carefully consider to what extent a bull spread would limit your mobility. The out-of-the-money spreads are the least confining in this respect, the on-the-money ones are fairly difficult, and there is almost no possibility of getting out of in-the-money options until the very end.

The one exception to all these statements is if the stock really takes off, rising substantially above the higher strike price. Then the future time value of both the options will rapidly decrease, and you will be able to get out sooner. For example, if you go into a 50 and 60 option bull spread, and you pay 13 for the 50 and are able to sell the 60 for 6 when the stock is 62, you have a 7-point debit. That spread is not going to increase very rapidly as long as the stock stays at 62. But, should the stock suddenly go up to 72, you will find that the 50 option may be at $22\frac{1}{2}$ and the 60 at 13, for a debit of $9\frac{1}{2}$. If there is still plenty of time in the options' lives, you might just as well put in a closing order for a credit of $9\frac{1}{2}$. If the order gets executed, you can surely find something better to do with your money than tying up $950 for weeks in expectation of making another possible $50. Remember, there is no guarantee that even on the expiration day you will actually be able to get 10 points, and in fact you should expect to have to take a small discount to get out.

Bull Spread Strategy

Here is a strategy tip for bull spreads: Think in advance of what you are going to do if things go wrong, especially for in-the-money and on-the-money options. This is my standard first rule, and it should be your first rule, because it is not only the most important one, but also the one most frequently overlooked. I often talk with investors who tell me that they think a certain stock is going to go up, and they ask my advice on the best way to utilize current option prices to realize the greatest profit. After I find out the time frame in which they expect the rise, and the approximate magnitude of the increase, it is a relatively easy task for me to recommend the appropriate option strategy.

Rarely indeed does anyone ask how we can get protection in case the stock goes down. So we execute and wait for the stock to go up. If it does, the rest is easy. The hard part unfortunately often faces us, because the stock goes in the wrong direction. And the reason that this is the hard question is that there is no easy answer. No matter what you do, you will probably be losing money, and you will be taking the chance of preventing yourself from ever recouping the loss if the stock comes back.

For example, let's say you put on a bull spread between the 60 and 70 options when the stock is 65, and the spread costs you 5 points. The stock moves down to 60, and the spread is now worth 3 points. Your choices are (1) to stay in your position and hope that the stock moves up before the expiration, in which case it must go up over 63 in order for the spread to be worth what it is now, or (2) to close out the position for 3 points, realizing a loss of 40% of your investment, plus transaction costs. The obvious advantage of the latter is that now, if the stock continues to move down, you are out and have salvaged most of your investment for what it is hoped will be a more successful investment in the future. But if the stock should start going back up, you have irrevocably lost the chance to recoup your loss, and what may hurt even more, the chance to make a good profit if the stock should go back up to 70. One word of advice is easy to give. If you do get out of the spread, and the stock starts going up, *do not* go back into the spread at the higher level. You are just begging to be whipsawed. Go on to another stock or wait until there is another strategy available for this one.

Now we see why it is so hard to decide what to do when things go wrong. But unless you do make some decision in advance, then you will just let the spread drift down in value until it expires.

Bear Spreads

A bear spread is a spread that will make money when the price of the stock goes down. Just as you sell a naked call to make money from the decline in the price of a stock, so a bear spread using calls is basically the sale of a call that brings in a substantial amount of money. Then, in order to obtain the advantages of a spread and to eliminate some of the strong disadvantages of selling a naked call, you buy another call on the same stock. But the call you buy is worth much less than the one you sell, so you are basically selling the substantial option mentioned. You hope to make your money from the decline in the price of the call you have sold, and you are willing to take a small loss on the expiration of the call you bought in order to get the advantages of a spread.

Let's take an example. Suppose a rather nonvolatile stock is now 69 and you believe that it is going to go down. You could sell the nearest-duration 70 call, which might be selling for 2 with about two months to go. If the stock stayed below 70 you would pick up the $2 as your profit. But you would have to put up margin of as much as $32 to do it, so your percentage return would not be very good. But even more important is the tremendous risk you would be taking. If the stock went up, you might be forced to buy back the option at $3 or $4, thus losing as much as you could have made. Furthermore, there is always the possibility that the stock might go up so fast that you could miss the chance to buy it back at $3 or $4 and have to buy it back for substantially more. Finally, you just might not want the risk hanging over your head that a naked option entails, or there might be reasons why you cannot sell naked options, such as that you are not approved for naked option writing by your brokerage firm. Using a bear spread instead of selling a naked option solves all these problems. And if the stock goes down you can make a much greater return on your investment.

In this example, let's assume that there is a 60 call available of the same duration, and it is $9^{1}/_{2}$. The bear spread consists of selling the 60 call for $9^{1}/_{2}$ and simultaneously buying the 70 call for 2. The result of doing this spread is that you have taken in a net amount of $7^{1}/_{2}$. Since you have more money in your account when you are finished with the spread than you had before, it is called a credit spread. All bear spreads using calls are credit spreads, and the amount of the credit is always the difference between the amount received for selling the expensive lower strike price option and the amount spent to buy the cheaper higher strike price option. Since they are done for a net credit, the way to execute such orders is to request your broker to try to do it at a credit of a certain amount.

Instant Credit? Some of you who are used to dealing with brokerage firms must find it a refreshing change to be able to do something that will immediately make your account richer. Your next question is probably whether you can withdraw this credit from your account immediately, and if the answer to that question is yes, then you will want to know how many of these you can do and when the next plane leaves for Brazil. Unfortunately, although probably not unexpectedly, the answer is that you cannot withdraw the credit from your account until after the transaction is closed out. But even worse is that, despite the fact that this is called a credit spread, you have to send in money to do it.

The money required is the difference between what you take in as a credit and the difference between the two strike prices. So, in this bear spread, where you are using the 60 and 70 strike prices with a difference of 10 and you are putting the spread on for a credit of $7^{1}/_{2}$, you must have margin of $2^{1}/_{2}$ in your account or send it in. This is the so-called exchange minimum requirement, and many brokerages will add an additional amount onto it.

The profit potential of a bear spread arises when the stock declines below the level of the lower strike price option, and both of the options used in the spread then expire worthless. When this happens, your spread will have no value, and it will expire without anything being expected of you. At that time the entire credit for which you originally did the spread becomes your profit on the transaction. Here you would make $750.

The investment was the amount of margin required, namely $250. You therefore would have a profit of 300%. Thus, in deciding whether to do a bear spread, you first figure out the credit you are looking for (here $7^{1}/_{2}$), then subtract it from the difference in strike prices (here 10) to determine the amount of margin you have to use up to do the spread ($2^{1}/_{2}$), and then you divide the credit by the amount of margin to determine your maximum rate of return. Here you would have divided the credit of $750 by $250 to get 3 (i.e., a maximum rate of return of 300%).

In the example we started with, the stock was 69 and we did the bear spread for a credit of $7^{1}/_{2}$. To find the break-even point, you add the credit onto the lower strike price. Hence, the stock must move down a point and a half to $67^{1}/_{2}$ just to break even. And of course that is before transaction costs. If the stock stays still, you will lose $1^{1}/_{2}$ points—a very substantial amount relative to your cost of putting this spread on, which was just $2^{1}/_{2}$.

Three Types of Bear Spreads

Bear spreads can roughly be divided into the same three subtypes as bull spreads (i.e., out-of-the-money, on-the-money, and in-the-money). The big difference is that the prices of the stocks are in the other direction from the option strike prices than they were for the bull spreads. While in an out-of-the-money bull spread the stock price is below the lower option strike price, the out-of-the-money bear spread has the stock price above the higher option strike price. If you are thinking of doing a bear spread with the 45 and 50 strike price options, and the stock is 54, that is an out-of-the-money bear spread. But once you get that difference digested, the result in the bear spread is quite similar to a bull spread. The out-of-the-money one is the one that requires very little money to do and can give a high percentage return if it is successful. The on-the-money spreads require more money to do and cannot make as high a percentage return, but do not require the stock to move as far to make a profit. Finally, the in-the-money spreads take a lot of capital, can result in a relatively large loss, and have limited profit potential.

Out-of-the-Money Bear Spreads. Now let's take a look at each of the subtypes of bear spreads. First is the out-of-the-money, which is the most popular type of bear spread and is the most similar in result to selling a stock short. If a stock is 64 and you want to do a bear spread selling the 50 call option and buying the 60, that is an out-of-the-money bear spread. With three months to go, the 50 option might be $14^{1}/_{2}$ and the 60 might be $5^{1}/_{2}$. Thus, you would be putting this spread on for a credit of 9, which means that you would have to put up $100 for margin, and you could make a profit of $900. But there are two problems. The first is that the stock will have to move down to below 59 before you even break even. At any point above 60 you will lose your $1 per share. But that's a problem that you should be prepared to face before you put on the spread. Of course, once the stock does get down to 59, you will be increasing your profit by 100% for every additional point that the stock declines.

The second problem is a bit nastier, and you might not be prepared for it. That is the danger of being exercised on the deep-in-the-money option, which you have shorted. Here you shorted the 50 option with three months to go when the stock was 64 and the option had a future time value of only $1/2$ point. As time moves on and the expiration date of the option comes closer, the future time value will naturally decline. Two other factors may hasten its decline. First, if you should be wrong about the future price action of the stock, and it goes up further, the future time value of the option will certainly go down. Second, if the stock is a dividend-paying stock, the future time value of the option will decrease very rapidly as the ex-dividend date of the stock nears.

This is easily explained, but not so easily counteracted. As the stock gets closer to going ex-dividend, the price of the stock may slightly increase in anticipation of the dividend, but it will certainly decrease in value on the ex-dividend date by the amount of the dividend. Naturally, all option buyers realize that the stock is going to decrease by the amount of the dividend, so on the day before the stock goes ex-dividend, the option will decline even further than normal to reflect this anticipated decline in the price of the stock.

Thus, if GM were paying a quarterly dividend of $1, its in-the-money calls would decrease by approximately that amount from their normal price on the day before the stock went ex-dividend. And if the amount of the dividend is greater than the future time value the option would normally have, the option might be selling for less than its intrinsic cash value, that is, at a slight discount from cash value. Once that happens, arbitrageurs will buy the option and exercise it, and sell the stock at the same time, making the $1/4$ point profit. Since they pay no commissions, it is profitable for them to do this.

Premature Exercise. The unfortunate result is that you may be exercised on your short deep-in-the-money call long before the expiration date. When this happens, you no longer are short your deep-in-the-money call. Instead you must pay a sales commission on the sale of the stock at the exercise price, and you are now short the stock, which may take more margin than you have. You can buy in the stock to cover your short position, but now you are long the higher strike price option and have no short position. This is exactly the opposite of what you want! You could sell the deep-in-the-money option all over again to reinstate your position, but before you do so, check the future time value of the option. If it isn't more than a small fraction, you are letting yourself in for an unwelcome exercise again. The conclusion is that before you put on a deep-out-of-the-money bear spread with calls, you must check the lower strike option to make sure (1) that there is still a decent future time value and (2) that if an ex-dividend date is coming up before the expiration date of the option, the dividend will not be great enough to more than offset the amount of the future time value.

On-the-Money Bear Spreads. The second subtype of bear spread is the on-the-money spread. This is something like shorting the stock, in that you can make quite a bit of money if the stock goes down, and something like selling a naked call, in that you may be able to do it in a situation where you can have the odds on your side—that is, you can make money if the stock stays still. For example, if a stock is 55, and you are selling a three-month 50 call for 6, you might be able to buy the 60 call for $1/2$. This means that you are putting this on for a credit of $5\frac{1}{2}$, which gives you a break-even point of $55\frac{1}{2}$. Thus, the stock can actually go up $1/2$ point at expiration before you begin to lose money, and if it stays still you will be making $1/2$ point. The spread is done for a credit of $5\frac{1}{2}$, which means that you are required to put up $4\frac{1}{2}$ as a margin call. Thus, you could make a profit of $5\frac{1}{2}$ on your investment (a profit of 122%). Notice that the potential return is much less than from the out-of-the-money spread, and note also that you are putting up much more money per spread. All the money you have to put up as margin is money you can lose. So, whereas you could have lost $1 per share on the out-of-the-money spread, here you can lose over four times that amount. Thus, this type of bear spread is not as popular as the other two subtypes.

In-the-Money Bear Spreads. The third subtype of bear spread is the in-the-money, which means that the price of the stock is already near or below the strike price of the lower strike price option. For example, where a stock is 69, you may sell the 70 call with three months to go for 4 and pay $1/2$ for the 80 call. Your credit for doing the spread is therefore $3^{1}/_{2}$, which is the maximum profit you could make; your cost of margin required, and also the possible loss, is $6^{1}/_{2}$. So you have a chance to make about half the amount you have to put up, while risking the possibility of losing twice that amount. Doesn't sound too appealing to you?

It can be, but it must be approached with the right expectations. This type of bear spread is actually very similar to selling naked options, but for margin purposes and suitability purposes it is not treated that way. Therefore, it can be very valuable for accounts that for either of these reasons cannot or will not do naked option writing. At many brokerage firms, anyone who is approved to purchase calls and write covered calls can do bear spreads. And if you shy away from naked options because of the unlimited potential losses and the risk of mushrooming margin requirements, in-the-money bear spreads provide an alternative. The margin is fixed when you put on the spread and can never get any higher. The loss is limited to the amount of margin you put up. Therefore, for those who are reluctant to get into the water of naked option writing, in-the-money bear spreads provide a good wading ground in which to experiment before taking on the currents of deeper water.

The other benefit of an in-the-money bear spread is that, depending on the price of the stock, it is possible to give yourself quite a bit of upside leeway. Thus, if the stock were only 66 when you did this spread, and you received a credit of perhaps 2 for the spread, your break-even point at expiration would be 72, which means that you have 6 points or almost 10% upside protection. And if the stock stays below 70, which doesn't sound too unlikely, you would have a profit of 2 points on your margin requirement of 8, for a profit of 25%. Furthermore, unless the spread turns out to be a disaster because the stock goes up too far, you don't have to worry about the short option being exercised prematurely.

The strategy for handling these spreads after they have been put on should be very similar to the strategy for naked calls. That is, one shouldn't just sit there and let the option go up and up. Decide on a price at which you will close out the position, and if the stock gets up that high, do it! If you have any luck, the option you own will have increased a little and will provide a small profit to offset your loss on the option you are buying back.

This concludes our discussion of bear spreads. While each of the three subtypes was a bear spread, in actual practice they are more different than they are alike. The out-of-the-money bear spread involves risking a small amount of money and can result in a great profit if the stock moves down, but it must make that move in order to just break even and must make a bigger move to give you a profit. These spreads also have the unwanted problem of early exercise of the deep-in-the-money call you have shorted. Next were the on-the-money bear spreads, where the stock is between the two strike prices. Here you can make about as much money as you can lose, but it may not be necessary for the stock to go down in order to break even. Finally, we looked at the in-the-money bear spread, where the stock was already below the lower strike price. This spread entailed quite a bit of margin and thus risk of a large loss, and had the promise of a smaller profit, but the stock could actually move up and the spread could still result in a profit. Thus, the in-the-money bear spread is very similar to selling an out-of-the-money naked call, and the strategy for following them once they are on is quite similar.

Calendar Spreads

The most difficult type of basic call spread to understand is the calendar spread. What is difficult to comprehend is how it is supposed to make money, and at times people who have done calendar spreads have asked themselves that very question after the spreads were unsuccessfully completed. Hopefully, that will not be your predicament after you have read this section. The big advantage of calendar spreads is that they are much more hedged than either bull spreads or bear spreads and it is therefore unlikely that there will be a complete loss of the cost of doing a calendar spread.

A calendar spread consists of buying an option and simultaneously selling a shorter-duration option at the same strike price on the same stock or index. For example, let us assume that it is now January 20, and you buy a July 35 call and sell the April 35 call. That is a calendar spread. If you paid 3 for the July call and sold the April call for 2, your cost of doing the spread would be 1. Therefore it would be a debit spread with no margin required, simply payment of the difference between the option prices, here $1, plus transaction costs.

Now for the more difficult question of how you make money on this spread. Let us assume the stock was at 35 when we put on this calendar spread, and to make matters easy, let's assume that it is still at 35 three months later, when the April 35 option expires. The

April option therefore expires worthless, and we have a profit of $2 on the April option. We close out the calendar spread by buying in the near-term option if this is necessary (and here it is not since it expires worthless) and at the same time selling the long-term option. The big question is what the July option will be worth with the stock at 35 and three months left to go. This is the question we must answer when we put on the spread, because the answer to that question will tell us whether there is a chance that the spread can be profitable.

When we are considering whether to do this spread, the best way to estimate what the July option will be worth when it has three months to go is to see what the current option with three months to go is worth. On January 20, when we put on the spread, the stock was at 35, and the April option, with three months to go, was worth 2. Therefore, we can make an estimate that if three months later the stock is where it is now, the option at that time that has three months to go will also be worth 2. We must remember that this is only a rough estimate, and the actual price of the July option three months from now could vary widely due to many factors, such as the tone of the market in general and the level of option premiums on other stocks. But this rough estimate is probably as accurate as any.

So we estimate that at the expiration of the April 35 call the July 35 will be worth 2. If we are later proven to be correct and we actually sell it for 2, then a spread that cost us 1 to put on is taken off for 2, for a 100% profit before transaction costs.

The mathematical theory behind the potential profitability of a calendar spread is related to the price action of options with the passage of time. This action is that as the price of the underlying stock stays constant, the prices do not decrease equally for equal-duration options. Rather, the price erodes very slowly for a long-term option, and the decline becomes more and more pronounced as the option gets closer to its expiration, until in the final weeks and days the decline is extremely rapid. (See Figure 6.3.) Obviously, an option with just one week to go will lose 100% of its value in that week if the underlying stock stays below the strike price, whereas an option with three months to go will suffer an almost imperceptible decline. The principle behind calendar spreads is that you sell an option which, if the stock stays where it is, will decline 100%, and you buy an option which under the same circumstances will decline by only a small percentage. You must pay careful attention to the fact that a decline of 100% in the near-term option may not be so much more than a decline of 30% in the long-term option,

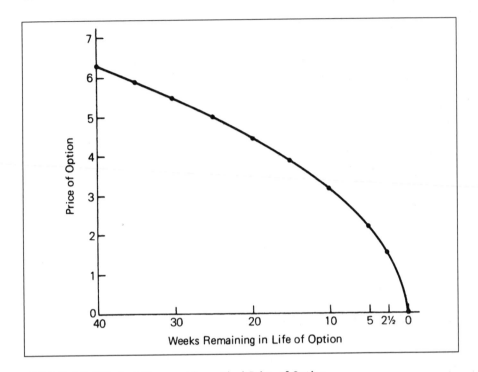

FIGURE 6.3 Effect of Time on Theoretical Price of Option
Chart assumes that the stock remains at the same price and the option is on the money. Note that in the first 10 weeks the option price declines $0.82, whereas in the last 10 weeks it loses $3.20. This provides the mathematical basis for profiting from calendar spreads.

since the price of the long-term option is so much greater to begin with.

Estimating Profitability of Calendar Spreads. Obviously the most important aspect of calendar spreads is whether they can be profitable, and if so, under what circumstances. Both these questions are difficult because both involve an estimate of the price of the long option on the expiration of the short option. And unlike the bull spreads and the bear spreads we discussed, there is no known method to come up with an amount that is more than a rough estimate. This inability to predict what the longer-duration option will be worth when the shorter-duration option expires makes calendar spreads less accurate than the others. However, there are two basic rules that can help.

The first is that a calendar spread is always worth the most when the underlying stock is at the strike price on the expiration of the shorter-duration option. As the stock goes up above the strike price, the short-term option begins to pick up a large amount of intrinsic cash value, and as its price goes up, the difference between it and the longer-duration option starts to decrease. In our previous example, if the stock had gone up to 40 when the April 35 expired, the April 35 would have been worth 5, and the July 40 might have been worth 6. The spread would then be 1, and there would be no profit on it. Even worse, if the stock went to 45, the April 35 would be worth 10, and, depending on the level of option premiums in general, the July 35 might be worth only $10\frac{1}{2}$, for a loss of one-half of your investment before transaction costs.

But calendar spreads are like Icarus, the Greek mythological figure who put on wings and attempted to fly. When he flew too high, the sun melted the wax that held on his wings, and when he flew too low the waves knocked him into the water.

So, too, a calendar spread is in an equally unhappy situation when the stock goes too low. Let's say the stock in our example goes down to 30, and the April option expires worthless. What will the July option be worth? It's anyone's guess, but certainly 1 is not improbable, especially since the stock has gone down 5 points from where it was. Thus, again, the spread is not a profit maker. Obviously, if the stock goes down to 27, the July 35 option is worth even less and we have a loss situation. So the first rule to apply when thinking about a calendar spread is to project what the prices of the two options are going to be if the stock is at the strike price when the near-term option expires. This will give you the *maximum* potential spread. If you can't see a really good profit at this price of the underlying stock, after deducting your estimated transaction costs, then for heaven's sake don't do the spread. Because your chances of having the stock end up just on or around the strike price are no better than your chances that the stock will go up when you do a bull spread, or that it will go down when you do a bear spread. And for every point that the stock is above or below the strike price you diminish your profit very significantly.

The second helpful rule to keep in mind is the mathematical formula that tells you the correct theoretical relationship between options of different durations. This theorem was discovered by the French mathematician Louis Bachelier in 1900. It is that the price of an option varies with the square root of the time remaining in its life. Therefore, if there is an option with 4 weeks left, and another one with 16 weeks, the correct mathematical relationship between the option prices should be the square root of 4 (2) to the square root of 16 (4), so we have a ratio of 2 to 4, or 1 to 2. The short-term option should be at least one-half the price of the long-term option. Note that if you simply took the ratio of the time periods, that is, 4 to 16, you would come up with a ratio of 1 to 4, and if you noticed that the options actually had a relationship of 2 to 4 you would be overjoyed. But you would be wrong.

In doing a calendar spread one is always looking for a relationship where the near-term option seems overpriced in relationship to the longer-term option. But many times, what seems on casual observation to be an overpriced near-term option is really not overpriced at all when subjected to Bachelier's theorem. The way to use his formula is with a pocket calculator that has a square root key. If yours doesn't have one and you intend to do calendar spreads, I would advise you to buy one that does. It's very simple to find the square root of the times left in the various options, and then divide the one number by the other to get the ratios of the proper mathematical price relationships. If your near-term option is priced higher than it should be, then the odds are on your side. If not, then the odds are not on your side.

Advantages of the Calendar Spread. So far we have discussed the possibilities for making money from a calendar spread, and you will have correctly gathered that in certain situations there is simply no way to make money from a calendar spread. In fact, you may be wondering what the point of a calendar spread is at all. The big advantage of a calendar spread over either the bull or the bear spread is that you are not likely to lose all your money. Properly set up, a calendar spread has a good probability of making money and a very small chance of losing more than a fraction of your money. Remember, with a bull spread, if the stock is below the lower strike price on expiration you lose all your money. Every single penny. And the same thing is true with a bear spread when the stock goes above the higher strike price. But with a calendar spread this is unlikely to happen because when it is over you are left with a three-month option. If the stock is way down, the option may not be worth very much, but it still will have some value. If the stock has gone up dramatically, the difference in the price between the option you are short and the one you are long may not be a very big difference, but in only extreme circumstances will there be no difference, and of course this difference is the value of the spread. The calendar spread can be said to be the most conservative of the three types of spreads we have discussed, because it is the only one in which it is unlikely you could lose all your money. And the right calendar spread can also make a lot of money on a percentage basis.

Three Types of Calendar Spreads

Calendar spreads may also be divided into three categories: in-the-money, on-the-money, and out-of-the-money. Just remember that in every case a calendar spread is its most profitable when the stock is at the strike price. With that in mind, you will have no trouble remembering how you make money from these three different types of calendar spreads.

In-the-Money Calendar Spreads. In an in-the-money calendar spread, the stock might be at 30 and you are buying and selling calls at the 25 level. Presumably you are putting them on for a very small debit spread, and of course your risk is limited to the amount of the debit you put up, since under normal circumstances the difference between the two options can never be less than zero. Your objective is to have the stock fall to 25. If the option you sell is at $5\frac{3}{4}$ and the longer-term option is $6\frac{1}{4}$, you hope that the stock will be at 25 on the near-term option's expiration, and that then the options' prices will be 0 and perhaps 2. Your spread will have increased from $\frac{1}{2}$ to 2, which is a 300% profit.

Nevertheless, these in-the-money spreads are the least frequently used of the three types. One reason is that the commissions are quite large. While the spread of $\frac{1}{2}$ is very reasonable, if you were doing 10 options, the commission on the $5\frac{3}{4}$ option could be 13.3 cents per share, and the commission on the $6\frac{1}{4}$ option could be 13.9 cents. So the total commission would be 27.2 cents, which is a commission cost of more than 50% of your cost of the spread! Worse, if the stock stays where it is, your commission costs for coming out of the spread will be approximately the same. This means that even if the spread stays at $\frac{1}{2}$, so that you theoretically will break even, you are still losing your entire investment in commission costs! It was spreads like this that led to the invention of the phrase "cemetery spread"—a spread in which you get buried by the commissions.

On-the-Money Calendar Spreads. More commonly used are the on-the-money spreads, where the stock is just about at the strike price. Here the biggest concern is whether it will be possible to make a profit. The difficulty is that the stock is already at the point where the spread is the largest, and the only element that can improve your spread is the passage of time. Any movement of the stock price either up or down will decrease your spread. So carefully figure out your maximum profit by the method outlined previously, and then be realistic with yourself and concede that it is not too likely that the stock is going to end up exactly on the strike price. Your most difficult aspect is to estimate how much of a decrease there will be in the spread for every point that the stock is above or below the strike price. While there is no easy way of doing so, the example in Tables 6.1 and 6.2 might be of some help. It is a computer projection of what a 30 strike price calendar spread would be on expiration of the near-term option with the stock at prices ranging from 24 to 36. Of course, different stocks will react in different ways depending on the volatility of the stock and hence the amount of future time value given to the premiums, but the general result will be similar.

Out-of-the-Money Calendar Spreads. Probably the most popular calendar spread is the out-of-the-money one, which is really very much like a bull spread in its purpose. The purpose is to make money when the stock goes up, and the benefit over a bull spread is that if the stock stays where it is, you may be able to get out on the expiration of the near-term option with a breakeven, instead of losing all your money as you do with an out-of-the-money bull spread. The biggest disadvantage is that if you are too successful in your prediction and the price of the stock goes up over the strike price before the expiration of the shorter duration option, the spread begins to lose value, and it could happen that if the stock goes up far enough you would actually lose money on the spread.

As an example, let's say your stock is at 30, and you sell a three-month 35 option for $3/4$ and buy the six-month 35 option for

TABLE 6.1 Prices When Spread Was Transacted

Stock	$28^7/_8$
July 30 call	$1^3/_{16}$
October 30 call	$1^3/_8$
Cost of spread	$^{11}/_{16}$ or $.6875

TABLE 6.2 Estimated Price of Spread Just before Expiration of July Calls

Stock Price	Spread	Profit or Loss
24	$.07	(.61)
25	.19	(.49)
26	.38	(.30)
27	.58	(.10)
28	.89	.20
29	1.36	68
30	1.64	95
31	1.54	86
32	1.22	54
33	.91	23
34	.60	(.08)
35	.28	(40)
36	0	(68)

$1\frac{1}{2}$, giving a spread of $\frac{3}{4}$. You hope that the stock will be at 35 in three months, at which time the near-term option will expire worthless, and you will sell the longer-term option for a price you estimate at about 2. This would give you a profit of 166%. If the stock just stays where it is, then in three months, when the near-term option expires, the longer-term option should still be worth about $\frac{3}{4}$, and you get out at a break-even point. Of course, if you are really wrong, and the stock goes down, then the long-term option could decline to any amount, and there would be a loss. Finally, in the unlikely situation that the stock goes up to 40, the near-term option will be worth 5 at its expiration and the long-term option might be worth $5\frac{3}{4}$ for a breakeven. One big advantage of the out-of-the-money calendar spread is that the commissions going in are so much less. In this case, if you were doing 10 options the total commission costs would be only 15.4 cents per share, and on the way out, with the stock at 35, the total commissions would be just 6.3 cents.

Calendar Spread Strategy

Strategy tip: The biggest cause of losses on calendar spreads is not treating them as calendar spreads after the near-term option has expired. Remember, a calendar spread exists only as long as there are a long-term option and a short-term option. When the short-term option expires, or loses so much value that it is providing no meaningful downside protection to the long-term option, then you don't have a calendar spread anymore. If you went into the spread because you liked the hedged concept of a calendar spread, then for heaven's sake when the calendar spread is over, close it out! This may seem easy, but in practice the temptation to hold on to the long option can be almost overpowering. It takes strong willpower, but I can tell you, from seeing many, many calendar spreads, that the big losses always occur when people are unwilling to close them out when they should.

What typically happens is that the stock will float downward somewhat, accompanied by what seems like an inordinately large loss in the price of the long-term option. Thus, if you have put on a spread at the 50 strike price for a debit of 2, when the near-term option expires the long-term option may be just $1^3/_4$ with the stock at 48. You now are in the position of owning a three-month option at what seems to you to be a ridiculously low price. How can the option be worth so little when this is a great stock, and it's only 2 points away from the strike price? Of course you know that you really should close out the spread and take your loss of a quarter of a point. But in this case the option seems to be so seriously undervalued that you decide to wait just one week to see if the stock won't rally a couple of points so you can get out with a small profit at least. So one week goes by, and the stock sinks to 47, the option declines to $1^1/_2$, and now you really are determined not to sell it out. And so it goes. Three months later the option may expire worthless and you will swear that you will never do a calendar spread again as long as you live. But was it the fault of the calendar spread or was it that you didn't treat it as a calendar spread? Of course, it was your fault, and the $^1/_4$-point loss you should have taken when the calendar spread was over would have been negligible, while the loss of your entire spread is both substantial and insulting.

So please remember: When you go into a calendar spread, you are doing so because you want the downside protection of a spread, and you want the relative safety of a calendar spread. Therefore, when the near-term option expires, be consistent in your thinking and get out of the spread! Take your loss now, and hope that the next spread will make more than enough profit to make up for it. As tempting as it is to stay with the long-term option, remember that you could have bought an option in the beginning. But you chose not to do so and to do a calendar spread instead for very good reasons. Stick to those reasons! Once you become the holder of an option, you are subject to all the hazards of that position, including not getting out until the option expires worthless.

Some people look on out-of-the-money calendar spreads as a means of buying longer-term options for a lower price. While this may be correct in some instances, one must always keep in mind that if the stock does move up over the strike price before the expiration of the near-term option, you will not make nearly as much profit as you would have with a bull spread.

Using Ratios on Call Spreads

There is a virtually limitless number of call spread varieties possible. Some of the most interesting ones involve simple variations on the three basic spreads we have already discussed. The simplest variation concerns buying a different number of options than you sell. For example, a bull spread that involves buying 10 May 40 options and selling 10 May 45 options can be varied to buying 15 May 40s and selling 10 May 45s. The purpose of this variation is to allow five of the 40 options to keep on increasing in value once the stock gets above 45 without having the profit increase cut off by the 45 options that were sold. In this case there would be an increase in the cost of the spread on a per-share basis, because you would not be getting the benefit of selling the 45 options on five of the options. This is the trade-off against the greater profit potential.

Or if you wanted an even lower cost by *ratio writing,* you could sell 15 of the 45 options and still buy only 10 of the 40 options. In this case you are taking in 50% more money from the sale of the extra 45s, thus reducing your cost accordingly. The risk is that now if the stock goes above 45, you will begin making less money because you actually have sold five naked options. In putting on this spread, you must be approved for writing naked options, and you must supply the margin for selling the five extra options.

Let's say that you bought the 40 options for 3 and sold the 45 options for 1, for a 2-point debit on a one-for-one basis. By selling the extra five 45 options, you took in 5 points more, which reduced your cost per spread by 50 cents, meaning that you were able to put on the spread for a $1^{1}/_{2}$-point debit instead of a 2-point debit, for a meaningful savings of 25%. Now let's see what happens when the stock starts going up. At 45 all is well, because your 40s are worth 5 points, and the 45s expire worthless, so you are making $3\frac{1}{2}$ points profit on each spread. If you had not sold the additional five options and your cost for the spread had been 2 points, you would have made a profit of 3 points per spread. The percentage profit on your investment when you sell the extra calls is 233%, but the percentage profit on the regular bull spread is only 150%, so the sale of the additional five calls can really pay off.

As the stock starts going up above 45, the 10 40 options that are covered by the 10 45s continue to be worth exactly 5 points. But you also have five naked 45 options, and as the price of the stock goes up, you must buy them back at some point. At 46 you are buying them back for 1, which is exactly what you paid for them, but for every point that the stock goes above that you are losing an additional point. Since you sold an extra half an option for each spread, you are losing $\frac{1}{2}$ point for every point that the stock goes above 45. Since your maximum profit per spread is $3\frac{1}{2}$ points at 45, and since you are losing $\frac{1}{2}$ point per spread for every 1-point increase in the price of the stock, you see that at 7 points above 45 you will break even on the spread. At any stock price above that (52) you will begin to lose money on the spread.

The general rule for determining how high the break-even point is in a spread where you have sold additional options is to figure out the total profit at the maximum profit point, which in this case was 45, and then to divide that by the number of naked options. Here your total profit on the transaction when the stock is 45 at expiration is $35 (disregarding hundreds). You are short five naked options. Dividing 35 by 5 gives 7, which you add to the strike price to get a break-even point of 42.

The Two-on-One Bull Spread

In fact, one of the most popular variations on a bull spread is the two-against-one spread, which involves buying one lower strike price option and selling two of the next higher strike price options. There were times when option premiums were fat and juicy that this could be done for almost no debit at all, or for only a very small fraction of a point. Those prices are hard to find today, but they may come back. And if they do, this can be a very interesting play. Let's assume that you do find such a zero-cost two-on-one spread, perhaps buying the 45s at 4 and selling the 50s at 2 when the stock is 47.

Note that in order to do this you must have the margin for selling the naked 50 options, and that as the price of the stock goes up you will be marked to the market on your margin and may be required to supply more margin.

The first advantage of this spread is that since it cost you nothing to put on, there is absolutely no risk on the downside. If the stock goes down to 45 or less, all the options become worthless, and you simply walk away without any profit or any loss. It is on the upside that this strategy becomes profitable. If the stock is at 50 on expiration, your 45 options are worth 5 points each and the 50s are worthless. So something that cost you no cash at all to put on is now worth 5 points a share. It's hard to compute a percentage return on zero, so let's take the margin you need. At 50, if you are on 35% margin, you would have to have $17.50 for each share, which means that a profit of $5 would be a percentage return of 28%.

The real risk in this type of spread is that the stock will go up too far. Since you have written two for one, you start reducing your profit a whole point for every 1-point increase in the price of the stock over 50. Applying the general rule, your maximum profit is 5, and therefore your break-even would be 5 points above 50, or 55. Above 55 you begin to lose an entire point for each 1-point increase in the stock price, so that at 60 you are losing 5 points, which is as much as you could ever have gained, and above that the loss just continues to mount. Obviously the proper strategy to use is the same one that is urged so strongly in Chapter 4 on naked option selling: Decide in advance exactly what you will do at exactly what stock price, and then do it. You could decide to close out the entire spread when the stock got to a certain price, or you could just buy back the naked options, leaving yourself with a straight one-on-one bull spread. You hope this will increase in value with the passage of time, provided only that the stock does not fall back again.

Although the unlimited theoretical liability of the two-on-one spread means that it is not everyone's cup of tea, it can provide a very wide band of potential profit. In the example we have studied, there is a profit anywhere from 40 up to 50, and there is no loss below 40. The only risk is if the stock actually goes above 50, and you can judge for yourself just how often a stock goes from 42 to 50 in three months or so. If it happened very often, there probably would be a lot more rich stockholders out there than there actually are.

Ratio Bear Spreads

Bear spreads can also be done in a ratio, but this is not as common. If you don't buy as many higher strike calls as you have sold lower strike calls, you face a serious risk of loss if the stock goes up, and those higher strike price options are usually pretty cheap, anyway. On the other hand, if you buy more higher strike price calls, then you are really offsetting the bearish nature of the spread and perhaps converting it into a neutral or bullish spread. If you buy two out-of-the-money calls for every in-the-money call that you sell, you can probably still do this at a credit, but you will have transformed your bear spread into a volatility spread. This is a spread in which you will make money if the stock moves far enough in either direction. The big disadvantage is that if the stock stays within a fairly wide band in the middle you will lose.

Suppose you sold 10 20 strike price calls for 4 when the stock was 23 and you bought 20 25 options for 1, for a credit of 2 points for each spread. If the stock goes high enough you will make enough money on the 10 extra 25 options to offset your loss on the 10 20 strike price options. At 25 you would have a loss of 5 points per spread (1 point on the 20 option, which you would buy back for 5, and 2 on each of the 25s, which are worthless). You have one extra 25 option per spread, which will make you a 1-point profit for every 1-point increase in the price of the stock, so that you start to make money above 30. On the downside, since you did this for a credit of 2, you will begin to make money below 22 (at which point you would have to buy back the 20 for 2) and your maximum profit on the downside would be the 2 points that were your original credit. Thus, your loss band is from 22 to 30; your profit below 22 is just 2 points, while your profit above 30 doesn't really get attractive until you reach 32 or 33. Of course, if premiums are different you might be able to find a combination that has a slimmer band of loss range, but often there are more direct ways of putting on a volatility spread. (See the sections on straddles and combinations at the end of this chapter.)

Ratio Calendar Spreads

Calendar spreads also lend themselves very well to a ratio variation. If you are bullish on the stock, you can buy more of the long-term options than you sell of the short-term ones. Then if the stock goes up over the strike price, your profit continues to gain, instead of being reduced as in the regular calendar spread. The disadvantage is that you lose downside protection, since obviously if you use a two-to-one ratio you will have only half the downside protection. When you consider that in some calendar spreads there isn't very much downside protection in the first place, I can only urge you to consider very carefully what you are doing.

A calendar spread that has a two-to-one ratio of long-term options to short-term ones is actually a substitute for a bull spread and can be preferable. Sometimes, such a spread will make as much money when the stock goes up to the next higher strike price as a one-on-one bull spread would, and will continue to make more money as the stock goes up further, while it will perform far better than a bull spread on the downside. In a bull spread you have to suffer a total loss when the options expire with the stock below the strike price, but with a two-to-one calendar spread you still have options that should be worth something. So the next time you're inclined to do a bull spread, work out the figures first on a two-to-one calendar spread.

Selling additional short-term options in a calendar spread is not very popular because of the margin problem that arises on the naked options, plus the fact that you begin to lose money rapidly once the stock goes over the strike price.

COMPLEX CALL SPREADS

Butterfly Spreads

In addition to the bull spread, the bear spread, and the calendar spread there are a number of complex spreads used by options traders that deserve mention. Perhaps the most exotic is the butterfly or sandwich spread. This is a theoretically beautiful spread that should appeal to the mathematician in everyone. When properly done, a *butterfly spread* theoretically cannot lose, and can make a very good return on a fairly broad band of stock prices at expiration. A butterfly spread consists of four options on the same stock with the same expiration date, with three different strike prices. You sell two calls at the middle strike price of, say, 40, and then you buy one with the higher strike price, here 45, and you buy one below, here 35. The name sandwich spread is derived from the fact that the short options are sandwiched in between a long option above and below. The beauty of the spread is that the long options give you protection against any excessive loss on the short options.

The ideal butterfly spread is done for a zero debit, but depending on the difference between the strike prices of the options (whether at the 5- or 10-point level), the time left before expiration (the less time, the more you should be willing to pay), and the volatility of the underlying stock (the more volatile, the less you should pay), it may be acceptable to pay up to 2 points for one of these spreads. To understand how a butterfly spread works, let's take an example. Suppose a stock is at 45, and you buy one 40 call for 6, sell two 45 calls for $3\frac{1}{2}$ each (taking in 7), and buy one 50 call for 1. You now have a zero debit for the spread. Let's see what happens to you at expiration. When the stock is at 40 or less, all the options expire and you are out with nothing.

As the stock goes up above 40, the 40 option you are long begins to increase in price, until when the stock reaches 45 it is worth 5 points. All the other options expire worthless, so the spread that cost you zero to put on is now worth 5. But, as the stock advances above 45, each of your two short 45 options begins to increase in value, and you will have to buy them back. So, for example, at 47, your 40 option is worth 7, but each of the 45s has to be bought back for 2, making a cost of 4, which reduces your profit to 3. At 50 you have to repurchase the two 40 options for 5 each, making a total cost of 10, which just exactly cancels out the value of your 40 option, so the spread is worth zero for a breakeven. At any point above 50, the 50 option you own begins increasing in value, so both your long options are going up in value point for point with the stock while the two 45s are going down. The result is that at any point above 50 your spread is worth exactly zero, as Table 6.3 shows.

TABLE 6.3 A Butterfly Spread

	Value at Options' Expiration		
Cost to Do (Stock at 45)	Stock at 40 or Less	Stock at 45	Stock at 50 or Higher
Buy one 50 option @ 1 = −1	0	0	0
Sell two 45 options @ $3\frac{1}{2}$ ^{ß}=+7	0	0	2 @ 5 = −10
Buy one 40 option @ 6 = <u>−6</u>	<u>0</u>	<u>+5</u>	1 @10 = <u>10</u>
0	0	+5	0

This table shows that in theory one cannot lose money, and that there is a maximum profit of 5 points. For every point that the stock is either above or below 45 at expiration, the value is reduced by 1 (e.g., at 47 or 43 the spread is worth 3).

Actually, a butterfly spread is just a bull spread (that is, buying the 40 and selling the 45 options) with a bear spread added on top (selling a 45 option and buying a 50 option). This is the reason that the butterfly spread is so beautiful from a theoretical viewpoint. When you are making a lot of money in the bull spread, it offsets the loss from the bear spread, and vice versa. And it just happens that if the stock ends up at the middle, or near the middle, you can make some money on both of them, or make much more on one than you lose on the other.

Butterfly spreads do require margin in addition to whatever they cost. The amount of margin is the difference in strike prices for the bear spread on the top. Since there is a difference of 5 points between the 45 and 50 strike prices, we get a margin requirement of 5. This does not change with movement in the price of the stock and is a relatively modest requirement considering the profit possibility of the spread and the very limited risk.

Thus, it is clear that a butterfly spread is a nonvolatility spread that reaches its maximum profit at the strike price of the middle options and decreases in value to zero as the stock reaches each of the outer strike prices. Still, if butterfly spreads offered a chance to make a profit without any chance of losing any money, there are many people who would use them all day long. Unfortunately, three practical considerations have a severe negative impact on the attractiveness of butterfly spreads, and we will discuss them here.

Disadvantages of the Butterfly Spread. The first drawback is that the premiums are a long way from making it possible to do many spreads at a zero or small amount of debit. There is simply no point in doing a butterfly spread unless you can do it for a very low or no debit. But premium levels could improve in the future, and for that reason it is worth discussing butterfly spreads.

A second and more inherent problem is the difficulty of executing butterfly spreads at costs close to what you want due to the cost of executing option trades on an exchange. Every option is quoted in three important ways. The price of the last sale, the bid price, and the offering price. The bid price is what the brokers on the floor of the exchange are willing to pay right now for at least a small number of options. The offering price is what they are willing to sell you a small number of the options for right now. Thus, an option may show last trade $2^3/8$, bid $2^1/4$, offered at $2^1/2$. If you come in with a market order to sell the option, you will receive $2^1/4$. If you enter a market order to buy an option, you will pay $2^1/2$. If you are willing to be patient, and don't expect the stock to move in the near future, you could enter your order to buy or to sell at $2^3/8$. The chances are that if the stock does not move, you will eventually be able to execute your order, but then again you may not be able to do so. The only certain way of getting an order executed is to be willing to buy at the offering price and be willing to sell at the bid price.

This discussion is appropriate to our consideration of butterfly spreads, because this is the first spread we discussed that uses three different options. Now, when you are buying one option you may not care very much whether you pay $1^3/8$ or $1^7/16$. At the end, the option will probably be worth either zero or perhaps 5 and it won't make any difference whether you paid one-sixteenth of a point more or less. But where you are dealing with four options, and trying to put on a spread for a fraction of a point, it can make an enormous difference. Let's use the example we started with of buying one 40 option for 6, selling two 45s for $3^1/2$, and buying one 50 for 1, which came out to a zero debit. If these were not too actively traded options, we might find that the 40 options were offered at $6^1/4$, the 45s were bid at $3^1/4$, and the 50s were offered at $1^1/8$. Putting these prices together means that you would have to do this spread at a debit of not zero but $7/8$. That's an enormous difference from zero.

Of course, butterfly spreads are always entered as spread orders, but because there are so many different things to do, there is no way that anyone on the floor can hope to pick up more than one of the three options for the last sale price. He must be willing to execute the other two at market order prices, because when he fills one part of the order, he knows that he must immediately fill the other two parts, or he will be stuck with the loss. So there is really no way that you could do this spread unless you were willing to pay at least $5/8$, and from my experience even that is rather unlikely. The question then becomes one of judgment as to whether you are willing to do it at $7/8$.

But unfortunately putting on the spread is only half of the execution morass. At least when you put the spread on you can decide on the maximum debit you are willing to pay, put in the order with that debit, and if it isn't executed you can go on to something else with nothing lost. But once you have the spread on, you eventually will have to take it off. And there you are in a position with almost no room for maneuvering. They've got you. As expiration comes close you must get out of that spread or pay enormous commissions when your short options are exercised. So your hands are tied. While in theory you should always be able to get out of a butterfly spread at expiration for a credit or at worst no cost, this just isn't always the case. Typically, the deep-in-the-money option you are long is selling at a discount, while the two options you have to buy back are selling at a premium over their cash value. But you are in no position to argue.

So you take off the spread, and if the in-the-moneys are at a $\frac{1}{4}$-point discount, and the middle options are at a $\frac{1}{4}$-point premium, and then you have to sell the in-the-moneys at the bid price and buy the middle options at the offering price, you might have to tack on another $\frac{1}{4}$ or $\frac{1}{8}$ to the price of each. So you could easily have to pay a debit of a point or more to take off the spread. When the maximum theoretical profit was 5 (and this only if the stock ends up exactly at 45 and you risk not buying back two 45 options) you can see that paying over a point to close out the position really hurts. Thus, while in theory you should be able to put on and close out a butterfly spread for zero cost, in the real world you might have to pay almost 2 points to do this.

A final problem, especially for the smaller trader, is commissions. We saw how troublesome commissions could be in spreads involving two options. Naturally they are about 50% higher when the spread involves three options. The cost of doing the spread we used as our example is 40 cents per share if you were doing 10 options. Naturally, if you did less the cost per share would be higher. When you are trying to keep the cost of the spread down to about zero, commissions of almost half a point are very substantial. If the stock goes up, let's say to over 50, your commissions will be substantially higher, so that commissions could easily total over 1 point. Thus, between the costs of doing your spread at the bid and asked prices and commission costs, your transaction costs could easily be $2\frac{1}{2}$ points per share. When you consider that the maximum possible profit is 5, you realize that fully half of your greatest profit is consumed by transaction costs.

It is due to these three practical problems—finding the right option prices, getting executions at good prices, and commissions—that butterfly spreads are not as good as their excellent theoretical properties would suggest.

Diagonal Spreads

One popular variation of the bull spread is to purchase a long-term option, and then rather than selling an option of the same duration, sell one of the shorter-term options. For example, in May you purchase a January 40 option and sell a July 45. The advantage of selling the July option compared to an October or January 45 is that your premium income on a per-week basis is probably going to be higher between now and July. The July option will lose all its future time value, while the January might decline only very slightly. The theory is that if the stock is around 44 when the July expires, you will sell an October 45, let that expire, and then if the stock is in the right place, sell a January 45 option. This way you have three chances to take in premiums from the near-term option, which should be the one with the highest future time value in it.

On the other side of the spread, the advantage of buying the long-term option as opposed to a short-term one is that you should be paying less future time value on a per-week basis. Also, if the stock should decline within the next few months, you will have something that will retain a portion of its value much better than a short-term option. In fact, when declining stock markets have caused very low premiums on short-term options, it is sometimes surprising how well the longer-term options have maintained their levels. This is due to the fact that option buyers often get somewhat pessimistic about near-term prospects but continue to believe that there could be an upturn in about six months or more.

Another way of perceiving a diagonal spread is as a calendar spread that uses two strike prices. The benefit is that if the stock stays up near the strike price of the short option, the spread should result in a bigger profit than a regular calendar spread could produce.

There is even another way of looking at a diagonal spread, which should appeal to the more conservative traders. This is to think of it as a substitute for covered writing. In covered writing you buy the stock and write an option on it. Here, in lieu of buying the stock, you buy a long-term in-the-money option, which is the closest that you can come to actually buying the stock in the option world. These long-term options typically have a very low percentage of their value tied up in future time value, which means that they are quite similar to the underlying stock itself, and because of their long duration you don't have to trade them as often. The obvious advantage over covered writing is that it requires so much less money, since even these options cost much less than buying the stock on margin. And less capital tied up means greater leverage and the chance for a much higher return. If you want a higher return than a covered writing program can give you, consider diagonal spreads.

Selling Two Different Options against One Option

Earlier we discussed buying one 40 option and selling two 45 options. This section discusses buying one 40 option and selling one 45 option and one 50 option, and perhaps even one 60 option, all with the same expiration dates. This type of spread works best when option premiums are high, but it offers a great advantage over the two-on-one option positions we discussed earlier: namely, that since you are short only one of the 45 options you do not begin to lose money at expiration until the stock gets up to the strike price of the next option, which here is the 50. Therefore, your band of profitability is greatly enlarged. Instead of having a spread that is a breakeven at 50 after declining in profitability every point up from 45, you have a bull spread, which will stay at its maximum profitability all the way from 45 to 50. Only when the stock reaches 50 at expiration does the spread begin to lose in value, and then only on a point-for-point basis, so that your breakeven is reached at 55. On the downside, your loss is limited to the debit at which you did the spread, and your spread is worth 1 point for each point that the stock is above 40.

Principles of Complex Spreads

It is impossible to discuss every possible spread, for the reason that the variety of spreads is limited only by the imagination of the trader who wants to put them on. But there are certain basic principles that should guide the option spreader. The first is that every complex spread is a combination of the three basic spreads: bull, bear, and calendar spreads. When you are considering a fancy spread you should ask yourself why you are combining these basic spreads—that is, what advantages you seek that you cannot get from the basic spreads. As we noted, a butterfly spread is simply a bear spread on top of a bull spread, but there was a very good reason for combining the two. In theory, because they counterbalanced each other, there was no potential loss, and there was a possibility of a good gain. Therefore, one could logically decide to put on a butterfly spread.

The only real answer to the question of why spreads should be combined that I have learned is that it makes sense if in one way or another the combination provides a greater range of profitability than does a single spread. That is, if one spread works better over a long period, and another over the short period, you might have a valid combination—or if one works beautifully when the stock moves up, and the other when it stays still. For example, I have often combined a bull spread with a calendar spread done on the lower strike price of the bull spread when I thought that there was little likelihood the stock would go down very far, but I was quite concerned that it might not move up above the level of the lower strike price in the bull spread. In that case the bull spread would be worthless, but the calendar spread would be producing a fat profit. On the other hand, if the stock goes up, the calendar spread will start to show reduced profits, but the bull spread will be coming on strong.

When you consider complex spreads, therefore, it pays to take them apart in your mind, reduce them down to their basic components, and then ask yourself whether the different parts complement one another. If they are just two different ways of doing the same thing, or if they are diametrically opposed, then maybe you shouldn't be doing the complex spread at all.

The other basic rule in considering complex spreads is that in options, as in everything else in life, the best is the simplest. You should strive to keep your spreads as simple as possible, consistent with accomplishing your objectives. We have seen how complex spreads cost money in three distinct ways: (1) They are more difficult and expensive to execute; (2) commissions are higher; and (3) the more options you are short, the greater the danger of an unwelcome exercise. Each of these three will take money right out of your pocket. So consider carefully. There are many benefits to complex spreads, but the benefits frequently are outweighed by the practical problems and costs associated with them.

PUT OPTION SPREADS

To summarize put spreads, you can do anything with puts that you can do with calls. Sometimes you may feel as if you were standing on your head and looking at them from upside down to figure out what's going on, but put spreads can be done, and often with distinct advantages over doing the same thing with calls. In this section we will not bother explaining each spread in detail, since that would just duplicate what we said about call spreads, but will limit ourselves to pointing out the differences between call and put spreads and emphasizing when it is advantageous to use the put spreads.

Put Bull Spreads

The first put spread we will consider is the put bull spread, which is what you do with puts if you think a stock is going up. If that sounds self-contradictory, remember that we had bear spreads done with calls. The simple way to remember what a put bull spread is, is by keeping in mind that in a bull spread you always buy the lower strike option and sell the higher strike option. This is true whether you are doing a call bull spread or a put bull spread. Thus, in a put bull spread you would buy the 40 put for 2 where the stock is at 40, and sell the 45 put for 6, for a credit of 4. One difference between a call bull spread and a put bull spread is that whereas the call spread results in a debit, as you will recall, a put spread results in a credit. Since it is a credit spread, you have to deposit margin. The same rule applies as in a call credit spread; the margin call is for the difference between strike prices, minus the difference between the prices of the two options. Here the difference between strike prices is 5, and since we took in a 4-point credit on the spread, the margin call is for 1 point.

Just how does a put bull spread make money? Let's take a look at the example where the stock was 40 and we bought the 40 put for 2 and sold the 45 put for 6, for a credit of 4. If we are right and the stock goes up to 45 or higher, the 40 put will expire worthless, and the 45 put will also expire worthless. Thus, it will cost us nothing to get out of this position, and we are left retaining the original credit of 4 as our profit. On the other hand, if the stock should decline to 40, at the puts' expiration here is what would happen: The 40 put, which we own, will be worthless, but the 45 put, which we have sold, will be worth 5 points, and we will have to buy it back for 5. Now our cost of getting out will be 5, and since we took in a credit of 4 getting in, we have suffered a loss of 1 point. The result is the same no matter how far below 40 the stock falls.

If the stock is 43 at the puts' expiration, the 40 put we own is worthless, and the 45 put we're short is worth 2, so we buy it back for

TABLE 6.4 A Put Bull Spread

At Initiation Stock at 40			Stock Price at Expiration					
			40	41	42	43	44	45
Sell 45 put	6	Buy 45 put	−5	−4	−3	−2	−1	0
Buy 40 put	−2	Sell 40 put	0	0	0	0	0	0
Credit	4	Debit	−5	−4	−3	−2	−1	0
Cost (Margin)	1	Original Credit	4	4	4	4	4	4
		Profit or Loss	−1	0	1	2	3	4

that. This gives us a profit of 2 points when subtracted from our original credit of 4. For every point that the stock is above 43 we make one more point up to our maximum profit, at 45, of 4, and for every point below 43 we make one less point, so that our breakeven is 41. Table 6.4 shows the actual number for each stock price.

At any stock price below 40 the loss continues to be 1, and at any price above 45 the profit will be 4.

The fact that a put bull spread results in a credit rather than a debit really doesn't make much difference to you. What does make a difference in deciding whether to use a put or a call bull spread is where you can get the greater leverage. And here is where you will just have to figure out what each spread can do for you. As a rule, put prices on individual stocks are often less than call prices, and this is especially so for out-of-the-money options. Where here the stock is 40 and the 40 put is 2, the 40 call might be 3, and where the 45 put is 6, the 45 call might be 1½. This means that to do a call bull spread would result in a debit of 1½, whereas the put spread can be done for a credit of 4, meaning that you are putting up just 1 point. A difference between a cost of 1 and 1½ means a 50% higher cost for doing the call spread. Hence the moral, be sure to find out the cost of doing a put spread.

There are two other factors you should take into consideration. The first is commissions. The call bull spread involves options costing 3 and 1½, whereas the put bull spread involves options costing 2 and 6, which would result in higher commission costs. More important, if you are correct and the stock goes up to 47, for instance, the put spread evaporates with absolutely no commission costs whereas the call spread requires commissions on calls costing 2 and 7.

Second, you must always keep in mind the hazards of being short in-the-money options. With the call bull spread here there is very little danger, since your short option is out of the money, and by the time it gets into the money, where it could be exercised, your position will be quite profitable. With the put bull spread, you are by its very nature selling a put that is deep in the money, here that 45 put for 6. It could easily be exercised on you, especially the day after the stock goes ex-dividend.

Put Bear Spreads

The put bear spread is like the call bear spread in that in both cases you are selling the lower strike price option and buying the higher strike price option.

Table 6.5 shows how a typical put bear spread works. Since it is done as a debit spread, it makes money when the spread increases.

At stock prices below 40 the profit remains 4 and at stock prices above 45 the loss will be 1. A call bear spread creates a credit, while a put bear spread results in a debit. But, as we noted before, this really doesn't make very much difference to you. What does make a difference is the leverage you can get from the spreads, and here a put spread should be preferable to a call spread. The main reason is that most call bear spreads have to be done at least partly in the money to make them profitable, because you have to take in a lot of money for the lower strike option that you sell. Since you are selling the in-the-money option, you are normally selling an option with low future time value. You are buying an option that is either out of the money or not so deep in the money as the one you are selling,

TABLE 6.5 A Put Bear Spread

At Initiation Stock at 44			Stock Price at Expiration					
			45	44	43	42	41	40
Buy 45 put	−2	Sell 45 put	0	1	2	3	4	5
Sell 40 put	1	Buy 40 put	0	0	0	0	0	0
Cost	1	Credit	0	1	2	3	4	5
		Less Original Cost	1	1	1	1	1	1
		Profit or Loss	−1	0	1	2	3	4

and this means that it is going to have a greater future time value. This in turn means that you are losing out on this buy and sell, which is to say that if the stock stayed still until expiration, you would be losing money. But with a put bear spread just the opposite is true. Here you are selling the lower strike price put, which is the one with the greater future time value, while you are buying the higher strike price put, which has the lower future time value. This means that you are getting more than you are receiving as far as future time value on options goes, and therefore you should be able to make money if the stock stays still.

All this is simply a way of explaining that if you will compare the costs of doing a bear spread with calls versus puts, you will probably find that it is better for you to use puts. In addition to the better cost-to-potential-profit ratio that puts give you, you also avoid the serious problem in call bear spreads of being short a deep-in-the-money option. Remember, when this option is exercised against you prematurely, you're in bad shape. You must now buy in 100 shares of stock for every call that was exercised, paying commissions on that purchase, and when you were exercised you were charged commissions on the sale of 100 shares of stock for every option that was exercised. After you have done that you are left dangling with the options you are long, which you will probably sell out, generating more commissions. And all this without the probability of making any money. So the absence of being short an expensive in-the-money option is a significant plus feature.

Put Calendar Spreads

Put calendar spreads follow exactly the same principles as call calendar spreads. Since put prices tend to be somewhat lower than call prices, you should be able to do put calendar spreads for a lower debit. But this is not the advantage you might think it is, because when it comes time to close out the calendar put spread, it will not be worth as much as a call calendar spread. So your percentage profit on a put calendar spread is not likely to be much higher than on a call calendar spread. One word of caution: As your put calendar spread gets into the money (the stock moves down to below the strike price) the likelihood of your short option being exercised starts to grow. Since put premiums tend to be less than call premiums, the chances of being exercised on the short in-the-money put are that much greater.

Any one of the complex spreads that were discussed for calls can also be done with puts, including butterfly spreads, ratio spreads, and diagonal spreads. There is really no point in discussing in detail the use of puts in each complex spread because there are so many variations. But if you are mathematically inclined, you might consider whether you could improve on the butterfly spread by using calls to do the bull spread on the bottom, and then using puts to do the bear spread on the top. Have fun with your calculations.

COMBINING PUTS AND CALLS: STRADDLES AND COMBINATIONS

So far we have discussed spreads using calls and spreads using puts. Some of the most interesting things one can do with options is to combine puts and calls in the same transaction. Basically these fall into two categories, buying combinations and writing them. Generally you buy a combination of puts and calls when you expect a stock to move by a large amount in either direction, and this is called a volatility spread. Or you can sell combinations of calls and puts, which generally work out to be nonvolatility spreads, making money when the stock ends up near the strike price. When you buy or sell a combination of a put and a call with the same expiration date and the same strike price it is called a *straddle*. When you use a combination that has different strike prices or expiration dates it is called a *combination (combo)* or *strangle*.

Straddles

The easiest of these to discuss is buying a straddle. The big advantage in buying a straddle is that you can make money whether the stock moves up or down. Either direction is equally profitable *provided* only that the stock moves far enough. For example, when a stock is 70 you might buy a January 70 call for 4 and a January 70 put for $3^3/_8$ when each has about six months to go. The cost of buying this straddle would be $7^3/_8$, and your initial cost is the most you can possibly lose. If your strategy is to buy the straddle and hold it until expiration, the stock must move by $7^3/_8$ in either direction for you to reach your break-even point. If the stock goes up by that much to $77^3/_8$, then your call will be worth enough to cover your costs. If the stock moves down that much to $62^5/_8$, then your put will be worth your original total cost. Thus it is rather easy to decide whether you want to do a straddle. What do you think the chances are that the stock will be either over 77³/₈ or below 62⁵/₈ six months from now?

Trading with a Straddle. Buying and holding is not the only strategy open to a straddle buyer, and perhaps it is not the best one. Suppose that the stock were to move to 75 within four weeks. Probably the call would move up to 7 and the put would still have a value of perhaps 2, so that you could get out of the spread for 9 at a modest profit. One point that must be emphasized is the difference in trading strategy that I believe should be used with a straddle as opposed to buying a call or a put outright. The difference is that when you buy a straddle you should, by its very nature, be expecting to make a more modest profit than when you simply buy an option. Since you are paying approximately twice as much for the straddle as you would to buy just one side of it, and since under normal circumstances only one side of the straddle is going to make money for you, it follows that you have twice the cost with the potential for no more profit than you would have made had you purchased the call or the put alone. Hence, it is unreasonable to expect that you will make the same percentage profit. In fact, your percentage return may be about half as much as on purchasing one option alone.

But to counteract this smaller anticipated profit is the basic fact that you can make money whether the stock goes up or down. You are therefore literally doubling the chances you have of making money. And it should not be surprising that in exchange for this larger number of instances in which you will make money, you must give up a portion of the percentage return that you can make from any price move. To summarize this comment, while the straddle is speculative because it can be worth nothing if the stock hangs in at the strike price, it is more conservative than buying an option, because this is the only circumstance under which your cost will entirely dissipate; whereas when you buy a put or a call, if the stock goes in the wrong direction, which it has a 50% chance of doing, you are out every penny you paid.

Thus, the cost of a straddle may be twice as high as buying an option, but the chances of losing all your money are much less than half as much as with an option—perhaps they are only 10% as much as with one option. Furthermore, the chance that you will lose less than half your money with a straddle is quite good: As in our example here, the stock has to move less than 4 points in either direction. Get out some stock chart books and see how often any stock has been at exactly the same place it was six months earlier. Not very often, you can be sure. Now that we have established that the odds of losing all your money on a straddle are far less than with buying an option, the corollary should also be clear: that you will be satisfied with and will expect less spectacular profits.

Your trading strategies should also be adjusted to this conclusion, so that instead of closing out half your position when your option has doubled, as was suggested when you bought an option, perhaps you should close out half your position when it has increased by 50%, and then close out the other half when it has doubled. But whatever you decide, use the one guideline that has been the theme throughout this book: Decide in advance what you are going to do and when you are going to do it. Holding a straddle until the last day can be as disappointing as anything else you can do. If you have a profit on the call side of your straddle, and you don't close it out of greed, and you see the stock slipping back down to the strike price, you are losing money just like a call owner, and the fact that you also own a put at the same strike price doesn't do you one whit of good unless the stock moves all the way down to the strike price.

Closing Out the Other Side of a Straddle. One frequently asked question is whether there is any point in not closing out the other side of a straddle when you take a good profit from one of the sides. Thus, in our example, if the stock went up to 80, and you sold the call for $10\frac{1}{2}$, making a nice profit, should you sell out the 70 put at the same time, when all you can get for it is a negligible $\frac{3}{8}$ point? There is something adventurous about holding on to this near worthless item in the vague hope that perhaps the stock will plummet, and you will realize the option trader's equivalent of a hole in one. This is also called trading against a straddle. If the stock goes down, first you sell your put at a profit and hold the call. Then when it goes up you sell out your call at a profit, too. You will make a big profit on both the call and the put, thus astounding everyone and really getting your money's worth out of the straddle, instead of wasting a full half of your straddle, as one usually does. Yes, it certainly has a lot of romance, but to reach a rational decision, simply ask yourself this question: With the stock at 80, would you buy a 70 put for $\frac{3}{8}$ when it had only a few months or weeks to go? I'm not going to answer the question for you, but if you would not be a buyer of that put, then you should sell it out when you close out the call side. It is not a free dividend that is left over after you have taken your profit out of the straddle. It is part of the profit you are entitled to and should be treated as such.

Ratio Straddles. Straddles don't have to be done on a one-for-one ratio, and I believe that ratio straddles are going to become more and more popular. Since most of us do have views on how the market is going to move in the next few months, it is natural that we will tend to favor the side we believe in. Of course, knowing that we are fallible, we may want to protect ourselves with a few options for the other side, but there is a big difference between a *hedge* and the main thrust of our anticipated profit making. Thus, if we are bullish on the stock in our example, we may decide to buy 10 calls and only 4 puts, reasoning that the stock will probably go up and our puts will expire worthless, so why throw away so much money on them? On the other hand, if for some reason we are wrong, and the stock plunges down to 60, it will be nice not to lose any money.

Using a 10 to 4 ratio, our cost for the straddle comes out to $4.97 for each share on which we own a call, versus the cost of a full straddle of $7.37, which is quite a significant reduction in cost. It means that our break-even point on the upside is reduced 32%, and our percentage profit will be twice as high at 70. On the downside it will be much harder to make a profit, but then we don't really expect to do that. All we are looking for is a self-liquidating feature to pay for the cost of the straddle. As it turns out, our break-even point on the downside now becomes 56.60, which is pretty low, but at 60, there would be a loss of only 1 point for each share on which we had a call, so the puts will have substantially accomplished their job of absorbing most of the cost of the straddle.

Combinations or Strangles

As has been pointed out, the cost of a regular straddle is substantial, and therefore the chance of a large profit is rather small, absent a really spectacular move in the price of the stock. One way of trying to overcome this is to use a combination, in which you buy a call with a strike price above the current price of the stock and a put with the strike price below the current stock price. For example, when a stock was $37^5/_8$, the six-month 35 call was $5^1/_4$, the 35 put was $1^1/_4$, and the 40 call was $2^3/_8$. Thus, to do a regular straddle at the 35 level would have cost 6³/₈, but to do a combination of the 35 put and 40 call cost only 3⁵/₈, or just over one-half as much.

The theory behind this type of combination is that you are going to make any real money on a straddle only if the stock moves by a large amount in either direction, so why not save money by cutting out the middle band of the straddle in exchange for a greatly reduced cost? In this type of combination if the stock moves much above 40 or much below 35 you will still make a profit, and since your total cost was so much lower than with a regular straddle, you can soon make a much larger percentage profit. With a volatile stock, with high prices for on-the-money options, this might make good sense.

The obvious disadvantage is that you are now losing a key feature of straddles—that the only way you can lose all your money is if the stock ends up exactly at the strike price. You now have a range of anywhere from 35 to 40 in which you will lose your entire cost of the combination if that is where the stock is at expiration.

Another popular type of combination is to buy calls of one duration and puts of another, depending on which way you believe the stock is likely to move. Thus, if you believe that a stock is going to go up, you might decide to buy the nine-month calls and also some three-month puts just in case the stock falls down in the near term. Your strategy might be to get out of the calls in three months if the stock goes down, in which case the puts will cut your loss or actually turn it into a profit, and if the stock goes up as you expect, then you can ride it for a long-duration gain.

Selling Straddles and Combinations

The easiest way to use straddles and combinations is to buy them, but there are also advantages to be gained from selling them, although selling straddles will probably not appeal to the same type of person. Let's make it clear at the outset that the effects of selling straddles are completely different from the results of buying them. The straddle buyer wants the stock to move in a large amount either up or down and limits his cost and maximum loss at the outset. The straddle seller, not surprisingly, wants the stock to stay just about where it is. But this is the least of the differences in terms of investment philosophy. The biggest one is that unlike the buyer, the seller is faced with an unlimited potential loss. This is not surprising because the straddle seller is actually a naked call seller, and in addition he is also a naked put seller with all the possible liability that naked puts bring.

Thus the straddle writer faces an almost unlimited loss if the stock goes either up or down too far! It is definitely not for the investor with limited resources because of this possible unlimited loss. Second, the straddle seller has to put up margin, and just as in the case of the naked option seller, the amount of margin can increase from day to day at an alarming rate. Finally, while the straddle buyer can always dream of striking it rich, the straddle seller can never make more than he originally took in on the day that he sold the straddle. And he will take in this much profit only if he is exceptionally lucky and the stock is just exactly at the strike price when the straddle expires.

Higher Income than from Naked Calls. Straddle writing does appeal to the person who may have considered writing naked calls but is a little afraid that he isn't getting enough premium to cover his risks. In selling a straddle, the writer may get up to twice as much money coming in as he could for selling a naked call, since he has the money from both the put and the call. And the beauty of selling a straddle is that although you take in up to twice as much money at the start, you should not lose any more if things go wrong than if you had sold only a naked call. That sentence must be read very carefully. It does not say that you have no more chance of losing money than if you had sold only a call; it says that you should lose *no more* than if you had sold only a call.

The reason is that by following the basic rule of strategy for selling naked options, you will close out the position at a predetermined stock price or option price for a predetermined loss. When the stock goes up, you will close out the position when it reaches your price, and the loss on the call will be no greater than it would have been had you sold the call alone. But you will then be able to buy in the put at what should be a good profit, since the put will now be way out of the money. Thus, you lost no more on the call than you would have selling a naked call alone, but you made a large profit on the put, which in some cases could actually wipe out your loss and even result in a net profit. So the straddle can be a big advantage over simply writing naked calls.

If this is so wonderful, then why does anyone still write naked calls alone? The answer is that while the amount of your loss may be no greater than with calls alone, the chances of having a loss with a straddle are about twice as great as they are with calls alone, for the obvious reason that with the naked put you now have the chance of losing money if the stock goes down. You must also select a price for the stock or the option on the downside at which you will close out the position and take your loss on the put. At the same time you should be able to close out your call position for a good profit.

Straddle Writing Strategy. The strategy in selling straddles involves first a careful consideration of whether you should sell a particular straddle at all. In order to do this you will want to know the percentage return on your margin. The amount of margin required for writing a straddle is determined by computing the margin for the naked call and then the margin for the naked put, and taking the greater of the two. To determine the amount of margin needed to write the straddle, you can subtract both the premiums you receive. So, actually, the margin rules for the sale of straddles are quite a break for the writer. He is getting up to twice as much premium income from the same amount of margin as he would have if he sold just a put or just a call. This should be an important factor influencing call sellers toward writing straddles. So, the first consideration is to determine the maximum profitability based on the stock staying at the strike price.

The second consideration is to decide what you can realistically expect to make on the deal. When a person writes naked calls, especially if they are out of the money, he can reasonably hope that he will retain the entire premium as his profit. But with a straddle this is somewhat fanciful, since the only way this could happen is if the stock is right at the strike price on expiration, and even then, since your brokerage firm may require you to close out the position by 3:00 P.M. eastern time, one hour before the stock exchanges close, you would probably have to buy in your position just to protect yourself from a move in the final hour of trading. So you must expect that the stock is going to move to some extent from the strike price, and you should come up with a reasonable figure. Now, subtract that amount from the total premiums you are going to take in from selling the straddle, and you will have some idea of what a reasonable profit would be.

The third step is to decide where your stop-loss positions are going to be if the stock moves strongly up or down. You do this in the same way you do for the sale of naked options, except that you might be able to stand larger moves against you because you have the profit on the other option to help you pay for your losses. In any event, once you have picked this price, you should then estimate what your loss on the entire position would be.

Having done these three things, you are now in a position to make a reasonable determination of what you should do. You know what percentage profit you can make, how much you can reasonably expect to make, and how much you can expect to lose if you are wrong. Of course, you will now consider the volatility of the stock to try to come up with a probability factor of how likely it is that the stock will move either up or down to your close-out points. If this sounds a bit complicated, it is, but not beyond the scope of any competent options trader. And who ever said that it was easy to make money? As everyone familiar with Wall Street knows, it is always very easy to lose money, but not so easy to make it.

As we have seen, one of the biggest drawbacks to selling straddles is that some cost of buying back one of the options at expiration is almost inevitable. And the loss could be fairly substantial. Wouldn't it be nice if there were a way of writing a straddle in which we had a good chance of getting away scot-free with a full profit on both the put and the call? There is such a way and it is called writing a combination, in which we sell the call with the strike price above the current price of the stock and we sell the put with the strike price below the current price of the stock. For example, if a stock is 37, we would sell the 40 call and the 35 put. This has a lot to recommend it, because it is really the closest analogy to selling out-of-the-money naked call options and out-of-the-money naked puts.

Margin for Combinations. To determine the margin required for this type of combination, we calculate the margin required for the put and then for the call, and use the greater of the two plus the current premium on the other option. Again we get a bargain, almost two for the price of one. Before deciding whether to set up one of these combinations we should go through the three steps recommended for the straddle, but we may not have to do anything about the second step of buying in the options if we can realistically expect that the stock will stay between the two strike prices until the options expire.

It seems to me that the sale of a combination is preferable to the sale of either naked calls or naked puts under most circumstances. The only exceptions would be where one has a strong viewpoint on which way the stock is going to move, or where the premiums for the two options are out of line. For example, a stock could have a very generously priced out-of-the-money call option that just begs to be sold naked, but because the public is so bullish on the stock, the put premium might be meager and therefore not worth writing. But generally put and call premiums are approximately in line, and a good call-writing opportunity should also be a good put-writing opportunity. And with little additional margin required to take in perhaps twice as much money, why not do it?

If one does have views on which way a stock is going to move, an alternative to a combination is to do a ratio combination. For example, if you thought that a stock now selling at 42 were overpriced and you wanted to write the 45 calls without writing the 40 puts, you might consider writing two or three puts for every 10 calls just to give you some additional income in case you are wrong.

To summarize the writing of straddles and combinations, they are definitely not for everyone. In the first place, you must be approved for naked option writing. In the second place, you must have the emotional temperament to be able to withstand the potential losses of naked option writing. Finally, you must be willing to accept a limited maximum profit with the knowledge that there is the possibility of an unlimited loss, because even with the best stop-loss plans, if a stock stops trading on news of a takeover, for example, and opens up 40 points higher, there is no way in the world that you can prevent what might be a catastrophic loss. But if you can accept all those caveats, then writing straddles and combinations can yield a relatively high return on your capital in good markets and bad. If a stock takes long enough to make a move, you will be a winner whether it goes up or down. It is only the sharp, sudden moves that will produce the large losses.

7

OPTION COMMISSIONS
Small Commissions
Can Swallow Your Profits

At a time when almost every Internet brokerage is advertising truly low commission rates for trading stocks, it may come as   learn that these bargain rates are simply not available o   this chapter we'll discuss why that is, and give you some   you can reduce your option commissions.

The good news is that anyone who wants to buy or sell *stocks* can do it at commission rates that were undreamed of just a few years ago. One commercial after another on Bloomberg TV, CNBC, and CNNfn announces that you can now trade up to 5,000 shares of stock for as little as (pick one): $17.95, $14.95, $8.95, $5, or in some cases for absolutely no commission at all. (See Appendix B for details.) This is truly amazing. Just figure it out: If you do trade 5,000 shares for $14.95, you are paying a commission of just three-tenths of a cent per share!

Years ago each stock exchange had legally binding minimum commission rates for all of its member brokerage firms. The lowest commission allowed for the New York Stock Exchange was 8.2 cents per share, and that was on a stock of under $2. Would you believe that if you had bought 1,000 shares of a $125 stock, the commission would have been 80.7 cents per share? That is a total commission of $807! So here is one expense that has really come down in price. And any brokerage that at that time dared offer a discount of even a penny from that rate would have been heavily fined and probably expelled from the brokerage business for violating one of the brokerage industry's core principles of business ethics! Let's all be thankful that today we are freed from those chains, which were first broken in May 1975.

I doubt, however, if you have ever seen a brokerage firm TV commercial spelling out how cheap its *option* commissions are. I don't recall ever seeing one and I don't expect to. The main reason is that there just aren't any bargains in commissions for options that are similar to the ones for stocks. While stock commissions range down to three-tenths of a cent or even zero as we just saw, options commissions go down to about a charge of $15 to $20 per trade and $1.50 to $1.75 per option contract. One Internet firm has no fixed charge per trade and charges $1.95 per contract. One firm that has a zero stock commission for customers with over $100,000 in their accounts charges an option commission of $40 per trade plus $2 per option.

Let's take an example to see just what you will pay in commissions for buying or selling an option. For our example, let's say you buy 10 calls at 2. This means you are buying options on 1,000 shares, costing you a total premium of $2,000. The commission would be (at a typical discount rate) $15 for the trade plus $1.50 times the 10 options ($15) for a total of $30. This works out to three cents per share. So you are paying three cents to buy an option that costs you $2 per share, when you could have bought the stock itself for $200 per share and paid a commission of just three-tenths of a cent. Does that make any sense?

As you have seen, the commissions on stock options are often extremely high for the average-priced call. This did not come about through a diabolical plot on the part of brokers but rather from the side effects of the fact that options, by their very nature, are priced at only a fraction of the underlying stocks. When the option exchanges were seeking a model for their original rate structure, they looked at the stock exchange rates and copied them.

As a general rule, the smaller the premium, the higher a percentage commission you will have to pay on a trade of a given total amount of dollars. The defense of this practice given by brokers is that it takes them just as much time, effort, and paperwork to process an order for a call whether the call sells for 12½ cents or $24. And of course there is some merit in this statement.

EXPIRING OPTIONS

The one time when the option trader must know the effect of commissions is when he is either the owner or the writer of a call or put that is in the money and just about to expire. If the option is in the money, it has an intrinsic value and will be exercised if it is still in existence on the expiration date. However, both the option holder and its writer have a choice. The option holder can either exercise the option on the final day or sell it on the last trading day. Similarly, the option writer can either buy back the option on the last day on which it is traded or let it be exercised against him and deliver or buy the underlying stock depending on whether it is a call or a put. In each of these decisions the amount of commission is of great importance.

Let us take the case of the call holder first. If the successful call holder wishes to make a cash profit on his call by exercising it, as distinct from continuing to own the underlying stock that he has obtained for the strike price, he must pay two commissions on the underlying stock at the regular rates. First he pays a commission when he acquires the stock through the exercise of his option, and then he pays a commission when he sells the stock on the open market. On the other hand, if he decides to sell his call, he pays only one commission on the sale of the call.

STOCK VERSUS OPTION COMMISSIONS

Thus it is necessary to make a comparison of the commission for one option trade with the commission for two stock trades. The option commission rates were discussed earlier in this chapter along with the new discount bargain stock commission rates. If you are trading with a traditional full-service brokerage firm, you will probably be charged a stock commission based on the old NYSE official rates prior to May 1975 and then they will subtract whatever discount your broker has agreed to give you. The NYSE rates are set out in Table 7.1. (A round-lot order is an order of 100 shares.)

In addition to the charges listed in the Table, there is another charge for each round lot: first to 10th round lot, $6 for each round lot; 11th round lot and above, $4 per round lot.

Finally, there is added a 10% surcharge on orders totaling $5,000 or less and a 15% surcharge on orders over $5,000.

You will immediately realize that the structure of the commission schedule is similar to that for options. To give an example of how the commissions work, let us assume that you own five call contracts on a stock that is now selling for $55 and your calls have a strike price of 50 and are trading at $5. First, you could sell your call, with the commission as follows: fixed commission of $12, plus $26 (1.3% of $2,000) plus $30 ($6 per contract times 5), for a total of $68, plus 10% equals $74.80. This is your total commission to transform your contract rights into cash.

Now let us compute the commission if you decide to exercise the

TABLE 7.1 NYSE Stock Commission Rates

On Single Round-Lot Orders		
Amount Involved in the Order	Minimum Commission	
$100–$799	2.0% of money involved	+ $ 6.40
$800–$2,499	1.3% of money involved	+ $12.00
$2,500 and above	0.9% of money involved	+ $22.00
On Multiple Round-Lot Orders		
Amount Involved in the Order	Minimum Commission	
$100–$2,499	1.3% of money involved	+ $ 12.00
$2,500–$19,999	0.9% of money involved	+ $ 22.00
$20,000–$29,999	0.6% of money involved	+ $ 82.00
$30,000–$500,000	0.4% of money involved	+ $142.00

call by buying the stock and then selling it, using the old fixed commission rate. The commission on buying 500 shares at $50 a share is: $82 plus $150 (0.6% of $25,000) plus $30 ($6 per round lot times 5), totaling $262 plus 10% equals $288.20. The commission to sell 500 shares at $55 comes to $304.70 for a total round-trip commission of $592.90. Since the amount of money that you would realize without any commissions from each method in this example is exactly the same, $2,000 profit, you would save yourself some money by going with the cheaper method. Using the old fixed rates, the cost of exercising the call and selling is $592.90. The cost of selling the call is $74.80. Thus you could save $518.10 by selling your call rather than exercising it. If you are using a full-service broker, its commissions are still probably based on this formula, although you normally can negotiate some discount from these rates.

In actual practice you might find that the difference between the two methods is closer than this, because the price of the call will be just a bit lower than the difference between the price of the stock and the strike price, in order to compensate for the amount of the commission.

If you are using a discount broker, then everything is upside down because it costs more to trade an option than it does to trade stock. So check what you are paying to sell an option and what the charge is for an assignment of an option. Then add in what you are paying to sell the stock. You will then know whether you are paying more in commissions to sell the option or to exercise it and sell the stock.

There are other considerations here that might outweigh the importance of the commission. That is that there is a natural advantage in selling the option, namely that it is a simple transaction in which you know exactly what you are getting. If you exercise the option, how do you know what you will be able to sell the stock for on the following day when you actually own the stock?

CHOOSING A BROKER

Are the deep-discount brokerage firms the best for you, or is there a valid reason why you should consider paying higher commissions at a full-service firm? To answer this question, we must first understand how discount stock brokerage firms are able to offer the bargain rates described earlier in this chapter. They have low overhead and keep expenses down by usually not engaging in stock market research or giving market advice to their clients. But most importantly they do not employ stockbrokers as most of us understand that word. They do employ registered representatives who are legally stockbrokers. But we think of a stockbroker as a person knowledgeable about the stock market, who knows his clients and gives them advice about what to invest in while keeping in mind the investment objectives and financial condition of the client.

From the point of view of the brokerage firms the brokers do something else—they bring in the clients. For these twin functions of bringing in the client and advising him on what to trade, the broker is paid a variable part of the commissions that his clients pay to the brokerage firm. The actual percentage of the commission that is paid to the broker depends on the firm he is with, the amount of business he does, and sometimes on the type of business and how many years he has been with the firm. A typical amount is 33%.

That is just the tip of the iceberg. Each broker needs to be in an impressive office, and he or she has to have support in the form of sales assistants who also need office space. This makes for an expensive rent bill. In addition to his commission payout, the broker usually receives health insurance, a pension plan, and other employee benefits, as does the sales assistant. Of course brokers make a lot of phone calls, many long distance, and nowadays all have state-of-the-art computer quote systems. All of this costs money. Then, since the broker has to have something to tell the client, the firms all have high-priced research departments and spend a large amount of money sending out research reports. Of course, the brokers require supervisors in the form of well-paid branch managers and so forth and a compliance department to ensure that all the regulations are followed.

Now imagine the savings to a brokerage if it can eliminate all these expenses. Most discount firms still have brokers but they can do a lot of trades because they do not spend any time discussing the pros and cons of buying stock and are not spending large amounts of time trying to woo new clients. Almost all their time is spent entering incoming orders. Furthermore, they are often paid by the month and not on commission. The new Internet firms don't even need brokers, because the order you enter can be passed directly to the floor of the stock or options exchange.

In short, these firms are simply order takers and executors. They cannot give you advice, they will not discuss alternatives with you, and they won't give you a feeling as to whether the market is going up or down. Now that we understand exactly what the difference between a full-service and discount brokerage is, we can return to our question of whether an options trader should use a full-service broker and pay higher commissions, or should he take advantage of the discount firms?

The answer depends entirely on who you are and what services you need. My advice is that the newcomer, or even a fairly knowledgeable new options trader, should definitely avoid the discount brokers. My reason is that the savings in commissions are not going to be very meaningful in relation to the total amounts involved.

To most option traders, the advice and expert execution that an experienced options broker can give are far more valuable than any discount could be. Remember that buying and selling options is a tricky business, far more difficult than the stock market, because the prices of options fluctuate so much more rapidly and because the liquidity of the market is so much thinner. If you ever needed a good person on your side, it is when you want to trade in options. But you must find a broker who has specific experience in options. Don't go with a stockbroker who has bought a call for a client only once or twice.

Don't be afraid to interview a broker before you hire him and ask him exactly what options experience he has had. One way of finding an options broker is to select a brokerage firm you like and then contact the branch manager. Tell him or her that you're looking for an experienced options broker and ask which of the brokers he or she would recommend. So, find someone with experience in options, and if he earns your trust and confidence, stick with him. His counsel and expertise will be worth many times his commissions.

If you eventually decide that you have learned as much as he or she knows and that the broker is not providing you with services that are of very much value to you, then by all means try out a discount broker. Their executions are generally just as good as regular brokers, and often quicker. And those commission savings can be quite substantial.

REDUCING YOUR COMMISSIONS

Now that we've discussed the nature of commissions, let's get down to the important point for all investors and traders: How can commissions be reduced without affecting your performance in a detrimental way? Here are four specific, concrete rules that can help you reduce commissions, and often by surprisingly large amounts.

Simplify Your Strategy

The more you simplify, the more commissions you eliminate. That sounds obvious, but it isn't always so easy to look at what you are attempting to do objectively and come up with a simplified version. Fortunately, the equivalency table in Appendix F can tell you in a moment if there is a simpler method of achieving your goal. If you find that you can do something with an option only, you may find that you will be far ahead in savings on commissions as compared with doing something that requires a position in the underlying stock as well as an option position.

One of the most dramatic examples of this is a covered call write. Covered call writing has become so popular that many people and institutions go into it without fully considering the alternative, which is simply to sell an uncovered put of the same duration and strike price as the call option in the covered write. There may be many reasons why accounts cannot write naked puts, and if there are such reasons, then they must continue with their covered call writing. But for the many investors who can write puts, it is well to stop and reflect on the fact that selling a naked put is the same as writing a covered call, and the commission cost may be only a fraction of that required for covered calls.

As an example, let's assume that the stock you are interested in is at 22, and you want to sell the 20 call option for 4, giving yourself a gross spread of 2 points. If you sell the 20 put for 2 you will have achieved exactly the same objective; that is, you can make a gross profit of $2 if the stock is 20 or better upon the option's expiration, and you have the downside risk of a decline in the price of the stock below 20 reduced, however, by the 2 of net future time value you took in with the original option sale. Some of the details will be different, such as collection of dividends if you own the stock, but on the other hand you may have to put up substantially more margin to do a covered call write. Of course, you may not be able to sell the put for 2 points. So there may be many valid reasons why you would prefer the covered call write, but you should at least be aware of the commission savings that could be possible.

Assuming you wish to buy 500 shares and write five calls, the commission at the old fixed minimum rate on selling the five calls at $4 is $68. The commission on buying 500 shares of the stock at $22 is $187.50. If we assume that the stock stays at the same price of $22, the easiest way to get out of the covered write is to let the stock be called away. This results in a commission on selling 500 shares at $20 per share, which is $176.50. (If we had bought back the option and then sold the stock, there would have been an additional commission on the purchase of the call.) These commissions total $432.

Now let's see what the commissions are on selling a naked put for $2. The commission on selling five puts at $2 is $55. If we assume, as we did before, that the stock remains at 22, then the put will expire worthless, and so there is no commission on closing it out. The comparison: commissions of $432 to do the covered call write as against commissions of just $55 to do the equivalent transaction with a naked put. That's a savings of 87%. Enough said. Note that even full-service firms should give you some discount from these rates today, and that the amounts will be completely different for discount firms.

Try to Do Your Transactions in Large Quantities

Option commissions are computed partly on the amount of money involved, but also largely on the amount of work that is required of the brokerage firm. To a large extent it costs the firm the same amount to execute an order whether it is for one option or for 100 options. The result is that the commission per unit of stock or option usually goes down markedly as the quantity goes up. For example, using the old fixed rates, the commission on two options at $3 is $31.80 or $15.90 per option. For five options it is $12.30 per option, for 10 options it is reduced to $10.90, and for 20 options it is just $8.80, a reduction of 44%.

The same reductions occur with stock if the commission is based on the old fixed minimum rate, as a quick look at the stock commission chart in Appendix H will show. For example, by buying 500 shares of a $20 stock instead of just 100 shares, one reduces the commission cost per share by 22%. And if one can afford to buy 2,000 shares of the stock at $20, the commission is reduced another 29% from that level. Thus the 2,000-share buyer is getting a savings of 44% over the 100-share buyer, based on the standard rates.

And you don't even have to be a big spender to realize savings by buying in quantity. Using the old fixed rates, two options at $1 have a commission of $13.30 each, but if you get five of them for $500 your commission is just $9.70 each.

The same rule applies equally to discount firms that have a fixed price per trade. If the charge per option is $1.50 but there is a charge of $15 per trade, then it costs you $16.50 to trade one option. Two options cost you $18 or $9 per option. That's a savings of $7.50 per option for a reduction of 54%!

So the second rule for reducing commissions is to take fewer positions and take a greater quantity of each position.

Concentrate on the Higher-Priced Options

Because of the nature of the formula for computing option commissions, the percentage commission you pay is much less for the higher-priced options. Thus, under the old rate, if you spend $1,000 to buy 10 options at $1, your commission is $85. But if you spend $1,000 to buy one option at $10, your commission is only $25. That's a savings of 70.5%, better than a discount store having its annual clearance sale. The new discount commissions work exactly the same way, in that the cost is always expressed as so much per option. Therefore, to reduce your cost in terms of a percentage of the money you are trading, trade the high-priced options. So if you want to save on commissions, take a look at the expensive options on the high-priced stocks. The biggest bargains in town, speaking strictly from the commission viewpoint, are the very high-priced stocks that have the highest-priced options. By concentrating on options of the expensive stocks and leaving the cheap options on the low-priced stocks to someone else, you can realize substantial commissions savings.

Never Trade One Option

The reason for this rule is that virtually every brokerage firm has a minimum commission per trade (also called a ticket charge). If you buy one option at $1 per share ($100) and the commission charge per trade is $25, that is an outrageous 25%. But as we saw in a previous example, if you buy two options at $1, the commission is increased only by a token amount of $1.60. Thus, the commission on two options is practically the same as for one, showing that you have grossly overpaid for the commission on one option. So that is why most options brokers will always buy at least 200 shares to write calls on and will try to do everything else in a minimum of twos. It is hard enough to make money in options without taking on the unfair burden of overpaying for commissions.

To summarize our rules for saving commissions, they are:

1. *Simplify*. Before you enter into any transaction requiring stocks and options, check the equivalency table in Appendix F to see whether there is an alternative that can be done with options only. Don't buy stock and write a call if you can sell a naked put. Don't buy stock and protect yourself by purchasing a put when you can get the same result by buying a call. This simplification will make it easier for you to get in and out of the positions and could save you up to 87% on your dollar commission costs!

2. *Trade larger quantities*. Remember, the commission rates are based on the fact that a brokerage firm does about as much work to execute an order for one option as for 100. This doesn't mean that you should risk more money; just use fewer positions.

3. *Stick to higher-priced options*. The same reasoning applies as for rule 2. Big savings result if you follow this.

4. *Avoid single options*. The fixed commission for each trade is just lurking in the wings ready to snare you with an excessively high commission.

8

TAXATION OF STOCK OPTIONS
How Your Net Profit Is Affected

The cry in every well-run corporation these days is, "What will it do to the bottom line?" What this means is that it is all very well to discuss a project that sounds good, but the acid-test question for every business idea is, "What will it do for the company's net profits?" It is on a company's net profits that it is really judged—not on its sales, not on its gross profits, not on its pretax profits. Similarly, the important question for the individual investor is, "What will puts and calls do to my bottom line—my net after-tax income?" There are so many complexities in dealing with stock options that it would be wonderful if one could just write a simple statement describing the tax consequences of all transactions involving stock options. Then after the investor had read that statement, he could go on about his business of trying to maximize his profits without altering his desired course of conduct because of the tax consequences.

Unfortunately this is not the case. Cynics have probably already said that it's impossible to name one case in which something involving taxes is simple. In the case of stock options the tax consequences are far from simple; in fact, they are very complicated. Even worse, they can be important. So, this may be one of the more significant chapters in this book. For while the rest of this book is concerned with earning money, this chapter is concerned with the equally vital function of keeping for yourself as much as possible of the money you do earn.

Since tax rules change virtually every year, be sure to check the current tax law with your tax adviser rather than relying solely on this book. First, a brief introduction to certain tax concepts is necessary. For tax purposes, income is divided into two basic types.

ORDINARY INCOME VERSUS CAPITAL GAINS

The money that you get paid from your job, earn in your business, or receive in dividends or interest is called ordinary income. It is normally taxed at the highest rates. If you lost money in your business, this would be an ordinary loss, and that loss could be deducted from any ordinary income you had, to determine your net ordinary income.

The other basic type of income is the profit that is made from the "sale or exchange" of a capital asset and this type of income is called a capital gain. If the "sale or exchange" results in a loss, it is called a capital loss. A capital asset is difficult to define, but it is sufficient for our purposes to say that it includes stock, and stock and stock index options. Capital gains and losses may be further divided into two types: short-term and long-term. Those that occur within one year—that is, where the date of the acquisition of the asset and the date of the sale or exchange of the asset are not more than 12 months apart—are called short-term capital gains or losses. In other words, if you have held a capital asset for exactly one year, it is still taxed as a short-term capital gain. A short-term capital gain is taxed at the same rate as ordinary income, which is the highest rate.

On the other hand, a short-term capital loss can reduce these highly taxed short-term capital gains and can also reduce long-term capital gains. Strangely, and importantly, although short-term capital gains are taxed at the same rate as ordinary income, neither short-term nor long-term capital losses can be used to offset ordinary income except to the extent of $3,000 a year. Watch out. The result may be that although you may have lost money from options, you will not be able to get a tax loss in the current year for it, because the capital losses cannot be deducted in full from ordinary income. This seems highly unfair, but the Internal Revenue Code was never noted for its evenness of application.

If the time elapsed between the purchase of the capital asset and its sale or exchange is more than 12 months, then the gain or loss is called a long-term capital gain or loss. Thus, if you own shares of a stock for just one year and a day, they qualify as long-term gain. Long-term capital gains (after subtracting capital losses) are taxed at a maximum tax rate of 20%. If you are in the lowest tax bracket of 15%, then your capital gains are taxed at only 10%.

Because you do not pay the full tax on a long-term capital gain, you also do not get the full benefit when you have a loss. It takes almost $2 of long-term capital gain to offset $1 of ordinary income if you are in the top tax bracket.

Now that we have these fundamentals out of the way, we can

begin to analyze the tax consequences to you when you engage in various option transactions. If you buy a call or put, it is considered a capital asset, unless you are a dealer in options. Assuming that you are not a dealer, the question that should first spring to your mind is whether you are going to have a long-term or short-term gain or loss. Assets have to be held for over one year in order to qualify for long-term capital gains treatment. Since the longest regular option available is for nine months, it is obvious that unless you buy a LEAPS it is impossible to ever hold an option long enough for it to become long-term. Thus, traders in regular options must resign themselves to having short-term assets and paying the short-term tax rate on any profits, unless they take advantage of the procedure described in the second paragraph after this. If you make money on your trade by selling the option for more money than you paid for it, then the profit you have made is a capital gain. The amount is determined quite simply by subtracting your cost, including all commissions and any fees, from the net amount that you received—that is, the amount after deducting all commissions and fees and transfer taxes, if any.

If you lose money by selling the call for less than you paid for it, you have a capital loss. If you lose money because your call has become worthless at its expiration date and you simply let it expire while you own it, then your loss is still considered to be a capital loss. In the eyes of the tax law you are considered to have sold or exchanged the option on the expiration day, for a price of $0.00. You thus have a capital loss equal to your net purchase price.

One procedure for possibly changing a gain on a call from short-term to long-term is that instead of selling your call when it is about to expire, you decide to exercise it. This means that you purchase the underlying stock at the strike price. Then the premium that you paid for the option is added onto the price that you paid for the stock. This total becomes your basis or cost for determining the profit or loss that you will make when you sell the stock. There is no separate taxation of the option. But you can not add the time you owned the call on to the time that you owned the stock in determining whether you held the stock for a long-term or short-term period. This means that in order to qualify for long term capital gain treatment, you must own the stock for a year and a day after you exercise the option. This of course means that you are subject to all the risk of having the stock go down in that time, thus erasing all the profit you originally made on the option. This procedure works best when you have a very large gain on a call, and believe that the stock is likely to go up even further in the months ahead.

CALL BUYER'S TAX STRATEGY

Let's illustrate that with a detailed example. Suppose that on May 15 you pay $5 to buy a December call and that the strike price of the call is 50. The end of December finally comes around and lo and behold the price of the stock has moved up to $65 and your call is now worth $15. At this point you have the choice of selling your call, or exercising it and buying the 100 shares of stock for $50 a share. As we already noted, if you sell your call, the profit of $10 per call is capital gain, and since you bought the call less than 12 months before you sold it, you will have a short-term capital gain this year. This is the expensive kind—the kind that can cost you maximum tax dollars.

If, on the other hand, you decide to take your alternate route, and exercise your option, you are purchasing the stock for $50. The $5 that you paid for the call is added on to your basis for the stock, which means that for tax purposes your cost of the stock will be deemed to be $55 a share. In other words, when an option holder exercises his option, the cost of the option is added to the strike price to determine the tax cost of the stock. Now when you later sell the stock, you will subtract $55 from your net sales price to determine your profit, and that profit is treated as a capital gain. Thus, the capital gain of $10 that you could have made by selling the call is carried over onto the stock. One advantage of this is that the profit of $10 that you made from your call is not taxed when you exercise the call. Rather, the tax is postponed until you sell the stock later. And of course you control the timing of selling that stock. If you happen to be in a high tax bracket in the year when the option expires, it would be to your advantage, taxwise, to exercise the option and hold the stock until the next year. You could sell the stock in early January and you would have delayed paying the tax for a whole year. In addition, you may be in a lower bracket next year. Since short-term capital gains are taxed at your regular tax rate, this will result in a tax savings for you. And even if you are not in a lower tax bracket next year, remember the old slogan of many tax experts that a tax delayed is a tax not paid. At least you have the use of the money for another year.

Achieving Long-Term Capital Gain

But an even bigger advantage than postponement of paying the short-term capital gains tax is that by exercising the option you have the opportunity to convert your short-term gain into a long-term gain. As we noted, it is not possible to obtain a long-term capital gain from an option unless it is a LEAPS. But when you exercise the option to purchase stock, the gain from the option is transferred to the stock. You can easily hold the stock for one year and a day, thus achieving long-term capital gain treatment on the stock and enabling you to have your profit from the option taxed as long-term capital gain.

Let's follow up on our example. You originally bought a December 50 option for $5 in May. December comes around and you exercise your option when the stock is $65. Your cost basis for tax purposes is the $50 you paid for the stock on the exercise plus the $5 you paid for the option, making a tax cost of $55. Your purchase date of the stock for tax purposes is the day of exercise in December.

Note that the date of purchase of the option now becomes irrelevant. The IRS says that although it was the purchase of the option that gave you the right to buy the stock, and although you might feel as if you owned the stock since the value of your January 50 call was going up and down with the price of the stock, you did not actually own the stock until you exercised the call. Therefore, for purposes of determining whether you have held the stock long enough to qualify for long-term capital gains you are not allowed to add on the time during which you owned the option. The *price* you paid for the option may be added onto your purchase cost, but the *time* cannot be added onto the holding period of the stock.

You now own the stock with a cost of $55 and a purchase date of December. You hold the stock for one year and a day after your purchase date and sell the stock. If we assume that the stock is still at $65 then you will be taxed on your profit at the preferential long-term rates. Your profit will be your tax cost of $55 subtracted from your sale price of $65 or $10 of long-term capital gains. By exercising your option and holding the stock you acquired for one year and a day, you have converted a short-term gain into a long-term gain.

Disadvantages of Exercising and Holding

There are, however, two disadvantages to this that should be discussed. The first is that you are tying up a relatively large amount of capital for an entire year without necessarily expecting to increase your profit during that year. You would undoubtedly prefer to take that money out of the stock and put it into other options where it could be giving you higher leverage. Unfortunately the very essence of long-term capital gains is that you must hold the asset for over a year.

The second disadvantage, and one that is more important than freezing your capital, is that you now face the risk of a decline in the stock for an entire year. You may have thought that the stock would go up to $65, but now that it's there you may be properly afraid that it will go down, and you don't want to end up a loser. Fortunately, there is a partial solution to both these problems.

The answer is to write calls on the stock. The deeper in the money you write, the more downside protection you get. But you cannot write really deep-in-the-money calls because the IRS has ruled that to do so is to cancel your risk in owning the stock. It is the very basis of the favorable long-term capital gains tax rate that in order to benefit from it the taxpayer must bear the risk of loss in his capital asset. The less deep in the money, the more future time value you will be able to take in from writing the calls. Writing calls does not give you complete freedom from downside risk, but it does give you protection to the extent of the premium you take in, and in normal times that should be enough to protect you from typical market fluctuations in the price of the stock. So here is a way to give yourself some downside protection, and to make a profit on the money you have tied up.

Writing on-the-money covered calls does not affect your holding period, which will continue to run from the day you acquired the stock. If the stock goes up, roll up the calls whenever you see that they are getting down to their cash values, because you do not want to be exercised. If you are accidentally exercised, you should buy in new shares to deliver against the exercise, retaining your old shares so that when you do sell them you will get long-term tax treatment.

Thus, exercising a profitable call can have two distinct advantages to an option holder. First, he defers paying the capital gains tax, and second, he can convert a short-term gain into a long-term gain. Here's another tip: The earlier you exercise the sooner your one-year holding period on the stock will be over. So once you have decided that you definitely are going to exercise, you might just as well do it early and not bother to wait for the expiration date. This is true even if the option sells at a premium above its cash value. Since you are going to lose that excess anyway by waiting, you might just as well do it now and start the clock ticking on your one-year holding period. You will receive any gain from a subsequent price rise whenever you decide to exercise.

TAX CONSEQUENCES TO CALL WRITERS

Now let's go through a typical call-writing transaction and see how it is taxed. You sell an October 50 call on June 15 for $5. First of all, it is comforting to note that the $5 that you receive for the option is not taxed to you at the time of sale. This can be important where you sell an option in the final months of the year, and the call does not expire or you do not buy it back until the next year. So, initially, the money you receive is not considered income to you and you pay no taxes on it.

Let us assume that the price of the stock was below 50 when you sold the call, and never goes above 50, with the result that the option expires unexercised. At that date, for tax purposes, you have received a short-term capital gain of $5. The next question should be what if you had sold a LEAPS and were short for over a year and a day, would that be a long-term capital gain? The answer is no, because our Congress has decided that no matter how long you hold a short position in any security, it can never be taxed as a long-term capital gain. Apparently our elected officials in Washington don't believe that shorting a stock is really contributing to building up the wealth of our great country. What a pity. And this even applies to shorting a put, which of course is just as much a vote in favor of our capitalistic society as buying stock.

Now let's get back to our example. If you decided not to wait for the option to expire and decided to close out your position by purchasing an October 50 call in September for $1, you would have a short-term capital gain of $4 on that date.

That's relatively straightforward, and it does give the call writer the chance to do a little tax planning by deciding when he wants to take his profit. For example, if you are short some January calls that have depreciated greatly, giving you a good profit, you should consider whether you would like to have the profit in December of this year or wait to take it in January and be taxed next year. The decision involves weighing the advantage of postponing the tax for one year against whether you think that your tax bracket will be higher or lower next year. If you had big losses this year, then it might be prudent to offset them with your profit.

Tax Choices

If you have not made a profit in your call writing, and the option has gone up in value, you have a choice of actions. You can close out your position by purchasing the identical call. In this case the difference between your original selling price and your purchase price is a short-term loss, tax deductible at the time you closed out your position.

Or you can acquire the underlying stock (or use stock you already own) and deliver it when your call is exercised. When you deliver the shares, the premium that you originally received from writing the call is added on to the exercise price of the call to determine your gain or loss. If you already owned the stock, then the gain or loss on the stock is long-term or short-term depending on how long you owned the stock. The length of time you were short the option is irrelevant to this determination.

Let's follow this through with an actual case. You sell an April 60 call for $9. The stock goes up to $65 by the end of April and you decide to deliver the stock, rather than to buy a call and close out your position. If you are a covered call writer you may have purchased the stock over a year ago at $80. When you deliver the stock you receive the strike price of $60. Your tax position is that your cost basis is $80. The amount you received for the stock is the $60 you got upon delivery plus the $9 premium, which makes a total of $69. Subtracting this from your $80 cost results in a tax loss of $11. This is a capital loss, and it is long-term if you had held the underlying stock for over a year.

If, on the other hand, you had purchased the shares for just $45 a share, you would have a profit of $15 per share when the call was assigned to you at the strike price of $60, plus the $9 you received for the call, making a total profit of $24. This entire profit would be taxed as a capital gain, and if you had held the stock for more than one year when the call was exercised the entire gain would be taxed as long-term capital gain.

Note that you would qualify for long-term capital gain on the entire transaction even though you had sold the call less than one year before the exercise date. The legal theory behind this result is that the $9 you received when you sold the call is simply added on to the exercise price, giving you a sale price of $69. The cost of $45 when subtracted from your sale price of $69 gives you your tax profit of $24. And since you bought the shares of stock more than one year ago, the gain is taxed as long-term capital gain.

It is fairly easy to remember these rules because they are similar to the rules we discussed previously that apply to option purchasers. In the case of both the option purchaser and the option writer, the original price of the option is added to the exercise price to determine the tax gain or loss on the underlying stock. For the owner of a call, this means that the premium he paid is being added to his purchase cost of the stock. For the call writer it means that it is being added to the selling price. In both cases there is no tax on the gain or loss in the option itself. And in both cases the length of time you held or were short the option is irrelevant in determining whether you have long-term or short-term capital gains. In both cases the only determining fact is how long you held the stock.

It is possible to make money on a call and still be in the position where it may be exercised against you. If you sell a call that is in the money, and then the stock goes down but is still above the strike price, the call will be exercised and you will make a profit nevertheless. For example, let's say that when a stock was $258 you sold a 250 call on it for $20. If the stock stayed at $258, the call would be exercised against you. You would lose $8 from buying the stock at $258 and delivering it for $250. Since you originally sold the call for $20, your profit would be $12. Whether you buy back the call or deliver the shares your profit is capital gain. Note, however, that the type of capital gain—long-term or short-term—depends not on how long you have been short the call, but on how long you have owned the stock.

TAX CONSEQUENCES OF PUTS

Put Holder

A put is classified as a capital asset and therefore the purchase and sale of a put creates a capital gain or loss. The longest put (except for a LEAPS) is for nine months, and a capital asset must be held for one year and a day in order to qualify for long-term capital gains treatment. It is therefore obvious that all purchases and sales of regular puts result in short-term gain or loss. As with calls, if a put expires worthless, it is deemed to have been sold for zero on the expiration date.

The more complicated question arises when the put holder decides to exercise his put and sell the underlying stock at the exercise price. The rule is that the amount of money that the put owner originally paid for his put is subtracted from the exercise price to determine his sale price for tax purposes. As an example, suppose an investor owns 100 shares of XYZ which he purchased for $47 and he is worried that the market may tumble and carry his XYZ down with it. To protect himself he buys a July 45 put which, being out of the money, is reasonably priced at 1. Sure enough, by the time the July expiration date rolls around XYZ is down to $41 and our investor decides to exercise his put and get rid of the stock for $45 a share. What are the tax consequences?

First let's see what really happened. He bought the stock for $47 and sold it for $45 for a loss of $2, and in addition he paid $1 for the put, so he actually had a loss of $3. The correct tax analysis of the transactions is that he bought the stock for $47; then he sold it for $45 minus the $1 paid for the put for a sale price of $44. A cost of $47 minus a sale price of $44 gives a loss of $3, so the tax effect squares with what actually happened.

The big question now is whether the loss, or gain as the case might be, is long-term or short-term. And here things are not as simple as they were for calls, because of a rule that if you own stock that has not yet attained long-term status (i.e., you have not yet owned it for an entire year), then the moment you purchase a put in that stock you immediately cancel your entire holding period in that stock. Your holding period is frozen at zero until you no longer own the put. Once you sell the put, your holding period then starts at day one. Thus if the XYZ had been owned for at least a year when the put was acquired, the loss is long-term; otherwise it is short-term. To explain this more fully let's look at another example.

Assume you buy 100 shares of GM on January 15. On December 15, 11 months later, you have a very good profit on the stock and are afraid that the stock might start going back down. You decide to protect yourself by purchasing a January put with the intention of selling the stock on January 16, when it will be long-term. That is not going to work.

Killing Your Stock Holding Period. The minute you purchase that put, your holding period in the GM stock becomes zero days. And it stays at zero until you either sell the put or allow it to expire in January. The day after you no longer own the put your new holding period starts. So the moral of the story is don't ever buy a put to protect stock you have held for a number of months but that is not yet long-term gain. If you had already owned the GM stock for one year, there would be no problem. Then you can buy all the puts you want and you will not change the status of the GM stock back to short-term.

The reasoning behind this rule is that you are permitted to get favorable long-term capital gains rates only as a reward for being a capitalist and taking the risks thereof. When you buy a put you have acquired absolute insurance against any risk of loss in the stock (below the strike price of the put and minus whatever future time value you paid for the put). Since you are no longer taking the risks of being a capitalist, the tax law says that you are no longer entitled to the rewards.

The solution to this problem of protecting a gain in a stock before it goes long-term is very simple. Sell a call. Unless it is really deep in the money, the IRS will not argue that this cancels your holding period on the underlying stock because you are still basically at risk if the stock price collapses. And by selling a call rather than buying a put you might even make some money instead of spending some. But remember that you only have downside protection up to the amount of money you took in from selling the call.

The One Exception. There is one exception to the rule that the holding period of stock does not run when you own a put on that stock. If you purchase a put on the same day that you buy stock and notify your broker that you intend to use the stock to satisfy an exercise of the put, you are then said to have "married" the stock to the put. Under these circumstances, the holding period of the stock starts to run on the day you acquired it. Of course, if the price of the stock declines and you sell the put but hold on to the stock, then its holding period for you would start on the day that you sold the put and not when you originally bought the stock. If, on the other hand, the price of the stock is up, then you do not recognize any loss on the lapsed "married" put, but simply add its cost onto the tax basis of the stock. In this case you get the benefit of this "married" put exception, because your holding period for the stock starts on the day you buy the stock and the put.

Put Writer

A put writer realizes a short-term capital gain or loss on the sale and subsequent purchase of a put just like a call writer. His sale price is whatever he received for the put originally and his cost basis is what he pays to close out the position. If the put lapses his cost basis is zero.

When a put writer is assigned his option, he is purchasing 100 shares of stock per option at the strike price. He will have a capital gain or loss on that stock when he eventually sells it depending on the price he receives. The date of acquiring the stock will be the date he will use to determine whether it should be long-term or short-term. The amount he originally received for the put is subtracted from the exercise price to determine his cost basis in the stock. Thus, if a person sold a September 40 put for $3, and was assigned on the put, acquiring 100 shares for $40 each, he would subtract the $3 from the $40, giving him a tax cost for the stock of $37.

Note that as with calls, the rule for determining the basis of the stock involved in put exercises is the same whether you are the writer of the put or the holder. In both cases, with puts you subtract the original price of the put from the exercise price to determine the tax basis of the stock. For the put buyer, this means subtracting the option premium from his sales price. For the put writer, it means subtracting the put premium from his purchase price.

TAX CONSEQUENCES OF SPREADS AND STRADDLES

The rule for determining the tax consequences on spreads is the epitome of simplicity: There is no such thing as a spread for tax purposes. Each component of a spread is taxed as if it existed all by itself. The same rule holds true for a straddle or a combination. So to figure out the tax consequence of any of these, just look at each particular side of the spread and work out the tax consequences.

WASH SALE RULE ON STOCKS AND CALLS

We have seen that the purchase of a put when you owned the stock canceled out the incomplete running of the long-term period because you no longer had the risk of loss from the stock. A similar rule applies on the other side when you sell a stock and take a loss. Under normal circumstances the wash sale rule states that if you sell a stock and claim a capital loss on the sale, you cannot buy the same stock within 30 days of the sale. The question has arisen as to whether it would be possible to avoid this consequence by purchasing a call on the stock instead of the stock itself.

Unfortunately, the IRS has already thought of this, and there is no doubt that the purchase of a call on a stock made within 30 days of the sale of the same stock will cancel out the ability to take a long-term capital loss on the stock. The reasoning is quite correct in that if you want to claim the loss you must be willing to give up the chance of making a profit on the stock if it should go up immediately. This is more of a nuisance and a trap for the unwary than a real problem. Simply buy your call more than 30 days before you plan to sell the stock and make sure you buy a call with more than 60 days before expiration.

TAX STRATEGIES

There is wide opportunity to use options in conjunction with tax planning, especially in the area of timing. And when it comes to capital gains and losses timing can have an unusually significant impact. The reason is that the Internal Revenue Code provides a rather strange method of computing capital gains and losses.

To review basics for a minute, you recall that long-term capital gains are taxed at a maximum of 20%, whereas short-term gains are taxed at the regular rate. On the loss side, a short-term loss can be subtracted directly from ordinary income (up to the $3,000 limitation) whereas long-term losses reduce ordinary income only by 50% for each $1 of loss. Thus, you want to get long-term capital gains and short-term capital losses, and each of these is worth, for tax purposes, twice as much as short-term gains and long-term losses respectively.

They are obviously quite different animals and worth quite different amounts of taxes to you. But here is how the tax you pay is figured. First, combine all your short-term gains and losses. Second, combine all long-term gains and losses. So far so good. But then the law requires you to combine the net short-term gain or loss with the net long-term gain or loss. This is exactly like adding oranges and apples (which we all learned long ago that we could not do) and arriving at a total number of "fruits." But that is the way the law is.

Now if you were in the fruit business and "fruits" were selling for $2 a dozen, and it cost you 10 cents to buy an orange and 20 cents to buy an apple, you would be damn careful that the "fruit" you sold would be made up entirely of oranges. And when you bought a dozen apples at 20 cents you would be careful not to let them find their way into the "fruit" boxes, but you would carefully segregate them and sell them as apples at the much higher price they commanded on the market. So it should be with capital gains and losses.

Avoid Long-Term Losses

The following section applies primarily to taxpayers who have very large capital gains and losses and are willing to spend effort and money to improve their tax situation. If this is not you, then feel free to skip this part.

The astute taxpayer will realize that he wants to end up with either long-term capital gains, on which he pays the 20% tax rate, or short-term capital losses, which give him a full deduction from ordinary income (subject to the $3,000 annual limit). What he does not want is for his valuable long-term capital gains to be swallowed up by short-term capital losses. You also do not want to end up with long-term capital losses, since they are worth only 50% against ordinary income, but if you have short-term capital gains in the same year, they are worth a full dollar for dollar in offsetting them. What you do want is for your short-term capital gains to be used up by your long-term losses. By doing this you are saving yourself $1 of taxable income for every dollar you lost, and you are only using up a loss that would give you 50% if applied to ordinary income or to long-term gains.

Therefore, the objective ought to be to have one year in which you will have net long-term capital gains, and in that year you try to avoid realizing any short-term capital losses. In the next year you might decide to realize a large number of short-term capital losses, but not realize any long-term capital gains. It is in effectuating this type of strategy that options can provide a wide variety of assistance.

We have already discussed how the owner of a profitable option can defer gain by exercising, and how the writer of an option can do the same by being assigned. The holder or writer of January options can usually decide whether he wants to close out his positions in the end of December or wait until the next year, and certainly the holder of long-term stock can easily determine whether he wants to realize his gain or loss in this year or next year. With the protection that covered calls offer, there is no longer a compelling reason for selling this year if next year is better from the tax viewpoint.

Now that we understand the basic principles of taxation that apply to options, let's see some specific examples of strategies that can actually reduce your taxes.

How Covered Call Writers Can Increase Their Long-Term Gains

Since it is desirable to get the maximum gains as long-term capital gains and to realize losses as short-term losses, especially if you already have short-term gains, this tip could be useful to the covered writer who has seen his stock appreciate since he wrote his call. Suppose that you already have about $2,000 in short-term capital gains. You also have 1,000 shares of a stock that you bought for $18 a share on which you sold the 20 option for $2. The stock is now long-term and has risen to 24. Absent tax considerations, you would normally let the stock be called away, since this is the method of getting out of the position with the smallest commissions (just one stock commission at 20 instead of a stock commission at 24 and an option commission at 4) and you don't have to worry about paying an eighth more when you buy the option and getting an eighth less when you sell the stock.

But when you consider the tax ramifications, you might well decide to buy back your option and sell out the stock. Here's why: If you let the stock be called away, you have a tax basis of 18, and a selling price of 20 plus the $2 premium you originally received, making a tax selling price of $22, for a long-term capital gain of $4 a share or $4,000. If you are in the 39.6% tax bracket, your tax at long-term rates would be 20%, or $800. The tax on the $2,000 short-term gain you had from before would be at the 39.6% rate for $792. The total tax would be $1,592.

If, however, you decide to close out the position before exercise, look at how you can reduce the taxes. You sell the stock for $24 a share, and this gives you a long-term gain of $6,000. You then buy back your option for $4, and since you originally sold it for $2, you have a loss of $2 a share. This is a short-term capital loss of $2,000, and wipes out the other short-term capital gain of $2,000, which you already had. The result is that you have a net long-term capital gain of $6,000, on which you are paying 20%, for a total tax bill of $1,200. By simply closing out the position in a slightly different manner you have reduced your taxes by $392, or 24.6%. Pretty good when you consider that a saving of $392 in taxes is equal to making an extra $649 in salary or short-term capital gains when you're in the top tax bracket.

Deferring Capital Gains with Spreads

Despite the best of planning there may be years in which you find yourself with an excess of realized short-term capital gains. If you already happen to be in a high tax bracket that year, it would be beneficial if you could somehow defer those gains into the next year. Prior to 1977 it was common for sophisticated investors to use commodity straddles to roll over capital gains, but on May 23, 1977, the IRS issued Revenue Ruling 77-185, which said that if a commodity spread had no economic risk and no reasonable expectation of profit, it would be declared void for tax purposes. Since the reason commodity straddles were so favored for tax rollovers was the very fact that there was hardly any economic risk, this ruling has squelched investors from relying on them.

This ruling on its face does not apply to stock options, and more importantly, the ruling's reasoning does not apply to option spreads to the extent that there is a real economic risk in the spread and the chance of making a profit. Since one can lose one's entire investment in a calendar spread if the stock moves too far in either direction, and since calendar spreads are recognized in both the CBOE and the American Stock Exchange (AMEX) explanatory booklets as accepted methods of attempting to make a profit, it may be assumed that the IRS will not apply the reasoning of the commodity ruling to calendar spreads.

Now, just how does a calendar spread work to defer a capital gain? Before explaining how it does so we must note a limitation, and that is that options are not suitable for deferring long-term capital gains; they can defer only short-term gains. To defer short-term capital gains you pick a spread where the economic risk of the spread is small in relation to the volatility of the stock. The usual type of spread is a calendar spread, and generally it is done with deep-in-the-money options.

Although calendar spreads are the favorite for tax deferrals, any type of spread with a low debit or high credit will do. The second most popular is a deep-in-the-money bear spread or bull spread with calls. As opposed to calendar spreads, these are available only when the market has recently risen substantially. If it has not, then there will not be any deep-in-the-money options to use as the bottom of your bull or bear spread. And if the spread is not deep-in-the-money, then the debit will be too high to put on the spread, which will both reduce your leverage and increase the risk of a loss from a subsequent diminishing of the spread. The deep-in-the-money bear spread is the safest, because if the stock keeps on going up you will lose only a small amount, and if by some stroke of luck the stock plunges, you could make a lot of money. The big disadvantage of the bear spread is that the option that is the most deep in the money is the one you are short, and there is probably very little future time value left in it, which means that risk of an unwelcome exercise is very high.

The advantage of the bull spread is that you are long the really deep-in-the-money option, so you don't have to worry about premature exercise. The disadvantage is that while you will make a little bit of money if the stock goes up, if by some chance it should plunge down, you stand to lose a huge amount of money, and it would be very large indeed in relation to the amount you put up to do the spread.

Which Kind of Spread? The controlling factor in your decision of which type of spread to use should be the factors of unwelcome exercise, the risk of losing economically from a decrease in the spread, and finally and most important, the amount of money you have to put up to do the spread.

In order to reduce the cost of commissions, one usually takes high-priced options. Let us therefore study in more detail one such calendar spread. If the stock is currently at 280, and it is now October 1, the January 260 might be 22 and the April 260 might be 25. This means that for a cost of only 3 points, plus transaction costs, you could put on this calendar spread. Let us now assume that the stock rises 10 points by mid-December and the January 260 is at 31. This means that you have a loss of $900 on each January option. Of course, this loss is offset by the fact that your April option has probably gone up by about 9 points. To defer a capital gain of $900, you would buy in your January option for 31 in late December, thus realizing a short-term capital loss of $900.

This, however, leaves you long the April 260 option and you are now at risk the full $3,400 value of the April option. Since you don't wish to take the risk, you must immediately hedge this position by shorting another option. Generally the best one to use would be the April 280. Although this gives you only limited downside protection, you do not intend to hold on to the option very long. The point is that you have realized your capital loss in the present year, and by selling the April 280 you have continued with a hedged position.

As soon as next year comes, you close out your current position by selling the April 260 and buying in the April 280. Unless the stock has moved in the few days between when you closed out the January 260 option and when you closed out the position, you will have a short-term capital gain of about 9 points on your 260 option and no appreciable gain or loss on the 280. If the stock has moved up or down a few points it doesn't matter, because the additional tax gain on one is offset by the additional tax loss on the other. So you have created a short-term capital loss in the current year and a short-term gain in the following year. Thus, you have deferred or rolled over into the next year $900 of short-term capital gain.

What If the Stock Goes Down? We assumed just now that the stock went up 10 points. What would happen if the stock went down 10 points instead? Fortunately, we will achieve the same result. If the stock declines to 270, we can assume that the January 260 would be about 13 and the April about 16. Toward the end of December you would sell out your April 260 option for 16 and since you had purchased it for 25, you would realize a short-term capital loss of $900 per option.

At that point you would be naked the January 260 option, which you had shorted, and in addition to being at risk if the stock went back up, you would be faced with a very large margin call if you did not immediately hedge it with another long option. The obvious answer is to buy the July 260, which will probably cost you a few dollars more than you received for the April. Your position is now short the January 260 and long the July 260, which is still a nicely hedged calendar spread.

Comes the first of the next year, you simply close out both sides of your new calendar spread. If the stock has not moved appreciably since closing out the April position, you will realize a short-term capital gain of about $900 on the January option and no appreciable gain or loss on the July. If the stock does move, the net tax result is still the same. So, once again, you have realized a capital loss in the current year but have had to realize a capital gain in the next year. Thus, you have deferred the capital gain into the next year.

Now we have seen how you can defer the gain if the stock goes up and how you can defer it if the stock goes down. But what happens if the stock just stays at about the same price? Alas, that is the one soft spot in this method. If the stock just stays where it is, you cannot accomplish a rollover or deferral. For that reason it is important to select a number of stocks, since the chance of a number of stocks all staying at the same price is obviously much less than for just one stock.

Points to consider. Points to watch out for in using option spreads to defer capital gains are:

1. Commission costs can be quite high in proportion to what is being accomplished. Remember, in these examples there were six commissions in each one! And each time there was a commission you were buying on the offering price and selling on the bid, losing an eighth or a quarter. All those little fractions add up when you multiply them by six.

2. The obvious danger is if the stock doesn't move, in which case the tax deferral is not accomplished. The three ways to minimize this risk are to pick volatile stocks, pick a variety of stocks, and give yourself as much time as possible before the year-end in which the stock can move.

3. The spread can narrow, thus losing your money. It is for this very reason that the reasoning in the IRS's commodity straddle ruling does not apply to option spreads, but it is also a reason why this can be an expensive proposition. In these examples I have assumed that the spread remained the same, but in real life it will tend to increase as the stock declines toward the strike price and to decrease as the stock goes up away from the strike price. When you are going into the spread for only 3 points, a decline to a point and a half means that you are losing half your money on the spread decrease alone, before even considering the commissions.

4. Since we are using fairly deep-in-the-money options for the reason of keeping the spread low and thus increasing your leverage, there is always the risk of unwelcome exercise on the short option lurking in the background. After all, we are short a near-term, deep-in-the-money option, and these are the very ones that tend to be exercised before they mature. So that is something that should be given careful consideration before you put on your spread. Pay special attention to any ex-dividend dates that might occur before year-end, since this is a natural time for surprise exercises. One solution is to do your spread on the SPX, which has a European exercise system so that you cannot be assigned until the last day.

Once you are exercised on the short option the net tax effect is as if you had closed out that position. Thus, if the stock has moved up sharply and you are exercised, all is well, since when you buy in stock to deliver against the exercise you are realizing the short-term loss you had been striving for. But if the option is exercised after the stock has fallen, then you're in trouble, because this produces a short-term capital gain, just the opposite of what you want! Fortunately, the option is most likely to lose its future time value, and therefore most likely to be exercised when the stock moves up, and not when it moves down.

How to Prevent a Stock from Becoming Long-Term

As we learned here, it is the most advantageous to take short-term losses in years in which you do not have long-term gains, but it is usually better to have short-term losses than long-term losses. What can you do if you have a stock that has been a sheer disaster and is just about to turn into a long-term loss, but you don't want to sell it this year because short-term losses will be much more valuable to you next year? Thanks to the application of tax laws to options, there is a very simple technique by which one can literally keep the loss on a stock as a short-term loss in perpetuity.

As we mentioned in talking about getting long-term capital gains, one of the dangers there was that if you inadvertently owned a put on a stock, your entire holding period disappeared. Now here's an opportunity to use that rule to your advantage. Just when your depressed stock is about to go long-term you purchase a put on the stock, which you can then sell a few days later. Presto, change-o! On the day you acquire the put, your stock, which had a holding period of 363 days, now has a holding period of zero and you have another 365 days in which to realize a short-term capital loss! Marvelous. One only wishes that the same principle could be applied to human holding periods. I for one would be very happy to purchase a put on myself the day before my next birthday if that meant that the birthday would legitimately be postponed until the same date next year. Ponce de León, we have discovered your fountain of youth! (Well, at least for stocks.)

Appendix A

WEB SITES
FOR OPTIONS TRADERS

Nothing in recent history has come close to having the impact of the Internet in bringing options information right into the home or office of investors quickly and inexpensively. Whether you are looking for option prices in real time, stock market opinions, information on underlying stocks, charts of stocks, or stock indexes, it is all there plus more on the Internet. And it is generally right up to the minute or the last 20 minutes, and either free or at very low cost.

It is exactly because the Web has been so successful that it can be bewildering. Unless you know which web sites to turn to, you can easily get lost and not find the information you are looking for. In this appendix I describe the sites I have found to be the most useful for option traders.

Anyone who knows the Internet realizes that it is changing as fast as a cloud pattern in a storm, so by the time you read this, some of the sites I recommend may no longer exist. These were all active as this book went to print, and hopefully many even better ones have appeared since then.

GETTING OPTIONS PRICES

If you are going to make money with options, the first thing you have to know is what their prices are. Fortunately, there are a number of sites that have very good option chains. Using an option chain means that you only have to type in the symbol of the underlying stock or index, click the Go button, and the site will print out every single option that exists on that security. In most cases this even includes the LEAPS. The chain starts with the current month, with the lowest-priced call, or puts and calls together depending on the type of chain you select, and then moves up by strike price.

Before we get to specific prices, you will notice that many of the sites that are free give you current prices on indexes but only prices delayed by 20 minutes on individual stocks or options. Do not blame the Internet sites. This situation is the fault of the options and stock exchanges that claim they own the news of prices. They demand that everyone who gets current prices pay them a monthly fee for this privilege. Whatever happened to free speech in America? In any event, when you pay an exchange fee for real-time quotes it goes right to the exchanges, not the web site.

My favorite site for option chains is www.pcquote.com. Its complete option chain is easy to find right on the home page, includes all strike prices, puts and calls, and LEAPS. It is also good for individual options prices and stocks because you can submit up to 20 symbols at a time. Costs for real-time prices are quite reasonable.

You also might want to compare this site with its main competition, www.quote.com, which is quite similar.

Other stock and option price providers that are reasonably priced are eSignal at www.esignal.com (800-575-2574) which provides Internet delivered, real-time, continuously updating market quotes, chats, news, fundamental data, and so on. Free 30 day trial, then $150 per month (prepaid annual subscription), and myTrack at www.myTrack.com, which provides extensive free services and real-time quotes for $19.98 per month plus exchange fees.

STOCK MARKET INFORMATION

A good starting place for any financial search is www.yahoo.com. This site has quotes, latest headlines from Reuters, and information on stocks. All of these features can be customized so that it will display headlines on the subjects you are interested in (e.g., Stock Market, International News, Tennis), and will give last prices on the stocks that you have in your own portfolio. One section I use frequently as my first source for financial information on any stock is the profile section. You find it by getting a quote on a stock and then clicking on the small "profile" heading you will find. This gives a compact one-page fact-filled summary of a company, including a description of the company in a few paragraphs and useful facts such as price/earnings ratio and price/sales ratio, latest reported sales and earnings, total capitalization, stock chart, and much other useful information. That may be all you need to make a decision about a stock. If you want to know what Wall Street is thinking about a company, just go back to the original quote you got and click on the heading "research," which will tell you exactly how many analysts are recommending the stock and what they believe it will earn in the coming quarters.

Another good general financial site is www.moneycentral.com, which is run by Microsoft and NBC. The latest improvement to this site is that it gives out real-time stock quotes for free after you have registered for its "passport," which is just a number you get after you have registered. Its stock research is excellent for beginners because its Research Wizard takes you through all the questions a good analyst would ask—questions such as what is its earnings growth, what is its debt to equity ratio, and so on. It explains both the importance of the questions and what to look for in the answers. Then it gives you the answers for the stock you are researching. It also has many other financial services.

The site of the *Wall Street Journal*'s Magazine of Personal Business does a top-notch job at www.smartmoney.com. It has an easy-to-read format and excellent commentaries on the market. Features include your own personalized investment calendar and real-time quotes (if you register and give your e-mail address).

Another general financial site is www.quicken.com, which has an interesting service. If you register which stocks you are interested in, it will alert you to any stock splits, earnings reports, and upgrades and downgrades of the stock by analysts.

If you want still more detailed information on a company, you can get the company's home page from Yahoo! and try that. My preference, however, is to go to www.hoovers.com, which for free will give you more detailed information on any company, including a detailed breakdown of the financials for each of the past five quarters. For a small subscription fee the site will give you far more information than you probably want.

If you want more in the way of analysts' research reports, try www.multex.com, which has many free research reports from a number of major Wall Street firms and also has its own summaries of Wall Street opinions.

The site with the most detailed chart information is a real gem, www.wallstreetcity.com. It starts with free real-time quotes once you register, and then gives you analytic tools that you would expect to pay for. Examples are moving averages, very precise charts of stock and index prices for any period from one day to 10 years, Bollinger bands, momentum charts, and even a calculator that tells you if it pays to hold a security until it becomes a long-term capital gain, plus complete options prices.

Other general stock sites include www.stockpoint.com, which gives you the 10 most active stocks and biggest gainers and losers in addition to real-time quotes, and www.investing.lycos.com, which has streaming live charts.

OPINIONS ON STOCK AND INDEXES

There are a number of sites that give very good comments on stocks and the stock market as a whole. The cbs.marketwatch.com site (discussed in the next section) has many excellent columnists.

An outstanding site for commentary on stocks and the market is www.investools.com, which features 32 advisers who give their opinions and comments. The site issues 10 specific recommendations every Friday.

A very thorough and detailed commentary on the market, stocks, and sectors can be had at www.briefing.com. The site issues a comprehensive market comment three times a day, an excellent way to keep up with what's moving the market and what stocks are playing a big role.

One of the primary Internet advisory services is www.thestreet .com, which has lots of fearless comments and predictions and offers a free six-week trial subscription.

A service that gained a wide following when Internet stocks were flying is the Motley Fools at www.fool.com. They have an irreverent viewpoint, which is often entertaining, as well as informative. And make no mistake about it; these guys are definitely not fools.

The www.clearstation.com site has excellent charts and personal portfolios for keeping track of your positions, plus discussion groups.

OPTIONS ANALYSIS AND OPINIONS

There is no question in my mind that the best starting point for information about options is the Chicago Board Options Exchange (CBOE) at www.cboe.com. It is here that you can find the Options Calculator, which you can download or receive when you get CBOE's "Options Toolbox." The site also has volatility figures for all optionable stocks for the past month in the Market Statistics section.

These are required to find out the various answers from the options calculator.

One of the top options sites is www.optionstrategist.com by Lawrence G. McMillan who is the author of two best selling books on options, *Options as a Strategic Investment* and *McMillan on Options*.

This site includes a commentary of current option topics such as put-call ratios. Free services on the site include calculators for covered call writing and probability, volatility data, stock trigger e-mails, e-mail newsletter, and free trials of his products including his newsletter, The Options Strategist.

The www.ino.com site bills itself as "the largest and most comprehensive website for futures and options traders," and it has some features: real-time quotes, options chains that you can speed up by saying you only want options near the strike price, late-breaking news, easy links to options on futures, excellent "Power Charts," and its own Options Power Analyzer.

www.optionsnewsletter.com is a clear options site that specializes in covered call writing and gives you its top 30 covered calls every day.

www.optionadvisor.com is published by Bernie Schaeffer, who puts out the best-known newsletter on options. His web site gives a lot of options information for free while encouraging you to subscribe to his well-written newsletter.

www.optionsanalysis.com has all the tools any serious options trader could ask for. The web site of Optionetics, it gives for free an analysis of any option including all the Greeks (i.e., *delta*, *gamma*, *theta*, etc.), recommends top trades, and analyzes them with risk graphs, volatility, and profit probabilities.

www.optioninvester.com says it is the #1 options advisory service on the Internet. It costs $39.95 a month, but you can get a free two-week trial that is e-mailed to you three times a week.

NEWS THAT IMPACTS OPTIONS

One of the best all-around financial news sites is cbs.marketwatch.com. It has dozens of departments, columnists, and regular daily features plus frequently updated stories on the market as a whole as well as recent news on any stock you select. I find that it is best of all in posting recent news events on its headlines page. This is particularly helpful if you are just turning on your computer around 8:40 A.M. and there was a major government news release at 8:30 A.M. Click to the headline page and you will find all the essentials of the government's release. In fact, it generally takes the site only about five minutes to get the news out, which is far faster than the other sites I am familiar with. Because the headline page automatically updates every five minutes, you can just leave on that page to keep up-to-date. And if you want more information about the headlines concerning individual companies, just click on the headline and you will get the whole story.

www.cnnfn.com, the Internet site of the cable television network, does a very good job of covering financial news.

www.bloomberg.com is the Internet site of the top news supplier to brokerage firms and professional traders through Bloomberg terminals. The best thing about the site is that you can actually hear, and watch in slow motion, what is being broadcast on the Bloomberg cable television network. (You may need to download some software to do this, but it is free and doesn't take very long to do.) Being able to get this TV can be important since many cable operators do not offer Bloomberg TV, which does an excellent job of giving out a lot of information in a businesslike manner. This is often a welcome change from the chattiness of CNBC.

Most financial sites seem to close down after the last market story is filed around 5:00 P.M., but the Bloomberg web site is clearly a 24-hour operation. If you are waking up early, or going to bed around 11:00 P.M., and want to find out what's been happening in the Far East or European markets, Bloomberg is the place to go.

Last but definitely not least, once you have checked out all the web sites we've mentioned, take a look at www.cyberinvest.com, which is "The Investors' Guide to the Net." And it is the best at doing just that. It describes practically every one of these web sites plus many more, and does so in a very serious way, listing all the features of each site on a checklist chart so that you can make a meaningful comparison of features and cost. It's well worth a look.

Appendix B

STOCK AND OPTIONS BROKERS

Is there anyone alive who hasn't already had his or her fill of discount broker advertisements? Unfortunately, most of the ads are long on originality and short on some of the important facts. So here are some of the facts on the leading brokers. Keep in mind that rates can and do change overnight, so check them out. One of the great advantages of the Internet is that it's easy to surf, and you don't have to answer to a salesperson asking if he can help you.

As noted elsewhere in this book, rates on stocks have really come down. But who offers the lowest rates on options? Like many important questions in life, there is no one clear answer, for the reason that most option commissions have two parts: (1) a fixed price per order plus (2) a price per contract. So if you are doing a large number of contracts, the price per order isn't as important to you as if you are doing only two at a time. Also, many of the lowest rates are for online orders only and perhaps you would rather talk with a broker than type in an order. So here is a discussion of those rates that are among the lowest. You'll have to decide which is best for you.

Certainly among the lowest is a new Internet-only firm called www.interactivebrokers.com, which charges $1.95 per contract with no fixed charge per ticket and no minimum charge per ticket. This is an outstanding bargain for small orders. It also has a very simple rate for stocks, namely $1 per hundred shares. As mentioned, the firm appears to accept orders only over the Internet. The firm is a member of the Timber Hill Group, one of the largest institutional options traders and very highly regarded on the options exchange floors.

E*Trade at www.etrade.com is one of the major online firms. Its option commission is a ticket charge of $20 and then $1.75 per contract. Stocks are $19.95 per trade. It has its own high-speed trading services using its own electronic communications network and can provide customers with a large amount of market data.

Brown & Company at www.brownco.com charges an option commission of $15 per ticket plus $1.50 per contract for online market orders up to 30 contracts. For online limit orders and over 30 contracts the cost is $15 plus $1.75 per contract. Its online stock commission is among the lowest at just $5 for up to 5,000 shares for market orders, and $10 for up to 5,000 shares of limit orders. The firm also offers broker-assisted option orders at a still-reasonable $20 per order plus $1.75 per contract. Brown & Company is a subsidiary of Chase Manhattan Bank, so we don't have to worry about whether it's going to be around for a while.

The biggest online broker is Charles Schwab at www.schwab.com (800-225-8570). It was rated number one in customer satisfaction for online trading by J. D. Powers & Co. The basic stock commission for Schwab One accounts is $29.95 per 1,000 shares online. Option orders have a minimum commission of $39. The commission is figured on a chart that charges a fixed price per contract and an additional amount based on the premium of the option. For example, to trade 20 contracts with a premium of 4, you would be charged $29 plus 1.6% of the premium, which comes to $157. For Web trades, the maximum charge is $40 per trade for one or two contracts and an additional $4 for each additional contract thereafter.

The first firm I know of that offers totally free stock commissions is American Express Online Brokerage at www.americanexpress.com (800-297-7378), but you do need a fairly high account balance to qualify. If your account balance (the total value of your cash and securities including options) is at least $100,000, then all online stock trades are completely commission free. If your balance is between $25,000 and $99,999, then all your stock buy commissions are free and sell orders are $14.95 up to 3,000 shares. If your balance is less than $25,000, then each stock trade is $14.95. Options commissions are $40 per trade plus $2 per contract.

Another online stock broker with free commissions on Internet equity market orders of at least 100 shares is www.freetrade.com. Limit, stop, and odd-lot orders are $5.00. This is a subsidiary of Ameritrade designed for people who are already familiar with Internet trading. Unfortunately at the present time they do not handle any options orders. All communication with freetrade is by e-mail only.

Another major online firm is TD Waterhouse at www.waterhouse.com (800-934-4448), which has a stock commission of $12 for up to 5,000 shares. Option commissions are shown on a chart. Examples are: 12 contracts at $2 is $29.25, and 50 at $3.50 is $179.78. The firm provides various kinds of free research.

One of the lowest stock commissions is charged by Firstrade (www.firstrade.com), which charges $6.95 for online market orders and $9.95 for online limit orders with no extra charges for postage, handling fees, or other hidden charges. Options online or by touch-tone phone are $20 per trade plus $1.75 per contract with a minimum charge per order of $28.75.

If you want to find out what people think about a particular brokerage before you open an account with it, you can click on to Gomez Advisor's Internet Broker Scoreboard at www.gomez.com. There you'll find ratings on just about every online brokerage and detailed comments on many of them.

Appendix C

COMPUTER SOFTWARE PROGRAMS

More and more option analytical tools are becoming available for free on the Internet, but for the time being if you want a really complete service you have to buy a software program. These programs can tell you the volatility of the underlying stock or index, the implied volatility of the option you are considering, the delta, theta, and vega of the option you are considering, what will happen to the option if the stock goes up or down by a certain amount and what will happen with the passage of time. It will do this for individual options, covered writes, and spreads of all types. Some of them will pick out the best covered writes, the cheapest options, the options most likely to make money, the best naked option writes, and so forth.

In short, these programs can make anyone into an expert on options. Just remember that no matter how much you know about an option and its underlying security, the success or failure of any option trade depends upon the subsequent movement of the stock. That is something that is unpredictable, regardless of the amount of information anyone knows.

The first computer program everyone should acquire and use is "The Options Toolbox" published by the Chicago Board Options Exchange. It covers equity options, index options, and LEAPS. Its Options Calculator lets you type in the elements of any option such as expiration date, strike price, and volatility of underlying security, and it will calculate for you the theoretical value of the option, and give you its delta, theta, and gamma. It also contains the options disclosure document, and definitions of all these terms. In addition to all of this, the reason I can recommend it with so much assurance is that the price is right. The CBOE will send you this very useful software for free, and you can get it either by calling the CBOE at 800-OPTIONS or going to the Internet site at www.cboe.com. You can either download it or get it on CD-ROM.

If you are going to be doing a lot of options calculations you will want to move up to the next step, which is getting a system that can get its information as to prices and volatility online. Here are three options programs listed in order of ascending price.

The Option Expert by AIQ searches out the best trades, lists most overpriced options, and gives likely outcomes and results of time. It is available with the quote provider myTrack for $39 a month with end-of-day prices or $59 a month with real-time quotes, plus exchange fees. There is a $61 trial offer with myTrack free for the month. You can find them at www.aiq.com or by phone at 800-332-2999.

OptionVue5 for Windows has a free demo version on its Internet site www.optionvue.com. It also has a fully functional program available for a one-month trial at $49 plus shipping of $10 that includes free quote service and can be applied to the purchase price. The program includes a free training video, DataVue, OpScan, and a free weekly background data base. The price is $995.

OptionStation 2000i by Omega Research has a large variety of options analysis software. It also has an extensive back-testing program. This means that if you come up with a strategy, you can plug it into this program and they will be able to run it over the past number of months or years and tell you how much money you would have made or lost. The program also features an "intuitive wizard" that guides you through the process of finding the most profitable option position. The program is $2,399.40 payable over 12 monthly installments and with a 30-day money back guarantee when you buy it. They are at www.omegaresearch.com or 800-328-1267, extension 6006.

Since the success of any options program is dependent on the price movement of the underlying security, options traders are naturally also interested in any program that can give some help with the underlyings. One that can produce virtually any kind of analysis you can dream of is Metastock by Equis International, Inc. From moving averages of all durations to Bollinger bands to stochastics to comparisons of various stock patterns, Metastock can do it. They also have

Option Scope to analyze options. To help you forecast stock prices, you can enter up to 100 of the indicators that you believe lead the market. Prices start at $395 for an end-of-day price version and go on up for real-time versions. You can contact them at www.equis.com or 800-882-3040.

Appendix D

THE ANSBACHER INDEX

The Ansbacher Index is an indicator of the bullish or bearish sentiment of options traders which can be useful in forecasting the future direction of the stock market. This sentiment is measured by comparing the price of a put approximately 40 points below the current price of the Standard & Poor's 100 index (OEX) with the price of a call the same amount above the OEX. The price of the call is then divided by the price of the put to obtain the current Ansbacher Index.

HOW IT WORKS

A 1.00 reading of the Index is the theoretical neutral. In practice, perhaps because so many owners of stock are natural buyers of puts to hedge their positions, neutral appears to be between 70 and 90. A figure less than 0.70 is regarded as bullish for the stock market, with the Index becoming more bullish as the number decreases. An Index of over 0.90 is bearish, with the Index becoming more bearish as it moves higher.

The relevance of the Index to future moves in the stock market is based on the contrarian theory that when most people are bullish, the stock market is likely to go down, and when they are bearish it is likely to go up. This is ascribed to the fact that when a person is really bullish, he has already bought all the stock and calls he or she is likely to buy, and therefore there is not much more the person can do to cause the market to rally. If, however, the market goes down, there is a lot of selling the investor will probably do, which will intensify the downturn. The reverse is true when a person is really bearish.

In The Ansbacher Index, the higher the price of the put that is compared to the price of the call, the lower the Index will be. For example, if a put were 2 and the call were 1, the Index would be 0.5. If the put and call were equal, the Index would be 1.0, and if the put were 1 and the call 2, the Index would be 2. Thus, the more people are willing to pay for puts, which is a way of indicating that they are bearish, the lower the Index will be, and based on the contrarian theory, the more bullish the Index is.

CALCULATING THE INDEX

To calculate the Index, one starts with the current price of the OEX. Then one goes down approximately 40 points to the put with a strike price at that level. Then go up the same amount from the OEX and find the price of the call there. Next, divide the price of the put into the price of the call. The options that have between three and seven weeks left until their expiration are the ones that are used.

Here is a simplified example: OEX is 800. Going down 40 points we come to the 760 put, which is $2^{1}/_{8}$. Going up 40 points from 800 we come to the 840 call, which is $1^{3}/_{4}$. All fractions must be converted to decimals: $2^{1}/_{8} = 2.125$; $1^{3}/_{4} = 1.75$. We then divide 1.75 by 2.125, obtaining 0.82, which is within the neutral band.

In an actual example, the OEX is unlikely to be exactly 40 points away from a strike price, which requires another step. Let's assume that the OEX is 801.50, and that the 760 put is still $2^{1}/_{8}$, that the 840 call is now 2, and that the 845 call is $1^{1}/_{8}$. By going down 40 points from the OEX we arrive at 761.5, which is not the strike price of any put. But it is nearest to the 760 put, so we will use that put at $2^{1}/_{8}$. But note that we had to come down 1.5 points to get there. Now, when we want to find the appropriate call, we must add the same amount to the OEX as we subtracted to get to the put. In other words, to keep the Index accurate, we must go exactly as far up for the call as we went down for the put.

Adding 41.5 to 801.50 gives us 843. Of course there is no 843 strike price call. What we must now do is to compute what the price would be if there were such a call. We do this by taking the appropriate average of the actual calls that are above and below this figure. Here the 840 call is 2, and the 845 call is $1^{1}/_{8}$ (1.125).

To calculate the approximate value of an 843 call, we subtract the difference between the two prices, here 2 minus 1.125 equals 0.875. Then divide this by 5, which gives 0.175. This is the average change in the price of the call for each 1 point change in the call's strike price. This figure is then multiplied by the amount by which our theoretical strike price is above the strike price of the lower call. Here we are looking for an 843 theoretical strike price, and the lower call is an 840, so the difference is 3. Multiply 3 by 0.175, which gives 0.525. This is then subtracted from the price of the lower call. Here that is 2 minus 0.525, which equals 1.475. This is the price of a call with a theoretical strike price of 843, which is exactly the same amount above the OEX as the 760 put was below it.

Now we can find The Ansbacher Index by dividing the price of the theoretical 843 call, 1.475, by the price of the 860 put, 2.125: 1.475 divided by 2.125 equals 0.69, which is just slightly bullish.

ROLLING OUT TO THE NEXT MONTH

One problem that arises if one keeps a record of the Index week after week is that the number of weeks left in the options' life has an impact on the result. The nearer-term options are likely to be more extreme in their reading, whether they are bullish or bearish, whereas the further out readings will be closer to neutral. Therefore, when one moves out from one month to the next, there is likely to be a large change in the Index.

In order to smooth this out, we must constantly take readings further out each week. Here's how this is done: Let's assume that we are seven weeks away from an expiration date, and we are using January options. The following week, instead of using only January options, we compute the Index using both the January and February options. Then we combine the two numbers, giving a 75% weight to the January figure, and bringing in the February figure with a 25% weighting. The following week, we decrease the weighting of the shorter term options by 25% to 50% and we increase the weighting of the further out option by 25% to 50%. This continues each week, so that the next week the January is weighted only 25% and the February is weighted 75%.

This method of constant forward rolling reduces the large changes that occur when one month is used for four weeks and then scrapped for the next month. Once a quarter there is no change, to allow for the fact that there are 52 weeks in the year rather than 48.

Appendix E

MANAGED OPTIONS INVESTMENT PROGRAMS

Even when you have finished reading this book and you understand fully the many different strategies described here, you may not want to manage your own account. There may be many valid reasons for this, such as a daytime occupation that does not permit you to spend the necessary time for real-time investing, or just lack of time to handle all the day-to-day details of managing money. In any event, there are professionals who are willing to undertake the management of your money using a predefined options strategy. Here are three of them with very different options strategies.

Ronald M. Berman, a managing director of Bear, Stearns in the New York office, has been managing discretionary accounts devoted to covered call writing for many years. He selects the stocks, writes the options, and then rolls them up or out as the market requires. Because he is a broker rather than a money manager there are no management fees, just the regular stock and options commissions. His phone is 212-272-2677, e-mail is rberman@bear.com, or you can write him at Bear, Stearns, 245 Park Avenue, New York, New York 10167.

One manager who has been successful in trading LEAPS is Del-Ray Capital Corporation of Florida. Because LEAPS have a much lower rate of time decay than regular options, this firm believes that LEAPS can make a good substitute for stocks while providing added leverage and limiting the possible loss per share. The firm couldn't resist the theme, "Investment strategies that are quantum LEAPS ahead." For more information phone 561-499-0411, fax 561-498-1193, or go to the web site www.leapsfunds.com.

And last but not least, the author of this book manages options accounts through his firm, Ansbacher Investment Management, Inc. based in New York City. We have been doing this for 10 years using the strategy of writing uncovered options on the S&P 500 stock index. The options are actually written in the futures market where the margin rate is lower. At press time we had over $30 million under management. For more information visit our web site at www.ansbacherusa.com. You can phone us at 212-332-3280, fax us at 212-332-3283, e-mail us at maxans@banet.net, or write to us at 45 Rockefeller Plaza, Suite 2003, New York, New York 10111.

Appendix F

PUT-CALL EQUIVALENCY TABLE

This table shows positions that are theoretically identical. These equivalencies will not necessarily produce identical prices because of the different interest costs involved in (1) putting up the money to buy stocks, (2) providing the margin requirements to be short options, which can be done with interest-paying Treasury bills, and (3) the dividends that are received by owning stock and must be paid to be short stock. Nevertheless, these equivalencies are valuable in determining if substantially the same objective can be accomplished in a more advantageous manner.

Long 1 call	= Long 1 put and long 100 shares of stock
Long 1 put	= Long 1 call and short 100 shares
Long 100 shares and short 1 call (covered writing position)	= Short 1 put
Short 100 shares and short 1 put	= Short 1 call
Long 1 put and long 1 call (long a straddle)	= Short 100 shares and long 2 calls
	or
	= Long 100 shares and long 2 puts
Short 1 call and short 1 put (short one straddle)	= Long 100 shares and short 2 calls
	or
	= Short 100 shares and short 2 puts
Long 1 straddle and short 100 shares	= Short 200 shares and long 2 calls
	or
	= Long 2 puts
Long 1 straddle and long 100 shares	= Long 2 calls
	or
	= Long 200 shares and long 2 puts

Short 1 straddle and short 100 shares	= Short 2 calls
	or
	= Short 200 shares and short 2 puts
Short 1 straddle and long 100 shares	= Long 200 shares and short 2 calls
	or
	= Short 2 puts

Appendix G

OPTION SYMBOLS

If you want to get current option prices from the Internet, you can ask for a quote on the entire chain of options. But it may be quicker if you only want to get a quote on one particular option to request only that one. In that case you will need to know the symbol of the option you want.

Option symbols start with a symbol for the underlying security. These are obtainable from the symbol directories available on most quote sites. Note that most listed stocks use the stock symbol for options, but all Nasdaq stocks have a special three-letter option symbol, and many stocks with a lot of strike prices have more than one option symbol depending on which strike price you want. The best way to find out which symbol is correct is to go to an option chain. Then you type in the symbol for the month of expiration, which depends on whether the option is a put or call, and last you type in the symbol for the strike price. Thus, a Ford July 50 call is FGJ, a GM October 60 put is GMVL.

Expiration Month Symbols

	Call	Put		Call	Put
January	A	M	July	G	S
February	B	N	August	H	T
March	C	O	September	I	U
April	D	P	October	J	V
May	E	Q	November	K	W
June	F	R	December	L	X

Strike Price Symbols

5	A	40	H	75	O
10, 110, 210	B	45	I	80	P
15	C	50	J	85	Q
20	D	55	K	90	R
25	E	60	L	95	S
30	F	65	M	100	T
35	G	70	N		

The symbols are repeated every 100 points so that 120 is D and 200 is T. The 55, 65, 75, 85, and 95 strike prices are not used on many stocks.

Appendix H

STOCK COMMISSION SCHEDULE IN CENTS PER SHARE

Based on official NYSE minimum commissions in effect April 30, 1975, these cents per share rates still form the basis of the commissions at most full-service brokerage firms. This schedule will allow you to determine whether your full-service firm is really giving you the stock commission discount you have negotiated with it.

Stock Price	Number of Shares								
	100	200	300	400	500	700	1,000	1,500	2,000
$1	10.0	10.0	10.0	10.0	10.0	10.0	10.0	8.8	8.2
2	12.4	12.4	12.4	12.4	12.4	12.3	11.6	10.2	9.4
3	14.7	14.7	14.7	14.7	14.6	13.8	13.0	11.3	10.9
4	17.1	17.1	17.1	16.9	16.2	15.1	14.0	12.9	12.0
5	19.5	19.5	19.5	18.4	17.7	16.2	15.1	14.0	13.2
6	21.9	21.9	21.1	20.0	18.8	17.3	16.9	15.2	14.3
7	24.2	24.2	22.7	21.1	19.8	18.3	18.0	16.3	15.4
8	26.6	26.6	24.2	22.2	20.9	20.3	19.1	17.4	16.5
9	28.2	28.2	25.5	23.3	22.0	21.4	20.2	18.5	17.6
10	29.7	29.7	26.5	24.4	23.1	22.5	21.4	19.6	18.8
15	37.4	36.2	31.9	31.0	29.7	28.1	26.9	24.6	22.5
20	45.1	41.6	38.9	36.6	35.3	33.7	32.5	28.3	25.0
25	52.9	46.9	44.5	42.2	40.9	39.3	36.3	30.8	27.4
30	58.2	54.6	50.1	47.8	46.4	44.4	40.0	33.3	29.9
35	63.6	60.2	55.7	53.4	52.0	48.1	42.5	35.8	32.4
40	68.9	65.8	61.3	59.0	57.6	51.8	45.0	38.3	34.9
45	74.3	71.4	66.9	64.6	61.4	55.0	47.4	40.7	37.4

50	79.6	77.0	72.4	70.2	65.1	57.5	49.9	43.2	39.9
60	80.7	80.7	80.7	77.6	72.5	62.5	54.9	48.2	44.8
61									
62	80.7	80.7	80.7	80.7	77.5	67.4	59.9	53.2	49.8
80	80.7	80.7	80.7	80.7	80.7	72.4	64.8	58.1	54.8
90	80.7	80.7	80.7	80.7	80.7	77.4	69.8	63.1	59.7
100	80.7	80.7	80.7	80.7	80. 7	80.7	74.8	68.1	64.7
125	80.7	80.7	80.7	80.7	80.7	80.7	80.7	80.5	77.1
140	80.7	80.7	80.7	80.7	80.7	80.7	80.7	80.7	80.7

Appendix I

WORKSHEET FOR COMPUTING RETURN ON INVESTMENT FROM COVERED OPTION WRITING
on a Cash Basis and on a Margin Basis

I. Cash Required for Position

Cost of stock per share	$ _____	
Multiplied by number of shares	× _____	
Cost of stock	$ _____	
Plus commissions on stock purchase	+$ _____	
NET COST OF STOCK	$ _____	①
If using margin, multiply by 50%	× .5	
CASH REQUIRED TO PURCHASE STOCK	$ _____	①M

Price of option sold	$ _____	
Multiplied by number of options	× _____	
Amount received from options	$ _____	
Subtract commissions on sale of options	−$ _____	
NET PROCEEDS FROM OPTIONS	$ _____	②
From (1) or (1M) stock cash		
requirement	① or ①M $ _____	
Subtract (2) net proceeds from		
options	②−$ _____	
Cash requirement for position	$ _____	③

II. Changes during Position

Indicated quarterly dividend per share	$ _____	
Multiply by number of shares	× _____	

To get total dividend per quarter $ _____

Multiply by number of dividends
   expected during life of option   × _____
     TOTAL DIVIDENDS EXPECTED $ _____ ④

If stock is purchased on margin, enter here
  ⑴ⓜ Cash required to purchase stock   ⑴ⓜ $ _____
    (Use this only as long as the margin
      requirement is 50%. If it is not,
      then multiply net cost of stock by
      whatever percentage the brokerage
      firm is lending to you.)

Multiply by current margin interest rate   × _____ %

To get the annual interest charge on
   your debit $ _____

Divide by 365   ÷ _____ 365

   To get daily interest cost $ _____

Multiply by number of days to
   option's expiration   × _____

   To get total interest cost $ _____ ⑤

Enter ④ , total dividends expected   ④ _____

Subtract ⑤ , total interest cost   ⑤− _____

To get NET CHANGE IN POSITION
   DURING DURATION (+) or (−) $ _____ ④ⓜ

III. Proceeds from Closing Out the Position

A. If stock is called away
   Exercise price of option $ _____
   Multiply by number of shares   × _____
   To get gross proceeds $ _____
   Subtract commission on sale of
     stock at strike price   −$ _____
   To get NET PROCEEDS FROM POSITION $ _____ ⑥
   If purchased on margin, subtract
     amount originally borrowed from
     brokerage firm   −$ _____
   To get NET PROCEEDS FROM POSITION $ _____ ⑥ⓜ

B. If writing out-of-the-money options,
   and you assume that the stock price
   rwill emain unchanged and you will
   sell the stock at expiration
   Enter original cost of stock per share $ _____

Multiply by number of shares	$\times$	
To get gross proceeds from sale	$ _____	
Subtract commissions on sale	$-$\$ _____	
To get NET PROCEEDS FROM POSITION	$ _____	⑥
If stock was purchased on margin, subtract amount originally borrowed from brokerage firm	$-$\$ _____	
To get NET PROCEEDS FROM POSITION	$ _____	⑥ᴍ

IV. Computing Return on Investment

Enter ⑥ or ⑥ᴍ net proceeds from position	⑥ or ⑥ᴍ	\$ _____
Add or subtract ④ or ④ᴍ , net change in position during duration	④ or ④ᴍ	$+$ or $-$ \$ _____
To get total revenue from position		\$ _____
Subtract ③, cash requirement for position		$-$\$ _____
To get PROFIT ON POSITION		\$ _____
Divide this by ③, cash requirement		$\div$\$ _____
To get percentage return on investment		_____ %
To annualize this, multiply by 365		$\times$ ___365___
And divide by number of days until expiration of option		$\div$ _____
To get ANNUALIZED RETURN ON INVESTMENT		_____ %

Appendix J

THE 10 BIGGEST OPTIONS MISTAKES

So much intense thought and effort go into the planning and execution of option strategies that it is a tragedy that ignoring a few very simple principles later ruins many of them. To help you avoid these pitfalls I have decided to list 10 of the most common mistakes.

Making one of these mistakes is like planning out a picnic down to the last detail including the thermos, antibug spray, napkins, charcoal lighter fluid, cooking equipment, ketchup, pickles, and relish and then not getting to the picnic because you run out of gas when you are halfway there. These mistakes are just as easy to avoid, and unfortunately, they are just as expensive as situations that are far more difficult to avoid. Like running out of gas, once they have occurred it is often too late to go back and do much about them. So that you can prevent them in advance, they are listed here:

1. *Putting on one side of a position now, and planning to do the other side later when the stock moves in the right direction.* Every day I hear investors say that a certain stock looks like a good covered writing candidate, but since there just isn't quite enough money in the call to make it worthwhile, they will buy the stock now, wait until it goes up a couple of points, and then they will sell the option when it has increased substantially. The problem with this is that the only reason a person sells a covered option in the first place is to make a profit in case the stock does not go up. If you know that a stock is going to go up, then you don't need to write covered calls at all. You can make a fortune by simply buying calls on those stocks. If you buy the stock now without writing the option, what happens if the stock goes down? Then you have lost money on the stock without the offsetting profit from the option. In short, just when you need the protection of the option, you don't have it. If you want to buy stock without writing an option, no one is going to stop you. But don't think that you are doing it as part of a covered option writing program. Unless you buy the stock and sell the option simultaneously you are not engaged in covered writing, you are simply buying stock. And if the stock goes down, you get stuck with the loss.

2. *Failing to close out a time spread when the near-term option expires.* In a time spread one buys a long-term option and sells the short-term option on the same stock usually at the same strike price. The positions are put on simultaneously and should be taken off simultaneously. But so often when the near-term option expires the remaining longer-term option is not worth what the owner believes it should be worth. The temptation is very strong to wait just a little while in the hope that the option will go up in price. But what is really happening is that what started out as a hedged position, with some downside protection, has been transformed into a very speculative unhedged position with no downside protection at all. And it is worth noting that there is no more chance of the stock going up in the next few days than there was that it would go up in the previous weeks when the spread was in existence. Unless it was part of your original plan to continue owning the long option, have the discipline to take a small loss by closing out the long position when the near-term option expires. If your calendar spread did not work out, have the maturity to accept that. They don't all work, but it is better to take a small loss now than to watch the option remaining dwindle down to nothing, as thousands have done.

3. *Calculating your return from covered writing without including all the costs.* Like every other security transaction, writing covered calls against stock involves transaction costs, such as commissions, fees, and perhaps margin interest costs. But unlike most other types of investments, the amount of profit that can be derived from covered writing is strictly limited from the beginning. This is especially true in the case of in-the-money covered writing, where the potential profit is usually limited to a very small profit relative to the amount of money involved. For example, a stock may be purchased for $22 and the 20 strike price option written for $3. Since this gives a gross spread of $1, at a quick glance it would appear as if this gives a return of 5.2% when buying the stock for cash (22 minus 3 gives a net cost of 19; $1 divided by 19 equals 5.2%) or 12.5% when buying the stock on margin ($22 times cash required of 50% equals $11; minus $3 means a cash requirement of $8 to do the trade; gross profit of $1 divided by $8 equals 12.5%). If this option had four months to run before expiration, the annualized rates of return would appear to be 15.6% and 37.5%, which are certainly well worth your while.

But look at what an enormous difference the "little" transaction expenses make. Let's assume that you are doing 200 shares against two options. Using the old minimum commissions, the commission to buy 200 shares of stock at 22 is 43.74 cents a share, and the commission to sell two options at $3 is $15.90 per option. If we assume that the stock is called away when the option expires, we are saved the commission on buying back the option, but there is the commission on selling 200 shares at 20, which is 41.6 cents a share. Adding up these costs gives $1.01 per share. Of course, the costs with a discount broker will be far less, and even a full-service brokerage firm probably will give you a discount from these rates. Still, you will almost certainly be paying some commissions, so the point of this section still bears attention.

With a maximum gross profit of $1, we find that with the commissions we used, the actual profit is a guaranteed loss of one cent per share! For the margin transaction one must also subtract the anticipated interest charges on the margin debit, although we can add any anticipated dividends. The lesson should be clear: The "little" transaction expenses cannot be ignored! They are an integral part of the transaction and will always have a profound effect on your return. Don't try to estimate them. You are talking about your money and it is well worth a few minutes of your time to find out just how much you will actually be earning. See Appendix I for a complete worksheet showing how to calculate the return.

4. *Failing to establish profit goals on long options.* If we were in a perpetual bull market there would be no need to establish goals for options purchased. Every option would simply be held until expiration because it would become worth more and more every day. But in the real world in which we are now living stocks tend to go up and down and option prices with them. The only rational way to deal with this phenomenon is to set a goal, and when the option reaches this goal, to sell it. Some investors will haggle over $1/16$ of a point when they buy an option, but when it comes to selling it they can't decide whether to try for 4 points or 6. Decide in advance what you want to do and then stick to that. And you don't have to have an all-or-nothing approach. There is nothing wrong, for example, in deciding to sell half your position if the option doubles, thus getting back your entire initial investment, and then letting the rest run. But at least you have some plan, instead of just drifting aimlessly and always telling yourself that you will sell as soon as the stock goes 3 points higher.

5. *Being too bullish on the market.* Probably it is natural that investors who are used to buying stocks in the expectation that they will go up have a bullish outlook on the market. But by using puts and with all the possibilities for selling naked calls and putting on bear spreads, there is no reason option traders should not take a more neutral view of the market.

No matter what one's fundamental view is of the market, such long-term views may not have much effect on the very short time span encompassed by the usual option trade. Therefore, short-term trends are frequently independent of long-term fundamentals. They are called countertrend moves. Unless you are a confirmed chartist or other technician, this means that over the short term the odds are the same that at times the market will go down or stay still as that it will go up. The conclusion to be drawn from this is that in addition to buying calls, speculators should be careful to include some underpriced puts in their portfolios and give consideration to bear spreads. A trader who puts all his trading money into one side of the market is likely to have no trading money if he is wrong. With the enormous profit possible from trading in options, there is no reason why some of it shouldn't be put into the other side of the market.

6. *Using covered call writing without providing some absolute downside protection.* Covered call writing is an excellent method of making a relatively small amount of money with a large degree of assurance that you will make that money. Especially if one writes in-the-money options, one can make a profit even if the stock declines by a moderate amount, such as 10%. The only way in which one cannot make money is if the stock declines by more than that amount.

The inherent danger in covered call writing is that one makes only a limited small profit no matter how great the stock performance is, but one can lose an almost unlimited amount of money if the stock goes down far enough. When one considers this basic premise of how covered option writing works, it follows as the night the day that one really bad collapse in a position can more than wipe out all the profit in six other positions. I remember well a broker who was making a very good profit for his customers in many different covered writing positions, until he decided that a hot stock then selling at 43 was an ideal addition to his customers' portfolios. It was highly recommended by an analyst in his firm's research department. After he had put most of his customers into the stock, it proceeded to go down from 43 to 40, then to 35 and on down to 30. At each stage of its decline the broker called the analyst who told him that all was well at the company, and that he should just hang in there for the inevitable rally back up to 45. The stock went down to 20 and the analyst left the firm. Many of the broker's customers had bought the stock on margin, and found their entire equity in that position completely obliterated. The result was that years of profitable investments became a disaster—all because of one stock.

So when you can make only a relatively small profit from a position, but you have the potential to have a large loss, you are playing with unfair odds.

The successful option writer modifies these odds to his favor by changing the rules of the game. He creates a situation in which, since he can make only a limited profit, he can also lose only a limited amount. One way to accomplish this is to place a stop-loss order to sell out the stock when it has declined to a predetermined price. This order can be entered on a good till canceled basis from the time that the covered writing position is begun.

Once that order is in you have done the best you can to limit your loss. There is no assurance that you will be able to sell the stock at the stop-loss price, because prices can gap down right through your limit, and you will sell at the next trade price, however low that may be. Nevertheless this is about the closest you can come to limiting your loss. You could also buy a put, but that tends to drain most of the profit out of the trade. If the stop-loss order ever goes off, then you should immediately buy in your outstanding option at the market price. When you close out the position by other means, remember to cancel your good till canceled order to sell the stock.

In summary, the Achilles' heel in covered option writing is that you can sustain a very substantial loss when the stock goes into a nosedive. With the limited profit potential inherent in covered writing, you simply cannot afford such a large loss. The covered option writer who wishfully hopes that his favorite stock will come back up to its original price so that he can recoup his paper loss is very likely to be disappointed. You should not let yourself be one of the people making this mistake, when overcoming it is so easy.

7. *Expecting an unrealistic profit from options.* Perhaps nothing is so important in any aspect of life as knowing what to expect. If a recent college graduate expects that his first job will be as a senior executive with responsibility for a $700 million division and a salary of $250,000 a year, he is doomed to disappointment. But even more important is that he will be so misguided by his false expectations that he will decline excellent job opportunities that could lead to such a job in the future. Instead, he will languish among the unemployed complaining about the lack of job opportunities and his bad luck in getting passed over for jobs. Finally he may become convinced that there is simply no future in business for him.

So it is in the option market. Options, it cannot be emphasized too often, are not magic. They usually do not create instant wealth. True, used in certain ways, they can give greatly increased leverage, but as this book has been at pains to point out, every increase in leverage is gained at a cost of increased risk of loss. And of course one could be lucky and make a great deal of money if one were leveraged at just the time that a certain stock made a big move in the right direction. But it is vital to understand that such a success would be attributable purely to luck. If anyone thinks that such a great profit is due to his skill alone, we will wait patiently to see whether he can repeat his feat of skill the next time and the next.

The fact is that options enable one to invest or speculate in the stock market through the use of many different techniques. But it is still based on the stock market, and in general the returns available to the options investor or speculator are roughly equal to the risks taken, perhaps offset by whatever the fancy of the public happens to be at that time. This means that if one approaches options with the idea of making a 100% profit every year, he or she will probably be disappointed with the results (unless they are extremely lucky). But worse is that because they believe that they ought to make such a high profit they will deliberately turn their backs on many opportunities to make a very good return.

And when one does, one risks not making any profit at all. For example, the person who buys options to see them double and triple without closing them out and realizing at least part of his profit is leaving himself wide open for a reversal in the price of the stock and a complete disappearance of all his profits, and, even worse, of his entire starting capital.

What should be a reasonable goal? The answer is that if any professional investment manager could devise a method of making 20% a year, year in and year out regardless of market conditions, he would be a hero without equal on the face of the earth. If a member of the public is willing to take much greater chances he might set a goal of slightly more, say 25% to 40% in a good market. But that amount would, in my opinion, be the upper limit that one could even reasonably have as a goal for the average year. This is not to say that in certain unusual years one could not make a great deal more, but if you are so fortunate as to do so, please recognize that this will not happen very often.

The mark of the unsophisticated options trader is a false expectation of high profits. Such an expectation can be as dangerous as being completely wrong on which way the market is going to go, because it not only leads to disappointment, but it automatically locks one out from many profitable opportunities. The most famous saying on Wall Street is, *"Bulls* can make money and *bears* can make money. But pigs never make money." The same thing applies in options. You don't want to be the kind of animal that is fat and short, has a large snout, a short curly tail, and oinks. They end up providing the bacon for others to enjoy.

8. *Unwillingness to use naked options.* The very phrase "naked options" has an unfortunate connotation. One sees himself or herself naked, shivering on an icy lake, while the frigid winds from the north chill one's bones to the marrow. So the average investor looks upon naked options as a good way to be stripped of all his money in case the stock goes in the wrong direction. Because of this poor imagery, I prefer the more neutral term "uncovered options" and this is what we will use in this section.

It is true that uncovered options can bring quick losses of a very large size and that there is no way to completely guard against such losses. But these arguments alone should not deter investors from giving careful consideration to the advantages of using them. If the odds in favor of using uncovered options are so favorable that they outweigh even the theoretically almost unlimited loss potential, then we should use them, just as in our daily lives we are willing to take enormous risks to obtain slight benefits if the odds against those risks are remote enough.

For example, many people routinely fly distances of 200 miles or less when they could take a train or bus. They are saving perhaps a few hours, but are willing to accept the unlimited risk of death which, however remote, is always a part of flying and certainly present in much higher degree than when taking the train.

Although uncovered options may present special risks, there are risks inherent in any investment founded upon stock prices. And in some cases the risks of uncovered options are no greater than the risks in other types of option strategies that are generally assumed to be quite safe. The most striking example is that the most conservative use of options is considered to be writing calls against stock one owns, or writing covered calls. This strategy is the exact equivalent of writing uncovered puts. Nevertheless, thousands of investors, including professional fund managers, gladly write covered calls all year long but would be absolutely aghast if anyone even suggested that they write a few naked puts.

Uncovered puts have a number of advantages over covered call writing. First, the commissions are less. Even if you own the under-lying stock and intend to keep it, unless you are writing out-of-the-money calls, you will likely incur a commission at the end of the transaction. Second, it requires more margin money to write the same amount of covered calls as uncovered puts. Third, in many cases by using Treasury bills to provide the margin for the uncovered puts, you are getting a higher yield on your money than you are from the dividends on the stock.

When used in conjunction with other methods of covered options, selling extra options, or ratio writing as it is called, can substantially increase the return from a position while increasing risk only if the stock moves by a very great amount. For example, if a stock is 38 and you write the 40 option for 4, you are getting a return of 10% without deducting commissions. If you can also sell a 50 option for $1^1/_4$ you would increase your return to 13% and begin to lose money only if the stock went above 50, which is a 31% move. Unless the stock in-creases by more than that, you will have boosted your return by 30%, a very significant increase.

The moral of this section is *not* that everyone should write uncov-ered options. They are clearly not appropriate for everyone, and many types of investors are not even permitted to use them, for good reason. But if you are one of the ones who is permitted to use uncov-ered options, then you should give careful consideration to using them in two ways: (1) substituting uncovered put writing for covered call writing to save commissions and decrease the amount of capital required to produce a given amount of options income, and (2) sup-plementing your covered writing and spreads with uncovered options to increase return while risking loss only if the stock moves by an ab-normally large amount.

9. *Refusal to realize losses*. The most difficult aspect of options is not devising the strategies or executing them. Nor is it deciding when to close them out after they have made money. While these ac-tivities may be challenging, they are also fun. The toughest thing to do in options is to close out a position when it has become a loser. This is definitely not fun. It is difficult to do because in most cases there is always the possibility that if the position is left alone it will reverse itself and what is now only a paper loss will become a gain. Once you have closed out the position, you have cast the loss in con-crete, never to be able to reverse. So the psychology is against you, because we are all optimistic by nature, and having thought that our idea would make money when we started out, we are more reluctant to admit that we were wrong when it is going to cost us hard dollars of real cash.

But the alternative to closing out loss positions often is to risk even greater losses. And while there is plenty of money available in any options program to afford small losses, there is not enough money to be able to afford big losses. Thus, in order to make money over any sustained period of time, it is necessary to ensure that there are no big losses. The only way to be certain of this is to take a lot of little losses that if not stopped have the potential of becoming big losses.

The clearest example is with uncovered options. Since the profit potential of each option is limited, while the loss potential is very great, it is clear that one huge loss could wipe out the gains from an entire year of successful trades. The same reasoning applies to other areas of options, including covered call writing.

It is also true when you are buying in-the-money options. If you don't try to rescue some of the premium when the stock starts to slide down, you may wind up losing more than you could reasonably have expected to gain.

The conclusion is that the only way to avoid costly losses is to take care of them when they are minor. You must realize that taking a loss is not a defeat. It is preparing for the next victory. In options as in war, "He who fights and runs away, lives to fight another day." If you don't, you won't.

10. *Not using a broker who is thoroughly familiar with options.* In today's market, there are basically two types of stock brokerage firms. There are the discount and/or online firms, which give no assistance, and there are the full-service firms, which do. While commission rates between full-service firms may differ, they are probably more alike than they are different. What can be a large variable is the amount of discount you are able to negotiate with your own stockbroker. And a broker who is knowledgeable about options may be willing to give as big a discount as one who knows almost nothing about options.

In short, once you decide to use a full-service firm, you may be paying about the same commission dollars no matter which firm you use and which broker within the firm you use. This means that if you are interested in options and you are dealing with a broker who is not well versed in options, you are paying for something that you are not getting.

It is a relatively easy matter to work with brokers who are thoroughly familiar with options. One way is that if your present broker is not familiar with them, ask him if there is an options coordinator at his local office. You can ask your broker to talk with the coordinator and relay the ideas to you, or you could ask to have this coordinator work with you directly.

If your brokerage firm is part of a national or regional firm, then there probably is a national options director at the main office of the firm. Ask your broker to contact this director for ideas. If you do a meaningful amount of business with the firm, you could ask to talk to the national options director yourself. Don't be bashful. Brokerage firms are in keen competition with one another and will go to quite some lengths to keep a good customer.

Finally, there is nothing wrong with opening an account at another firm for the specific purpose of doing options where you can get the advice and benefit of a broker who really understands options. Most large investors have more than one account, and unless you are very small, there is no reason why you can't as well. By having two accounts you will be able to compare ideas and services provided by the two different brokers and thus get a better idea of what the standard of service ought to be.

In summary, your commissions are paying a broker to help you in options and to give you options ideas that are useful to you. To the extent that you are using a broker who merely executes orders that you must conceive, you are not getting the help you are entitled to. Since, as this book has emphasized, making money in options is not easy, you ought to see that you get all the help you are entitled to—especially when it costs no more.

Appendix K

OPTIONS STRATEGIES RANKED FROM EXTREME BULLISHNESS TO EXTREME BEARISHNESS

Very Optimistic

Buy call with strike price above market.
Buy call with strike price at market.
Buy call with strike price below market.
Buy stock on margin.

In conjunction with any of these strategies, to make them more speculative:

Sell put with strike price above market.
Sell put with strike price at market.
Sell put with strike price below market.

Moderately Optimistic

Buy stock, sell put.
Buy stock, sell call with strike price above market (covered call).
Buy stock, sell call with strike price at market (covered call).
Buy stock, sell call and put, both at market.
Buy stock, sell call and put, both with strike prices *away from the market*.

Neutral

Buy stock, sell one call with strike price above market, one at market.

Buy stock, sell two or more calls with strike price above market.

Sell put and call both with strike prices at market (straddle).

Sell call with strike price at market, put with strike price below (combination).

Buy stock and one put with strike price at market (call).

Moderately Pessimistic

Buy stock and buy two puts.

Sell call with strike price at market or lower, buy call at higher strike price (bear spread).

Sell naked call with strike price above market.

Sell stock short, buy two calls.

Sell stock short, buy one call at market (synthetic put).

Sell naked call with strike price at market.

Buy one call and two puts, all with strike prices at market.

Very Pessimistic

Buy put with strike price at market.

Sell naked call with strike price below market.

Sell stock short, buy call with strike price above market (partial put).

Sell stock short.

Buy put with strike price below market.

Appendix L

GLOSSARY OF TERMS

Adjusted strike price. The new strike price after a stock declares a stock dividend or stock split, also accompanied by an increase in the number of shares per option. The purpose of the adjustment is to keep the value of the new options the same as they were before the split. If a stock is 100, and it splits 3 for 2, the old 100 strike price option will now be a $66^5/_8$ strike price option, and each option will give the holder the right to buy 150 shares.

American style options. Options that can be exercised at any time. The opposite of European style options which can only be exercised at the expiration date.

Asked. As used in the phrase "bid and asked prices," it is the price at which a potential seller is willing to sell; in other words, this is the asking price for what is for sale.

Away from the market. A stock option for which the strike price is a substantial distance from the current price of the stock. *See also* **in the money** *and* **out of the money.** Also used when an order is entered at a price that is not near the current price, as placing an order to buy an option at 8 when it is offered at 10.

Bear. An investor who believes that stock prices will decline. His strategies are to buy puts, sell naked calls, and sell stock short.

Bear spread. A spread that makes money when the price of the stock goes down. A bear spread consists of selling the option with the lower strike price and buying the option with the higher strike price. A bear spread with calls is a credit spread; a bear spread with puts is a debit spread.

Beta. A figure that indicates the historical propensity of a stock price to move with the stock market as a whole. The lowest theoretical beta is 0, which indicates no movement, and the highest can go up to 4 or more, indicating wild gyrations for small movements in the market.

Bid. The price at which a potential buyer is willing to buy; the buyer is bidding that amount to purchase the security offered. If you want to sell a security immediately, this is the price you will receive. As used in the phrase "bid and asked prices," the two prices give the current market for an option or stock.

Bull. An investor who believes that stock prices will rise. He buys calls, sells puts, and buys stocks on margin.

Bull spread. A spread that makes money when the price of the stock goes up. It consists of buying the lower strike price option and selling the higher strike price option. A bull spread with calls results in a debit, and with puts in a credit.

Butterfly spread. A spread consisting of being short two options, being long one option of a higher strike price, and being long one option of a lower strike price, all with the same expiration date (e.g., long a January 30 and a January 40 and short 2 January 35s). In theory it can never be worth less than zero and is most profitable when the stock is at the mid strike price on expiration.

Calendar spread. Buying a long-duration option and selling a shorter-duration option of the same strike price on the same stock. A calendar spread makes money by the expiration of future time value in the short option at a greater amount than the loss in value of the longer-duration option.

Call. An option giving the buyer the right to purchase 100 shares of the stock for a given price within a given period of time.

Cash value. The value an option has if it were to be exercised now. It is the amount by which an option is in the money. If a stock is now 22, the 20 call has a cash value of 2. Also known as intrinsic value. Out-of-the-money options do not have any cash value. *Compare* **future time value.**

Cemetery spread. What happens to a spread when the stock goes in the wrong direction. The spreader gets buried alive. An example of the humor (?) of Wall Street.

Chicago Board Options Exchange (CBOE). The CBOE opened April 26, 1973, as the first exchange in the world for stock options. In order to have an exchange of options, the CBOE had to make two major modifications to options as they had previously existed: Standardize the expiration dates and standardize the strike prices. By offering liquidity, the CBOE vastly increased the popularity of stock options.

Closing transaction. The sale of an option by someone owning it or the purchase of an option by a person who previously sold it short. This transaction terminates the investor's position in the option.

Combination (combo). A strategy involving calls and puts on the same security with the same expiration date but with different strike prices surrounding the underlying security. If an index is 725, to be long both the September 700 puts and September 750 calls is to be long a combination. The option owner hopes that the index will move to below 700 or above 750 by the expiration date so that one of the options will be worth more than the cost of the position. One can also be short a combo in which case the objective is to have the index end up between 700 and 750 so that both options expire worthless. *See also* the synonym **strangle.**

Conversion. Converting puts is transforming them into calls. This can be done without risk by buying a put, selling a call, and buying the underlying stock. Conversions are made because the supply of puts normally exceeds the demand.

Cover. To close out one's position. A call writer who is short 2 XYZ April 25s may decide that he has made a mistake and that he had better get out of the position. He will cover his position by purchasing those identical calls. This can also be done when most of the profit has been realized.

Covered call writer or seller. A call seller (writer) who owns the stock underlying the calls being sold. Owning the stock gives protection from any loss due to an increase in the price of the stock during the duration of the call.

Credit spread. (1) A spread that produces money upon its execution (e.g., selling a 35 call for 4 and buying a 40 call for 1). A credit spread has a margin requirement and makes money when the credit decreases because when you close out the position you will have to pay the amount of the credit. (2) The amount of the credit resulting from doing a credit spread. For example, when placing an order for the spread in (1) one could request that it be done at a credit spread of 3 points.

Debit spread. (1) A spread that produces a debit upon execution (e.g., buying a 30 call for 4 and selling a 35 call for 1). A debit spread makes money when the amount of the spread increases because when you close it out you will receive the amount of the debit. (2) The amount of the debit resulting from doing a spread. The aforementioned spread could have been executed with the request that it be done at a debit spread of no more than 3 points.

Deep in the money. An option that has a large cash or intrinsic value because the price of the stock has moved far beyond the option strike price. A call is deep in the money when the stock is much higher than the strike price, and a put is deep in the money when the stock is far below the strike price.

Deep out of the money. An option that has no current cash value because the strike price is significantly far away from the current price of the underlying security. In the case of a call, it is deep out of the money when its strike price is far above the current price of the security. The security must move up substantially if the call is to have any value at its expiration date. A put is deep out of the money when its strike price is far below the current price of the security. The security must move down substantially if the put is to have any value at its expiration date.

Delta. The amount by which the premium of an option changes for each 1-point change in the price of the underlying security. If a call goes up 37 cents when the underlying security goes up by 1 point, it has a delta of 0.37.

Diagonal spread. A spread in which a long-term option of one strike price is purchased and a shorter-term option of another strike price is sold. A common example is to purchase a long-term call at, say, a 40 strike price and sell the shorter-term 45 call. Basically a bullish spread.

European style option. An option that can only be exercised just prior to its expiration. The opposite of American style options which can be exercised at any time.

Ex-dividend. The date on which a purchaser of a stock does not receive a dividend. For example, if a stock goes ex-dividend on the 15th, anyone purchasing the stock on the 14th will receive the dividend, but those purchasing on the 15th will not. Usually the opening price on the 15th will be reduced from the previous day's close by the amount of the dividend. A call owner who exercises the day before a stock goes ex-dividend is entitled to the stock and the dividend, notwithstanding that the call writer will learn of the assignment only after the stock has gone ex-dividend.

Exercise. To do what a stock option gives one the right to do—that is, to purchase stock for the strike price in the case of a call and to sell stock for the strike price in the case of a put. Exercising an option requires paying a commission on the underlying stock. Options need not be exercised since they can always be sold for approximately the same profit that would be made by exercising them and immediately closing out the stock position.

Exercise price. The price at which the buyer of a call can purchase the underlying stock during the life of the call, and the price at which the buyer of a put can sell the underlying stock during the life of the put. *Also called* **strike price.**

Expiration date. The date on which the option becomes null and void. The expiration date is the Saturday following the third Friday of the month. Note that trading in the option ceases at 3:00 P.M. central time of the business day immediately prior to the expiration date and that notice of exercising an option must also be given the day before.

Future time value. That part of the option price that does not represent cash value. Future time value is the excess that option buyers are willing to pay in order to obtain leverage and to limit exposure. It is the only part of the option price that produces a profit for the covered writer. In the case of out-of-the-money options, the entire option price is future time value.

Good till canceled (GTC). An order to buy or sell an option that remains in effect until it is executed or is canceled by its originator. For example, a GTC order would be to buy 5 XYZ July 45 calls now trading at 4 when they reach 3.

Hedge. A transaction consisting of two or more separate options and/or stocks with the objective of providing a greater chance of making a profit, although perhaps a smaller one, than a single transaction. *See* Chapter 6 for a complete discussion.

Horizontal spread. A spread involving options with the same strike prices and different expirations. When connected in the daily newspaper report they make a horizontal line.

In the money. An option that is worth money because of the current market price of the stock. A call would be in the money if the current price of the stock were above the strike price of the call.

Intrinsic value. *See* **cash value.**

Legging. Legging into a position is executing one side of a position first, in the hope that the stock will then move in the right direction so that the other side of the position can be executed at a more favorable price. One can also leg out of a position with the same objective. Legging is the opposite of executing something as a spread, which means doing both sides simultaneously. Legging entails the risk that the stock will move in the wrong direction, leaving the position only half executed.

Long. To be long is to own something.

Margin. The amount of money that must be deposited with a broker in order to buy or sell a security. *See* Chapter 7 for the requirements.

The market. As applied to an options exchange, the market for a particular option is the current bid and offer prices on the floor of the exchange. This tells the potential customer the probable price if he wishes to buy or sell a call.

Mark to the market. The process of adjusting a margin account each day to the current prices of the underlying stocks.

Naked option writer or seller. One who sells (writes) a call without owning the underlying stock, in contrast to a covered call writer; the naked call writer may be able to make a higher return on the money, but faces an unlimited liability if the stock rises. *See*, however, the section in Chapter 4 on selling naked calls for ways in which to help control this liability. Also, one who sells a put without being long a put of equal or longer duration and of equal or lower strike price.

Open interest. The number of calls or puts that are outstanding at any time. Unlike shares of stock that are issued by corporations, usually via a registration statement, options are issued anytime an investor decides to write one. Thus the open interest fluctuates daily.

Option. A legal right allowing the owner to buy or sell 100 shares of stock at a specific price during a specific period of time. A **call** is an option allowing its owner to buy stock at a specific price, and a **put** is an option allowing its owner to sell stock at a specific price. A person who is short an option is under a legal obligation to comply with the option owner's request.

Out of the money. An option that, because of the difference between the strike price and the market price of the underlying stock, will be worth nothing unless the stock moves in price. A call is out of the money when its strike price is above the current price of the stock.

OTC (over the counter). When applied to stock options, this means all options other than those traded on an exchange. Generally OTC options expire 90 days, or 6 months and 10 days from the date of purchase, and the strike price is usually the same as the price of the stock at the time the option was written, although the options may be for any duration and written at any strike price. Now these options are rarely used.

Parity. When the price of an option is equal to its cash value. Thus, if a stock is 22, the 20 strike price call is at parity if it is 2. Useful in executing orders on a volatile stock, when you can request a purchase at no more than parity plus a given amount, such as parity plus a half. Especially useful in closing out covered writing positions.

Point. One dollar.

Premium. The price that the buyer pays the writer for an option contract (the term is synonymous with the price of an option).

Put. An option giving the owner the right to sell 100 shares of the underlying stock for a specified price within a stated period of time. The purchaser of a put profits from a decline in the price of the stock.

Ratio writing. Writing more than one option against each long position. Involves the use of uncovered options with its margin requirements.

Short. To be short an option or a stock means to owe it to someone. Whereas the investor who is long buys a security and then sells it, hopefully for a higher price, the short seller sells the security first, and then buys it back later, hopefully for a lower price.

SIPC (Securities Investor Protection Corporation). Established by Congress to protect customers of brokerage firms, it insures the customers' accounts of brokerage firms that belong to SIPC for loss if the firm goes bankrupt or otherwise cannot pay its customers' claims. Limits are $500,000 for each customer for losses of securities and $100,000 to the extent the loss is in cash that the firm was holding in the customer's name. All firms that are members of the NYSE, AMEX, or CBOE are members of the SIPC. Many brokerage firms also have commercial insurance policies which provide their clients with substantially higher limits.

Special puts and calls. Those OTC options that dealers have in their inventory. This is different from the normal method of trading OTC options, which is to find a seller in response to a particular request from a potential buyer. Now rarely used.

Spread. A combination of long and short positions in options of the same underlying stock, which have different strike prices or different expiration dates.

Straddle. A position consisting of a put and a call on the same stock for the same strike price. Each option may be exercised separately but they are sold as a unit.

Strangle. *See* the synonym **combination** for a full explanation. Whether the strangle buyer or writer ends up being strangled or being the strangler depends on which way the underlying security moves.

Strap. Two calls and a put on the same stock with the same strike price and expiration date.

Strike price. The price at which the buyer of a call can purchase the underlying stock during the life of the option, and the price at which the buyer of a put can sell the stock during the life of the option. *Also called* **exercise price.**

Strip. Two puts and a call on the same stock with the same strike price and expiration date.

Theta. The amount by which the future time value of an option declines with the passage of time, usually measured per day. It is the enemy of option buyers and the friend of option writers. It increases as the time shortens to the expiration date.

Time spread. *See* **calendar spread.**

Uncovered. *See* **naked option writer or seller.**

Vertical spread. Buying one option and selling another option on the same stock with a different strike price, usually with the same duration. Bull spreads and bear spreads are examples. When seen in the daily newspaper report they form a vertical line.

Writer. The grantor of an option contract; also called the maker or the seller; further divided, with respect to call writers, into covered writers, who own the underlying stock, and naked writers, who do not.

INDEX